Michael Price

Windows 7

in easy steps

special edition

In easy steps is an imprint of In Easy Steps Limited
4 Chapel Court · 42 Holly Walk · Leamington Spa
Warwickshire · United Kingdom · CV32 4YS
www.ineasysteps.com

Notice of Liability
Every effort has been made to ensure that this book contains accurate
and current information. However, In Easy Steps Limited and the
author shall not be liable for any loss or damage suffered by readers
as a result of any information contained herein.

Trademarks
Microsoft® and Windows® are registered trademarks of Microsoft
Corporation. All other trademarks are acknowledged as belonging to
their respective companies.

In Easy Steps Limited supports The Forest Stewardship Council (FSC),
the leading international forest certification organisation. All our titles
that are printed on Greenpeace approved FSC certified paper carry the
FSC logo.

MIX
Paper from
responsible sources
FSC® C020837

Printed and bound in the United Kingdom

ISBN 978-1-84078-444-2

Contents

1   Reviewing the basics   11

Versions of Windows	12
Editions of Windows 7	14
Basic controls	16
Working with programs	18
Libraries, folders and files	20
Accessing the Internet	22
Networking	24
Security and maintenance	26
Email and instant messaging	28

2   User account controls   29

User accounts	30
Create an account	31
Add an account password	32
Change the account picture	33
Turn on guest account	34
Fast user switching	35
User account control (UAC)	36
Adjust UAC settings	38
Password reset disk	39
Parental controls	40
Using the controlled account	42

3   Configure the desktop   43

Screen resolution	44
Make text larger	46
Multiple displays	48
ClearType	50
Personalize Windows	52
Get more themes online	54
Create a theme	56
Sound scheme	58
Screen saver	59
Save the theme	60
Other theme types	62

4   Windows your way   63

Customize the Start menu	64
Configure the taskbar	66

Notification area   68
Toolbars   69
Language bar   70
Pin programs to Taskbar   71
Pin programs to Start menu   72
Jump lists   73
Automatic logon   75
Automated shutdown   76
Change shortcut icon   78
Add keyboard shortcut   79
Mouse settings   80

5 Manage files and folders   81

Files, folders and libraries   82
Windows Explorer   83
Windows Explorer layout   85
Windows Explorer toolbar   86
Folder contents   87
Change your view   88
Sort contents   89
Windows 7 libraries   91
Add a location   92
Location unavailable   94
Arrange library contents   95
Create a library   96
Adjust properties   97
Customize folders   98

6 Searching techniques   99

Computer search   100
Start menu search   101
Address bar   102
Navigation pane   104
Folder and search options   106
Indexing options   108
Enhanced search   110
Using search filters   112
Favorites   113
Save searches   114
Move and copy   115

7 Built-in programs   117

Windows applications   118
Text management   119
Other text applications   121
Image management   123
Computations   126
Dis Writers   128

Utilities 130
Command Prompt 132
Windows PowerShell 133
System Tools 134
Administrative Tools 135
Desktop Gadgets 136

8 Windows Live Essentials 137

Getting started 138
Windows Live Essentials 139
Select and download 140
Completing installation 142
Other Windows Essentials 144
Adobe Reader 145
AVG Antivirus Free Edition 146
Irfanview 148
Notepad++ 149
OpenOffice.org 150
Paint.NET 152
µTorrent 154

9 Enhance your email 155

Email (electronic mail) 156
Windows Live Mail 157
Create Windows Live ID 158
Add email accounts 159
Add another email account 160
Windows Live Mail window 162
View messages 164
Attachments 166
Adding contacts 168
Junk email 169
Mail Calendar 170
Windows Live Calendar 171
Instant messaging 172
Newsgroups 174
RSS feeds 176

10 Internet Explorer 177

Internet Explorer version 9 178
Internet Explorer window 180
Page back and forward 182
Search for web page 183
Change search provider 184
Open in new window 185
Tabbed browsing 186
Home page 188
Favorites 189

Pinned sites   190
Browsing history   191
RSS feeds and web slices   192
Managing add-ons   194
InPrivate Browsing   195
Zoom and Print   196
Compatibility View   198

11 Manage digital images   199

Digital images   200
Image file formats   201
Digital camera   202
Install the software   203
Transfer the Photos   205
View the imported images   207
Transfer more images   208
Create panoramic image   209
Import with Windows   211
Windows Live Photo Gallery   212
Edit photos   213
Print your photos   215
Video clips   216
Edit your video clip   217
Create a movie from photos   218
Save and publish your movie   220

12 Music and media   221

Audio connections   222
Play CDs   223
Copy CD tracks   224
Media Player Library   225
Download media files   226
Internet radio   228
Home media streaming   230
Play to device or computer   231
Windows Media Center   232
Dictate to your computer   234
Text to speech   236

13 Devices and printers   237

Add a printer   238
Updating device drivers   240
Sharing the printer   242
Share printer with XP   244
Wireless printer   246
Virtual printers   249
Generic/text only printer   251
Location aware printing   253

Add a scanner — 254
Using the scanner — 256

14 Networking Windows — 257

Create a network — 258
Create a HomeGroup — 260
Network and sharing center — 262
Connect to wireless network — 264
Dual network access — 266
Manage wireless networks — 267
Network versus HomeGroup — 268
Network map — 269
Sharing folders — 270
Monitor network — 272

15 Laptops and Multitouch — 273

Portable computers — 274
Power management — 275
Portable power management — 276
Battery meter — 278
User interface for portables — 280
Windows Mobility Center — 282
Mobility Center functions — 284
Netbook computers — 286
Touch and Tablet PCs — 288
Taking advantage of Touch — 290

16 Sync with smartphone — 291

Smartphones — 292
Windows Phone 7 — 293
Set up Windows Phone — 294
Windows Phone software — 296
Set up software and phone — 298
Choose what to sync — 300
Enable Wi-Fi — 302
Networked Windows Phone — 304
Play To TV or Computer — 305
Outlook Hotmail Connector — 306
Copy Contacts and Calendar — 308
Update Windows Phone — 310

17 Troubleshooting — 311

Windows error reporting — 312
Troubleshooting settings — 314
Windows Troubleshooters — 315

Troubleshooter in action 316
Problem Steps Recorder 317
View the report 319
Get help from a friend 320
Connecting and sharing 322
Easy Connect 324
System Restore 325
Start in Safe Mode 327
Safe Boot 328
Program Compatibility 329

18 Backup and recovery 331

Copy files and folders 332
Copy libraries 334
Windows Backup 336
The first backup 338
After the backup 340
Scheduled backup 341
Create a manual backup 342
Manage space 343
Restore files 344
Previous versions of files 346
Recover your computer 347
System repair disc 349

19 Virtual machines 351

Windows Virtual PC 352
Install Windows Virtual PC 354
Install Windows XP Mode 356
Setup Windows XP Mode 358
The XP Mode system 360
Install an XP application 361
Run the XP application 362
Add existing XP applications 364
Add a virtual system 365
Create the virtual machine 366
Setup the virtual system 367
Install the virtual system 368
Install Vista as guest 369
Install and use Vista 370
Predefined VHD 371

20 Security and Encryption 373

User account management 374
Set password to expire 376
Hide user list 378
Encrypting files 380
Using EFS 381

Backup encryption key 383
Bitlocker to Go 385
Access the encrypted drive 387
Access from Vista 388
Access from XP 389
Whole system encryption 390

21 Command Prompt 391

Open Command Prompt 392
Select a folder 394
Open as administrator 395
Administrator shortcut 396
Adjust appearance 397
Changing window properties 399
Using the Command Prompt 400
Command line changes 402

22 Update and maintain 403

Windows Update 404
Update Settings 406
Microsoft Update 408
Update categories 409
Update history 410
Upgrading Windows 412
Windows Anytime Upgrade 413
Apply the upgrade 414
Disk management 416
Disk cleanup 417
Error checking 419
Defragmentation 421

23 Windows performance 423

System Properties 424
Windows Experience Index 426
Improving performance 428
Data execution prevention 430
Advanced system settings 431
Advanced tools 432
WinSAT and Event Viewer 433
Windows monitors 434
Information on the system 436
Other advanced tools 438
Boosting performance 439
32-bit versus 64-bit 441

24 Windows Registry 443

The Windows Registry	444
Registry backup	446
Open Registry Editor	447
Example Registry change	448
Finding a key	450
Backup before changes	451
Change a value entry	452
Using a standard account	453
Scripted updates	455
Applying an update	456
Resize taskbar thumbnails	457
Remove shortcut suffix	458
Adjust Aero Peek	460

25 Where next for Windows 461

Internet Explorer 10	462
Preview IE 10	464
Windows Live Essentials	466
Windows Blogs	468
Windows 8	469

Index 471

1 Reviewing the basics

This chapter outlines the versions of Windows that have been developed, leading to the current Windows 7 with its various editions, and reviews the features that allow you to work with programs, networks and the Internet.

12 Versions of Windows

14 Editions of Windows 7

16 Basic controls

18 Working with programs

20 Libraries, folders and files

22 Accessing the Internet

24 Networking

26 Security and maintenance

28 Email and instant messaging

Versions of Windows

There have been many versions of Microsoft Windows. The operating system was initially designed for IBM-compatible PCs, but was later extended to support larger computers such as servers and workstations. A derivative version Windows CE was also developed for smaller devices such as PDAs and cell phones.

The main versions of Windows that have been released include:

Date	Client PC	Server	Mobile
1985	Win 1.0		
1987	Win 2.0		
1990	Win 3.0		
1993		Win NT 3.1	
1995	Win 95		
1996		Win NT 4.0	Win CE 1.0
1998	Win 98		
2000	Win Me	Win 2000	Win CE 3.0, Pocket PC 2000
2001	Win XP		Pocket PC 2002
2003		Win Server 2003	Win Mobile 2003
2006	Win Vista		
2007		Win Home Server,	Win Mobile 6
2009	Win 7	Win Server 2008	
2010			Win Phone 7

The first three versions of Windows listed were designed for the 16-bit processor featured in the PCs of the day. Windows 95, 98 and Me added support for 32-bit processors. Windows NT was for 32-bit only while XP and 2000 were initially 32-bit but added 64-bit support later. Windows Vista and Windows 7, and the newer server editions are provided in versions to operate with either 32-bit or 64-bit processors (see page 441). They will also support the multiple processors that are often incorporated in modern personal computers.

Each version of Windows builds on the functions and features included in the previous versions, so that the knowledge and experience you have gained will still be valuable, even though the appearance and the specifics of the operations may have changed.

At the same time, each new version adds new facilities or new ways of carrying out tasks. Windows 7 for example includes:

- Action Center - helps you manage maintenance and security through notification messages including suggestions for fixes

- Device Stage - acts as a home page for portable devices such as music players, smartphones and printers, supporting tasks like battery life, file downloads and printing options

- HomeGroup - makes it easy to share music, pictures, videos, documents and printers on your home network of two or more PCs running Windows 7

- Improved Desktop - larger buttons, previews and jumplists provide shortcuts to files, folders and programs, while Snap, Peek, and Shake options help manage all your open windows

- Internet Explorer 9 - includes new browser controls, address bar searches and taskbar shortcuts to websites

- Internet TV - gathers programming from sites all over the Internet and, with a TV tuner, turns your PC into a digital video recorder to watch, pause, and record live TV

- Performance - Windows 7 takes up less memory and minimizes background services, to run your programs faster and to sleep, resume, and reconnect to wireless networks quicker. It also takes full advantage of 64-bit processors

- Smart search - locate files and programs by typing a keyword in the Start menu search box, with results displayed instantly. Searches within a folder or library use filters to fine-tune your search, and the preview pane shows contents of the results

- Windows Live - provides free functions to allow you to create photo albums and movies, chat in HD, send emails and share your media files anytime and anywhere

- Windows Touch - with a touchscreen PC, use your fingers to browse the web, view photo albums, or open files and folders

- Wireless networking - select and connect to an available wireless network with just a couple of clicks, and Windows will connect automatically, the next time you are within range

Don't forget

Windows 7 was initially shipped with Internet Explorer 8, but Windows Update will replace this with Internet Explorer 9.

Hot tip

Windows 7 includes true multitouch technology, with gestures for zooming, rotating and selecting.

Editions of Windows 7

Windows 7 is provided in a number of editions designed to suit particular types of user. For home and small office users there are three editions:

- Windows 7 Starter
- Windows 7 Home Premium
- Windows 7 Ultimate

Two editions are provided for businesses and large organizations:

- Windows 7 Professional
- Windows 7 Enterprise

There is an edition that is designed for the users of personal computers in emerging technology markets:

- Windows 7 Home Basic

This edition is not available for PCs in the developed technology markets such as United States, European Union and Japan.

Requirements

If you want to run Windows 7 on your PC, you need:

1 GHz or faster 32-bit (x86) or 64-bit (x64) processor

1 GB RAM (32-bit) or 2 GB RAM (64-bit)

16 GB available hard disk space (32-bit) or 20 GB (64-bit)

DirectX 9 graphics device with WDDM 1.0 or higher driver

There will be additional requirements to use certain features:

A TV Tuner for some Windows Media Center functions

Touchscreen for Windows Touch and Tablet PCs

Network adapter for HomeGroup

Optical drive for DVD/CD authoring

Trusted Platform Module (TPM) 1.2 for BitLocker

USB Flash drive for BitLocker To Go

Audio output for Music and sound functions

Beware

Starter Edition is for pre-installation only, and has a number of restrictions including no support for Aero and no Personalization.

Hot tip

Windows XP Mode requires an additional 1 GB of RAM and an additional 15 GB of available hard disk space.

There are some features of Windows 7 that are included only in specific editions, for example:

Features / Editions	ST	HB	HP	Pro	Ult	Ent
Aero Snaps	Y	Y	Y	Y	Y	Y
Aero/Peak/Shake	-	-	Y	Y	Y	Y
Anytime Upgrade	Y	Y	Y	Y		
Backup to network	-	-	-	Y	Y	Y
Basic Games	Y	Y	Y	Y	Y	Y
Bitlocker	-	-	-	-	Y	Y
Bitlocker to Go	-	-	-	-	Y	Y
Encrypting File System	-	-	-	Y	Y	Y
Fast user switching	-	Y	Y	Y	Y	Y
HomeGroup Create	-	-	Y	Y	Y	Y
HomeGroup Join	Y	Y	Y	Y	Y	Y
Internet Connection Sharing	-	Y	Y	Y	Y	Y
Location aware printing	-	-	-	Y	Y	Y
Max Memory (GB) - 32 bit	4	4	4	4	4	4
Max Memory (GB) - 64 bit	-	-	16	192	192	192
MultiTouch	-	-	Y	Y	Y	Y
Premium Games	-	-	Y	Y	Y	Y
Retail pack	-	-	Y	Y	Y	
Snipping Tool	-	-	Y	Y	Y	Y
Sticky Notes	-	-	Y	Y	Y	Y
Tablet PC	-	-	Y	Y	Y	Y
Taskbar Previews	-	Y	Y	Y	Y	Y
Virtualization	-	-	Y	Y	Y	Y
Windows DVD Maker	-	-	Y	Y	Y	Y
Windows Flip	Y	Y	Y	Y	Y	Y
Windows Flip 3D	-	-	Y	Y	Y	Y
Windows Journal	-	-	Y	Y	Y	Y
Windows Media Center	-	-	Y	Y	Y	Y
Windows XP Mode	-	-	-	Y	Y	Y

Make sure that the edition of Windows 7 that you choose will support the particular features that you want to use.

WindowsAnytimeUpgrade.exe

Basic controls

There have been many versions and releases of Windows, with considerable changes to the appearance and the functions offered. However, the basic principles of operation have remained quite consistent, especially since Windows 95, the first version that was truly independent of MS-DOS.

Starting Windows
Switch on the PC and Windows displays the Windows logo, the Starting Windows message and then the Account selection screen.

1 Select the user account required, to get the Logon screen

2 Enter the password (if one is specified) and press Enter

The Welcome message is displayed, while the Windows desktop for the selected user account is being prepared.

The Windows desktop

The specifics of the desktop contents depend on the way your PC has been set up, but it will typically contain these elements:

Desktop Icons   Windows Background   Windows Gadgets

Active task (Live Thumbnail)

Show Desktop

Start Button   Shortcuts Pinned to Taskbar   Active Task (Shortcut)   Notification Area

Ending Windows

As always, you need to explicitly select Shutdown to ensure that all open files are properly saved.

The messages Logging off and then Shutting down are displayed, then Windows is ended and the PC is powered off.

Working with programs

As in all versions of Windows, you click the Start button to display the Start menu, from where you can select the programs included with Windows or installed separately.

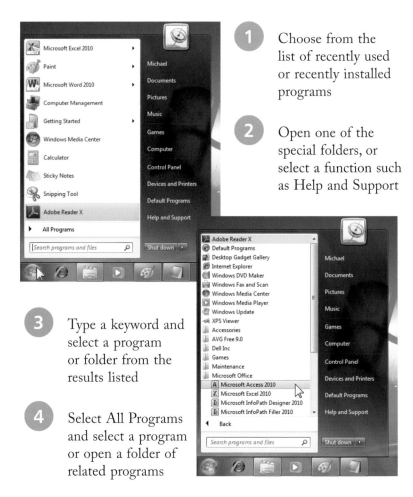

1 Choose from the list of recently used or recently installed programs

2 Open one of the special folders, or select a function such as Help and Support

18

3 Type a keyword and select a program or folder from the results listed

4 Select All Programs and select a program or open a folder of related programs

At the left of the Taskbar is a predefined set of program shortcuts, and you can add or remove entries to provide your own selection.

The right hand section of the taskbar contains links to programs that are preloaded when Windows starts up.

The shortcuts and the central part of the taskbar contain links to the windows for the programs and folders that you have opened.

Move and resize windows

You manage open windows the same way as in previous versions:

1 To move the window, click the title bar area, hold down the mouse button and drag the window

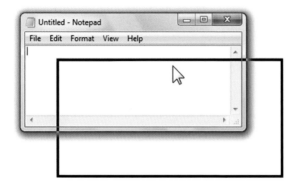

2 To resize the window, move the mouse pointer over any border or any corner until it becomes double-headed

3 Click and drag until the window is the desired size

4 To make the window full screen, select the Maximize button. Select the Restore button to return to the original window size

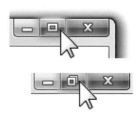

Snap, Peek and Shake

For Windows 7, the Aero Snap, Peek, and Shake options add new ways to resize and reposition your active windows.

Libraries, folders and files

There are sets of data folders for each user account, so Windows uses standard names such as My Documents, and My Pictures to refer to the particular folders for the current user account.

Windows 7 goes a stage further and defines a Library for each type of file. The library displays the contents of the relevant folder for the current user account and for the shared or Public account.

To see the contents of a library:

1 Select Start and choose the library type, e.g. Pictures

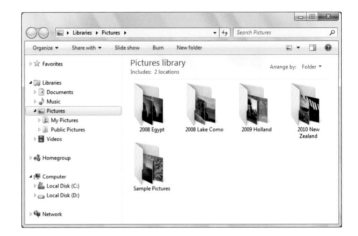

2 If you have similar files in other folders, right-click the folder and select Include in Library, then select the library

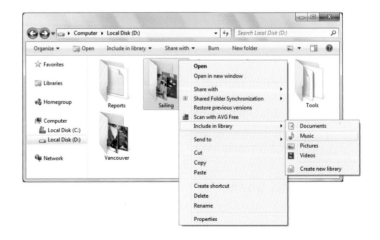

To locate a particular folder within a drive:

1 Click Start and select Computer, or select Computer from any open folder

2 Double-click the drive, for example C:, then double-click a folder, for example Users

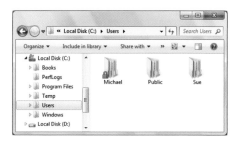

3 Double-click other folders, for example the user folder Michael, and the Pictures folders, to explore their contents

4 The hierarchical folder structure is displayed in the navigation pane

Hot tip

The folder path is displayed in the address bar, for example
C: > Users > Michael

21

Don't forget

You can click the white triangle ▷, which is added when there are folders within a drive or folder. Click the black triangle ◢ to collapse the display.

Accessing the Internet

Windows 7 will automatically detect and set up any available connection to the Internet during installation.

To check the status on your system:

1 Select Start, Control Panel, and click View Network Status and tasks, in the Network and Internet section

Don't forget

This opens the Network and Sharing Center which in this example shows a home network with a broadband router giving Internet access.

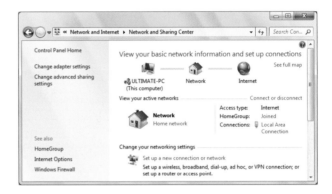

2 If no Internet connection is shown, choose the option to Set up a new connection or network

Don't forget

Windows will detect all the connection methods available on your system, network, wireless or dial-up, based on the hardware configuration.

3 Select Connect to the Internet, and click Next

4 Select the appropriate connection method and follow the prompts to define your Internet connection

When you have your Internet connection defined, you can surf the Internet using Microsoft Internet Explorer.

1 Select the Internet Explorer icon in the shortcut area of the taskbar

Hot tip

You can of course install a different browser, for example Firefox, Chrome, Safari or Opera.

2 In the original release, all editions of Windows 7 included Internet Explorer version 8.0, as shown above

Don't forget

This version of Internet Explorer is described in more detail starting on page 178, and is used for all web page examples throughout the book.

3 Microsoft released Internet Explorer 9.0 in April 2011, for installation using Windows Update (see page 404)

Networking

If you have two or more computers, you can connect them together in a network, and share resources such as files, printers and other devices. Each computer needs a network adapter, which is connected by cable or wireless to a network hub. This is usually the same device that provides you with broadband access for the Internet.

Windows 7 can automatically detect and configure your network devices. To view the network components on your system:

Don't forget

You could also click the Network icon in the notification area then select Open Network and Sharing Center.

1 Open the Network and Sharing Center from the View Network Status link in the Control Panel

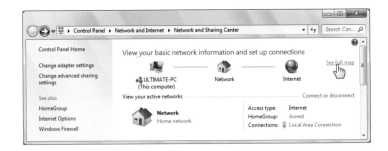

2 Select the link See full map, to display a network diagram showing all detected network devices

Hot tip

Here some devices are connected via network cables, and some are wireless devices, including the All-in-One printer shown separately.

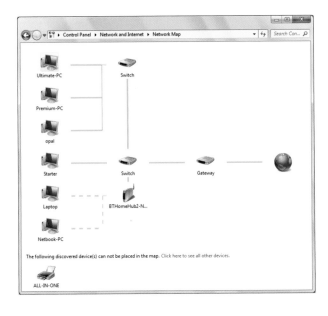

3 Click the network type, in this example Home network

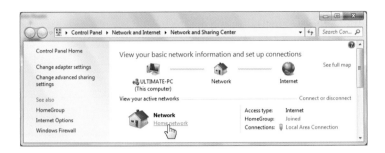

4 You can define the network as Home, Work or Public, depending on the location and types of users connected

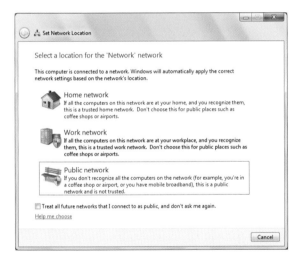

Windows 7 computers with a Home network defined can create or join a HomeGroup where libraries and printers can be shared with the other users in the same group.

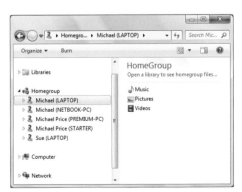

Beware

If you connect to a network with unknown or untrusted users, define the network as Public so your files are not put at risk.

25

Hot tip

Media files may be shared in the HomeGroup even if the particular user is currently logged off.

Don't forget

You can extend your network to include computers running other versions of Windows, or other operating systems (see page 268).

Security and maintenance

Your computer is susceptible to problems, accidental or deliberate, but too often users only become aware of the problems after the event, too late to apply the protective measures available. For this reason, Windows includes options to automatically monitor your system and warn you if anything needs to be done. This was the function of the Windows Security Center in previous versions. In Windows 7, you find the Action Center.

1 Left-click the Flag icon in the Notification area

2 Note any messages listed, then select Open Action Center

The detailed messages related to Security and Maintenance are displayed, along with buttons to carry out the suggested actions.

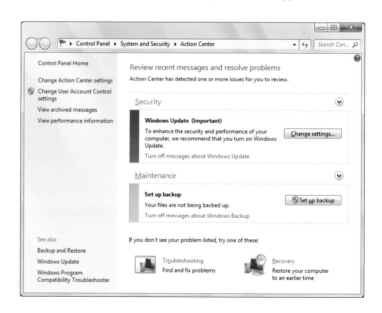

3 Click Change Settings for example to adjust the Windows Update settings (see page 406)

4 Click the Expand button to view the full list of Security options being monitored

26

Action Center keeps track of the status for Network Firewall, Windows Update, Virus Protection, Spyware and other Malware, Internet Security Settings and User Account Control.

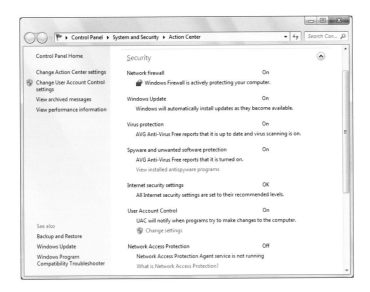

Hot tip

Click the Up Arrow (collapse) button to hide the details of Security options.

5 Click the Expand button to view the full list of the Maintenance options being monitored

Action Center manages Backup, Problem Reports, Windows Update actions and Systems Maintenance.

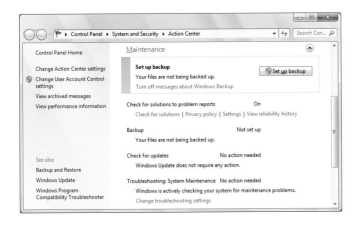

Don't forget

If you have issues not identified by Action Center, you can find and fix problems with Programs, Hardware, Network etc, using the Troubleshooting function at the foot of the Action Center (see page 315).

27

Email and instant messaging

Windows has always offered services such as email and instant messaging, but that has changed with Windows 7. There is no email or messaging program included.

However, there is a way to obtain replacements for these and other applications that are no longer included as part of Windows.

1   Select Start, Getting Started then Go online to Get Windows Live Essentials (see page 138)

28

2   Click Download Now, and Windows will offer to install all or part of Windows Live Essentials

If you still have an XP machine, you can get XP versions of these programs by visiting http://download.live.com and selecting Learn about Windows Live Essentials for Windows XP.

2 User account controls

Setting up user accounts is key to the safe and secure use of your computer, especially where you share the system with other users, or when guests need temporary access. Windows 7 provides the user account control facilities you need, along with parental controls needed for children's user accounts.

30   User accounts

31   Create an account

32   Add an account password

33   Change the account picture

34   Turn on guest account

35   Fast user switching

36   User account control (UAC)

38   Adjust UAC settings

39   Password reset disk

40   Parental controls

42   Using the controlled account

User accounts

The user account tells Windows which files and folders can be accessed, what changes to the computer can be made, and what choices of desktop background, color theme or desktop gadgets should be applied. This allows individual users on a shared computer to have their own files and settings.

There are three different types of user accounts, each giving the user a different level of control over the computer.

Standard account

This allows use of most of the capabilities of the computer, but permission from an administrator is required to make changes that affect other users or that impact the security of the computer. For example, you can't install or uninstall software and hardware, delete files that are required for the computer to work, or change settings on the computer that affect other users, unless you provide an administrator password.

Administrator account

Administrators can change security settings, install software and hardware, and access all files on the computer. They can also make changes to other user accounts.

When Windows is initially set up, an administrator account is created and used to set up the computer and install any programs that are required.

Guest account

There is a predefined guest account in the Windows system. This is the only account that never has a password and is intended for casual users such as visitors who don't have a permanent account on your computer. It allows them to use your computer without having access to your personal files, but they can't install software or hardware, change settings, or create a password. By default, this account will be turned off.

Don't forget

You always need a user account of one type or another to use the Windows computer. A password is not essential, though it is much wiser to add a password to every account you create.

Hot tip

Once you have finished setup on your computer, you are recommended to use a standard user account for your day-to-day computing, and reserve the administrator account for special tasks.

Create an account

1 Select Start, Control Panel, and click Add or Remove User Accounts, in the User Accounts and Family Safety section

2 Select the link to Create a new account

3 Type the name for the user account, choose the type (Standard is recommended) then click Create Account

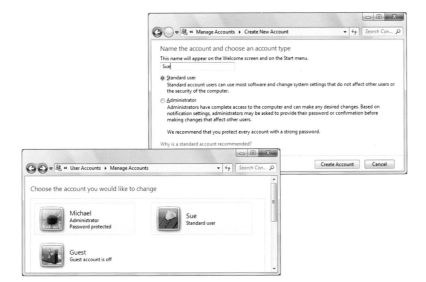

4 The user account as named is created, initially with a default picture and with no password specified

Add an account password

1 Select Add or Remove User Accounts and click the account you want to manage

2 Select the option to Create a password

3 Type the password, then type the password again

To create a strong password, specify at least eight characters, avoid proper names and complete words, and use a mixture of upper case, lower case, numbers and standard symbols.

4 Provide a password hint that will remind you of the password in case you forget, then click Create password

Change the account picture

1 Having set the password, you can then click the option to Change the picture

Don't forget

You can make further changes at any time by selecting the account you want to manage, as shown on the previous page.

2 Choose one of the images and click Change Picture

Hot tip

Select Browse for more pictures to choose an image from one of your picture folders. Windows will crop and scale it, to convert it into an account picture.

DSCF0022

Sue
Standard user
Password protected

3 The selected image becomes the new account picture

Turn on guest account

1 Open User Accounts, Manage Accounts and select the Guest account

2 Select Turn On to confirm you want this account active

3 The guest account is no longer shown as switched off

4 Now you can change the picture, or turn off the guest account

Fast user switching

If a user wants temporary access when another user is currently signed on to the computer, it isn't necessary to shutdown or logoff or even close files and programs You can simply switch users.

1 Select Start, click the arrow next to Shutdown and click Switch User to display the account selection screen

2 Select the additional user account that requires access

3 Enter the password for the user account and press Enter

4 To choose an active session, or to add another user account, select Switch User from the Shutdown list as shown above

5 Select an active user, entering the password when prompted, and click Logoff on the Shutdown list to end that user account session

6 When all but one of the sessions have been closed, you can select Shutdown as normal to terminate the last user account session

User account control (UAC)

The actions that a user account can perform depend on the account type. For example, see the options available for working with user accounts.

1 Select Start, Control Panel, and then click User Accounts and Family Safety

2 Select User Accounts

For Standard and for Administrator accounts, the same set of options will be offered:

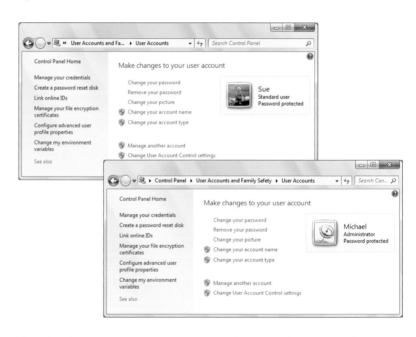

For the Guest account, there is a smaller set of options offered:

To illustrate the use of restricted functions:

1 From a standard account, open your User Accounts panel and select the option to Manage another account

2 Before carrying out the task, Windows asks you or an administrator to authorize the action

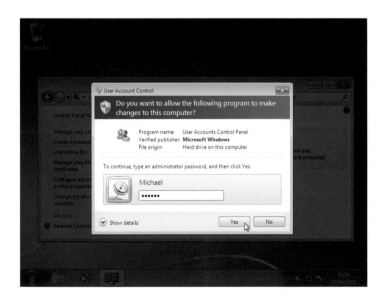

Adjust UAC settings

The default UAC setting notifies you when programs try to make changes to your computer, but you can change how often UAC notifies you.

1 Open your User Accounts panel and select the option to Change User Account Control settings

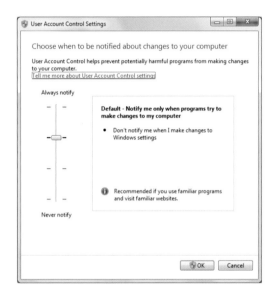

The default is to notify only when programs try to make changes, but not when the active account changes settings (assuming that account is an administrator).

2 Change to Always notify, if you frequently install new software or visit unfamiliar websites

3 Choose Never notify, if you need to use programs that do not support User Account Control

Note that you may receive a UAC prompt when you select OK to save the changes that you've made to the settings.

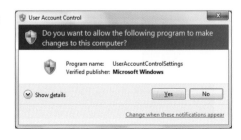

Password reset disk

The User Accounts panel also provides a link for creating a password reset disk that will allow you to regain access to your computer when you forget your password (and the password hint doesn't succeed in reminding you).

1 Insert a USB flash drive or floppy disk

2 Open User Accounts and select the option to Create a password reset disk

Beware

Make sure to store the reset disk in a safe place, since anyone could use it to access your system.

3 Click Next to select the drive then follow the prompts to enter the current password and create the reset disk

Don't forget

You use a removable drive, either a USB flash drive, or a floppy disk if available.

Hot tip

No matter how many times you change your password in the future, you only need to create the reset disk once.

If you forget your password at any time, you can reset it to a new value.

1 Select Reset password

2 Insert the reset disk and follow the prompts to create a new password and password hint

Parental controls

Don't forget

You use Parental Controls to help manage how your children use the computer, setting limits on their access to the web, the hours that they can log on to the computer, the games they can play and programs they can run.

Hot tip

You can apply parental controls to standard user accounts only, not administrator accounts.

To turn on Parental Controls:

1 Select Start, Control Panel and click the option to Set up parental controls for any user

2 Choose the standard user account you want to control (or click Create a new user account)

3 Click the button to turn On Parental Controls and enforce current settings, which will initially be set to Off

4 Select Time limits and drag to mark times where the computer is not be used, e.g. between 9 pm and 7 am

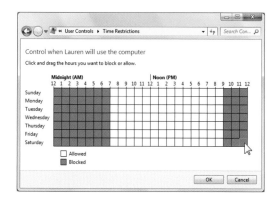

5 Select Games and indicate if games are allowed and at what level, and block or allow specific games

6 You can allow or block specific programs on the computer

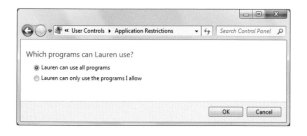

41

Using the controlled account

To see the effect of parental controls:

1 Log on to the computer using the controlled user account

2 Select a restricted program, in this case Adobe Reader

3 The user is told that the program has been blocked by Parental Controls

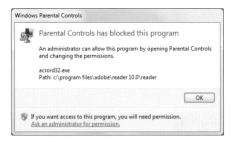

4 Click OK to abandon the attempt

5 Select Ask an administrator for permission, to invoke UAC and request authorisation to carry out the action

3 Configure the desktop

You can control how Windows sets up the screen so that it displays text and graphics at the right size. You can also take advantage of multiple monitors if available, and you can choose a desktop theme with the style, appearance and features that appeal to you.

44 Screen resolution

46 Make text larger

48 Multiple displays

50 ClearType

52 Personalize Windows

54 Get more themes online

56 Create a theme

58 Sound scheme

59 Screen saver

60 Save the theme

62 Other theme types

Screen resolution

To adjust the screen resolution:

 Right-click the desktop and select Screen Resolution from the menu

2 Alternatively, select Start, Control Panel and click the option to Adjust screen resolution

Hot tip

The screen resolution controls the size of the screen contents. Lower resolutions (e.g. 800 x 600) have larger items so fewer can be displayed. Higher resolutions (e.g. 1920 x 1200) have smaller and sharper items, and more can be viewed on the screen.

3 Click the Resolution box, select the desired resolution, then click OK to apply

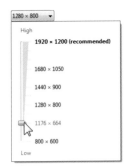

Hot tip

Intermediate values will appear individually when you drag the slider to that part of the bar.

4 Click Keep changes to confirm the revision

Don't forget

You can also change the orientation from Landscape to Portrait, useful for tablet PCs and for a monitor that can be rotated.

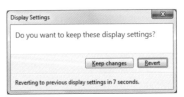

The values that are offered depend on the configuration. The laptop screen shown offers four settings at the physical aspect ratio (8x5) plus the minimum 800x600 and intermediate values at other ratios. Using these may distort the image, e.g. make circles appear oval.

Screen size	Aspect ratio
1920 x 1200	**8x5**
1920 x 1080	16x9
1768 x 992	16x9
1680 x 1050	**8x5**
1600 x 1200	4x3
1440 x 900	**8x5**
1280 x 1024	5x4
1280 x 800	**8x5**
1280 x 720	16x9
1176 x 664	16x9
1024 x 768	4x3
800 x 600	**4x3**

To illustrate the effects of changing screen resolution:

1 View a picture folder full screen at 1920 x 1200 screen resolution, with image files shown as extra-large icons

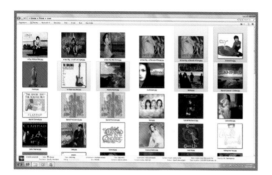

The full resolution and 8x5 aspect ratio lets you see the largest number of image file icons, and they appear as squares.

2 View the same folder full screen at 1280 x 800 resolution

This mid-level resolution shows fewer but larger file icons. Note that all of the components are enlarged, including for example the Start button and taskbar icons. Since the aspect ratio remains at 8x5, the image icons are still square.

3 Finally, view the same folder at 800 x 600 resolution

The lowest resolution has a different aspect ratio, so the image file icons are shown larger again but in an oblong form. Other windows components are also misshaped, for example the Start button is oval.

45

Make text larger

You should normally use the recommended resolution for an
LCD monitor or laptop screen. To enlarge the screen image in
these cases, you can change the text size. To demonstrate, start
with an example application (WordPad) and a picture folder.

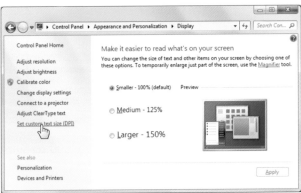

1 Display the Screen
Resolution option and
select Make text and
other items larger or smaller

2 Select Set custom text size (DPI)

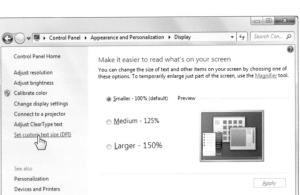

3 Select a percentage
from the list, or drag
the ruler with the
mouse

4 Click OK to continue

Your selected percentage is added to the options displayed.

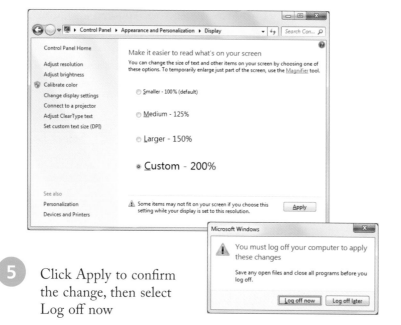

Hot tip

The text resizing applies only to the user account in which it was reset. If you switch users to another account, that will have the default smaller text, or its own reset text size.

5 Click Apply to confirm the change, then select Log off now

6 When you restart the user account, you'll see many of the Windows components have increased in size

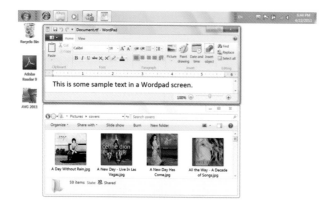

Don't forget

You will note that the image file icon size is not affected by the change in text size (DPI). You'll find a similar effect in web pages, where text is resized but images remain unchanged. In some cases, this can make the web page more difficult to work with, since placing can be upset.

7 To restore the normal sizing for the user account, open Screen Resolution, and set the text size to Smaller (100%)

Note that the text resizing applies only to the active user account.

Multiple displays

The graphics adapter on your computer is often capable of handling more than one monitor, having for example both VGA (analogue) and DVI (digital) connectors. You can also attach a second monitor to a laptop. To see how Windows handles this:

 Display Screen Resolution, then attach a second monitor

Beware

Your monitor may have both VGA and DVI cables, but you should never attach the monitor to two connections on the same computer.

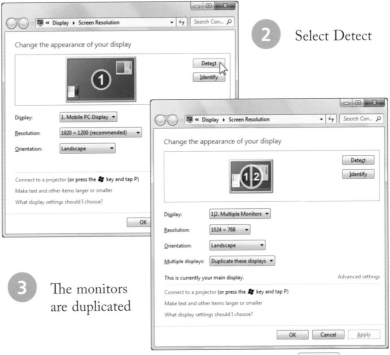

 Select Detect

 The monitors are duplicated

Beware

If you pick a resolution that is not supported by one of the monitors, you will get a warning message and the change will not be applied.

Cannot Display This Video Mode

Windows resets both monitors to a low resolution, that both are sure to handle. If you want to continue duplicating the display, you can choose another more suitable resolution that both monitors can support.

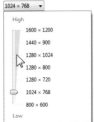

To use the monitors for different information:

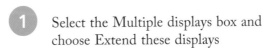

Select the Multiple displays box and choose Extend these displays

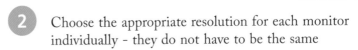

Choose the appropriate resolution for each monitor individually - they do not have to be the same

48

3 By default, the first monitor is the main display, but you can assign the second monitor instead

4 Click Identify to display the numerals 1 and 2. The selected background appears on both monitors, but the task bar appears on the main display only

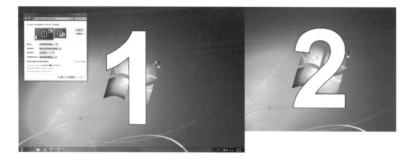

5 Drag one of the monitors to rearrange them, stacked, in the reverse sequence or with a different overlap

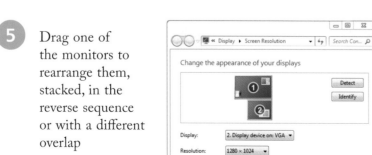

ClearType

ClearType font technology makes the text on your screen appear as sharp and clear as text that's printed on paper. It's on by default in Windows 7, but you can fine-tune the settings.

1 Select Start, Control Panel and Appearance and Personalization then click Adjust ClearType in the Fonts section

2 Click the Turn on ClearType text box (if not already selected)

3 Click Next and Windows checks that you are using the native resolution for your monitor

4 Click Next to run the ClearText text tuner

5 Click the text box that looks best to you, then click Next

Hot tip

To simply review the settings on each of the four pages, click Next to accept the default selection.

Don't forget

Any changes apply only to the current user. Each user account has its own ClearType settings recorded separately.

6 Click Finish to end the ClearText text tuner

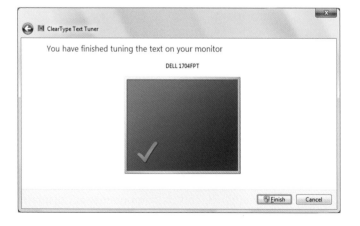

Personalize Windows

You can give your computer a personal touch by changing the computer's window color, sounds, desktop background, screen saver and other aspects. You can change the attributes individually, or select a prepackaged Aero theme.

There are several ways to view and change the current theme:

1 Right-click the desktop and select Personalize

2 Select Start, Control Panel and click Change the theme, in the Appearance and Personalization section

3 You'll see the current theme, initially the Windows 7 theme, with its desktop background, Windows color, sounds and screen saver (if any is assigned)

4 Select any of the suggested Aero themes, and it is immediately applied, and its components are displayed

5 For example, select the theme for your location, in this case the United States theme

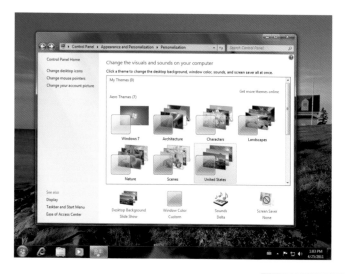

6 Close Personalization and the last selected theme will be retained

7 Right-click the desktop and select Next desktop background to see the next picture in sequence

Get more themes online

You can find many Windows themes at the Microsoft website.

1 Open Personalization and select the link to Get more themes online

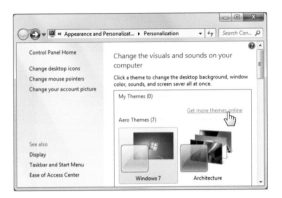

2 The Personalization Gallery opens and displays the Windows 7 themes

3 Review the categories and themes offered

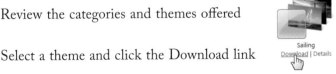

4 Select a theme and click the Download link

5 When prompted, select Open to download the theme

6 The theme is installed and activated on your computer

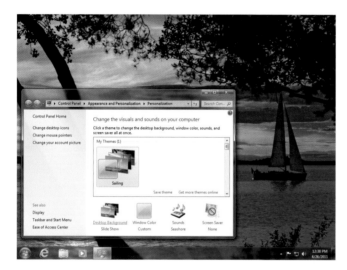

Hot tip

Themes you download are added to the My Themes section, as are themes that you modify.

7 Select Desktop Background to view the set of pictures included in the theme, and to adjust display sequencing

Don't forget

You can select which images get displayed, how frequently images are changed, and whether the display is random or sequential.

55

Create a theme

1 Open Personalization, select the existing theme, then select Desktop Background for that theme

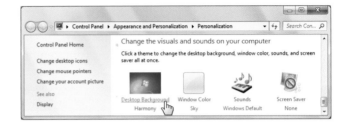

2 Click Browse, select the picture folder containing the images required and click OK

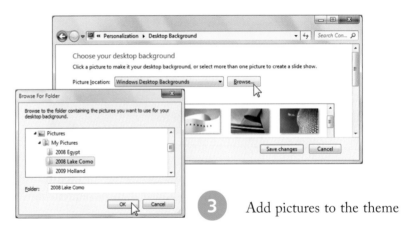

3 Add pictures to the theme

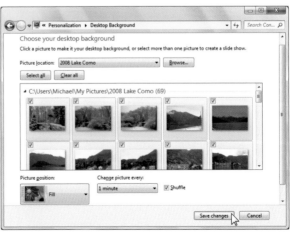

Hot tip

The modified theme is added to My Themes section, as an unsaved theme.

4 Select Windows Color to view the settings, and click Save changes, if you make any revisions

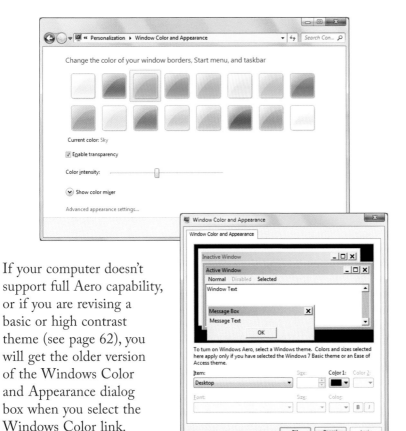

Don't forget

You can enable or disable transparency and adjust color intensity. Click Show color mixer, to adjust the hue, saturation and brightness.

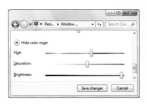

If your computer doesn't support full Aero capability, or if you are revising a basic or high contrast theme (see page 62), you will get the older version of the Windows Color and Appearance dialog box when you select the Windows Color link.

Sound scheme

1 Click the Sounds link for the scheme you are creating, to change the sounds associated with Windows actions

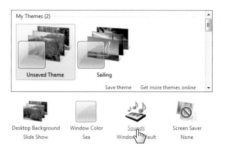

2 Select the Sound Scheme box and choose from the predefined sound schemes to find which you prefer

3 Select a program event such as Windows Logon and click Test to listen to the sound

4 Click Browse to associate a different audio file with that Windows action

5 Click Save As to save a revised sound scheme under a new name

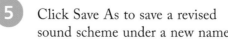

Screen saver

In the days when a static image could burn into the screen, a screen saver with an animated display was an essential. This is no longer a problem, but the screen saver can still improve security and privacy by hiding your information when you leave the computer. To add a screen saver to your theme:

1 Click the Screen Saver link for your theme

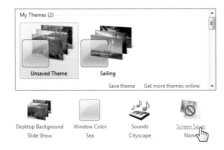

2 Click the Screen saver box to show the list available

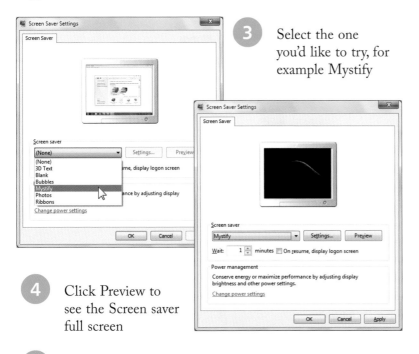

3 Select the one you'd like to try, for example Mystify

4 Click Preview to see the Screen saver full screen

5 Set the delay time, click Settings to review adjustments, and click OK to add the screen saver to the theme

Don't forget

To ensure that the password will be required to access the account and applications, select the option On resume, display logon screen.

Save the theme

Don't forget

The Unsaved Theme is stored as the Custom theme, until you choose to Save theme.

1 When you have finished amending your theme, select the Save theme option

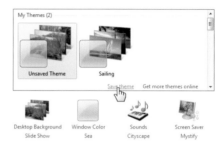

2 Provide a name for your new theme and click Save

3 The theme remains in My Themes, under its new name

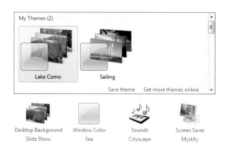

Hot tip

If you cannot see the AppData folder in your User folder, you may need to Show hidden files and folders (see page 106).

The theme file is stored in the user's applications data area e.g. c:\users\Michael\AppData\Local\Microsoft\Windows\Themes, along with any Windows 7 themes that have been downloaded.

To make the theme available to other users:

1 Right-click the theme and select Save theme for sharing

2 Specify the name and folder for the theme and click Save

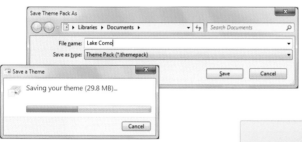

Don't forget

If you have a number of photos as background images, the theme can be quite large.

3 The background images, colors, sounds and other settings for your theme are saved in a file of type .themepack

Lake Como

Downloading this file or selecting it on a shared network drive will make the theme available to the other users.

You can remove themes from My Themes when they are no longer needed.

Hot tip

By default the themepack file will be saved in your documents folder, but you can choose any location, for example a HomeGroup folder.

1 Make sure that the theme is not currently selected

2 Right-click and select Delete theme

3 Click Yes to confirm the removal

Other theme types

Windows 7 also provides a number of basic and high-contrast themes. These may be used where performance is an issue or where the computer does not support Aero operation, or when improved readability is desired.

 In Personalization, select the Windows 7 Basic theme

Note that there is no transparency with this theme.

2 Select a high-contrast themes, for example High Contrast White, to see how the display is simplified and clarified

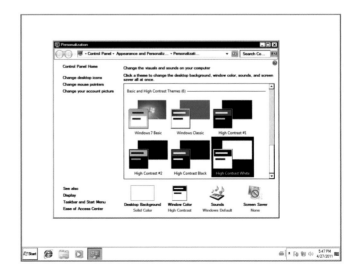

4 Windows your way

Set up Windows the way you like it, by configuring the Start menu and the taskbar, pinning applications to make them easier to access, using jump lists , setting up automatic logon or shutdown, and using shortcut icons and keyboard shortcuts. You can also optimize the way that the mouse operates for you.

64 Customize the Start menu

66 Configure the taskbar

68 Notification area

69 Toolbars

70 Language bar

71 Pin programs to Taskbar

72 Pin programs to Start menu

73 Jump lists

75 Automatic logon

76 Automated shutdown

78 Change shortcut icon

79 Add keyboard shortcut

80 Mouse settings

Customize the Start menu

You can change the default Start menu to make it easier or more convenient to use.

1   Right-click the Start button and then select the Properties option

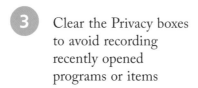

2   The Taskbar and Start menu properties are displayed, with the Start Menu tab selected

3   Clear the Privacy boxes to avoid recording recently opened programs or items

4   Clear then reselect the boxes, to empty the lists and restart the records

5   Click the Customize button to adjust the way the links, icons and menus operate in the Start menu

6   For items such as Computer and Control Panel, there are three options offered:
    ● Display as a link
    ● Display as a menu
    ● Don't display this item

7   Items such as Connect To and Default Programs are either selected (displayed) or not selected (omitted)

8   Options such as Open submenus when I pause are enabled when selected

9   If you have made any changes now or previously, click Use Default Settings to restore all the original values

To illustrate the use of menus versus links:

1 Select Start and click the Computer button to display the computer folder

2 Open the Start menu properties, click Customize and select Display as Menu for the Computer item

3 Click OK to save changes then OK to close Properties

4 Select Start then click the Computer button, and the drives are now displayed in the list format

Don't forget

A right-arrow is added to the Computer button, to indicate that it will reveal a list. You'll see this same convention on program buttons.

65

Hot tip

Note that for clarity the Desktop background in this illustration has been changed to plain white.

Configure the taskbar

You can view and change the Taskbar properties also.

1 Right-click the Taskbar and select Properties

2 The Taskbar and Start menu properties are displayed, with the Taskbar tab selected

3 Unlock the taskbar, from the menu or the properties, to allow moving and resizing

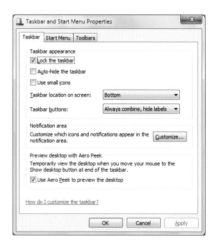

4 You can also select the Location bar and choose a position

By default, the Taskbar uses large icons for the shortcuts and tasks, but always combines similar tasks and hides labels.

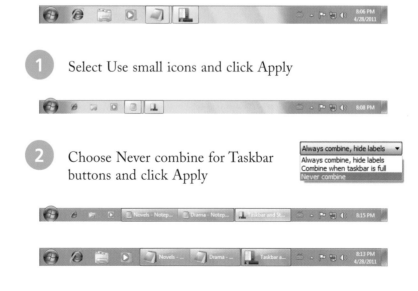

1 Select Use small icons and click Apply

2 Choose Never combine for Taskbar buttons and click Apply

From the Taskbar properties you can enable Aero Peek to preview
the desktop and show the desktop icons and gadgets.

1 Assume you have a number of applications open, with
their windows distributed across the desktop

You get a similar effect
if you move the mouse
over the thumbnail for a
task, but in this case the
window for the selected
task does appear

2 Move the mouse pointer to the Show desktop button, at
the end of the Taskbar, on the right

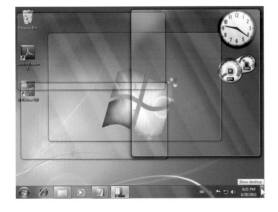

3 The open windows are replaced by outlines, and you can
see the remaining contents of the desktop

4 Click the Show desktop button to minimize all open
windows, so you can select icons or gadgets

Hot tip

Click the Show desktop
button again to redisplay
the application windows
that were open initially.

Notification area

There are two ways to configure the Notification area:

1 Click the Customize button in the Taskbar properties

2 Click Show hidden icons in the Notification area and select Customize

3 Select which icons and notifications appear on the taskbar

4 Click Turn System icons on or off, to specify which system tasks will put notifications on the Taskbar

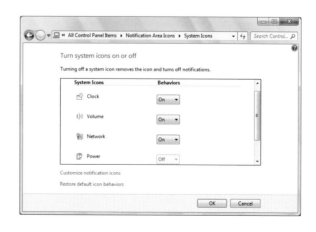

Toolbars

You can add toolbars to the Taskbar to give quick access to various features in Windows.

To add a toolbar:

1 Right-click the Taskbar, select Toolbars and click the toolbar you want

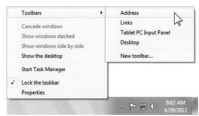

2 The toolbar, in this case Address, is added to the Taskbar

You can enter a web page address and go straight to the website, or you can enter folder paths to open a folder on your hard drive.

3 If there's no room on the Taskbar for the full contents of the toolbar, an up-arrow is added next to the name

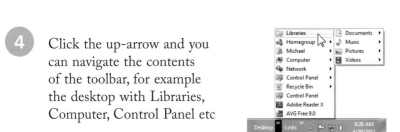

4 Click the up-arrow and you can navigate the contents of the toolbar, for example the desktop with Libraries, Computer, Control Panel etc

You can also manage toolbars from the Taskbar properties page:

1 Open the Taskbar properties and click the Toolbars tab, then set or clear the box for any toolbar

Don't forget

The toolbars that have been selected for display on the Taskbar will be flagged with a tick.

69

Hot tip

Click New toolbar from the Toolbars menu and assign any folder as a toolbar, for example, the Network folder.

Language bar

If you have multiple input languages or keyboards installed on your computer, Language bar icons are added to the taskbar.

1 There are multiple keyboards (US and UK) available for the computer - left click the icon to see the details

2 Multiple input languages (US and UK English) have been specified on this computer

3 Multiple input languages (English and French) and multiple keyboards have been defined

To view or change the language bar set up:

1 Right-click either icon, language or keyboard to list the options

2 Select Settings, then click the Language Bar tab

3 Click the General tab to amend language or keyboard details

Pin programs to Taskbar

You can pin a program directly to the taskbar so you can open it quickly, without browsing for the program in the Start menu.

To add the program:

1 Click Start, navigate to the program in the Start menu, right-click the entry and click Pin to Taskbar

2 Alternatively, click and drag the program or program shortcut, and drop it on the Taskbar

3 If the program is currently running, right-click its task button, and select Pin this program to taskbar

4 The programs are added as shortcuts on the Taskbar

71

To remove a program from the Taskbar:

1 Right-click the Taskbar shortcut and select Unpin this program from taskbar

Folders and drives do not have the Pin to taskbar option on their right-click menus, but there is still a way to add them to the shortcut area of the Taskbar.

1 Locate an icon or shortcut for the folder or drive, and drag it onto the Taskbar

2 Drop the item onto the Windows Explorer shortcut

Pin programs to Start menu

You can add programs to the Start menu, where they appear above the recently used programs on the top level.

To add the program:

1 Locate the program in the Start menu, right-click the entry and then click Pin to Start Menu

2 The programs are added at the top of the Start menu pane

3 A line is inserted between the pinned entries and the most recently used programs

You can add a folder, but again you need to use drag & drop:

1 Drag the folder or shortcut over the Taskbar

2 Drop the folder onto the Start button

To remove an entry that you have pinned to the Start menu:

1 Right-click the entry and select Unpin from Start Menu (for programs) or Remove from this list (folders)

Jump lists

Lists of recent items, i.e. files, folders or websites, can be displayed for individual programs in the form of Jump lists, so called because of the way that they appear. You'll find Jump lists on the Start menu and on the Taskbar.

1 Select Start to display the top level pane with the most recently used programs and any added entries

Hot tip

If you have cleared the option to Open submenus when I pause, then you should click the arrow to display the Jump list.

☑ Open submenus when I pause on them with the mouse pointer

2 The arrow indicates that a Jump list is available

3 Hold the mouse pointer over an entry, and the Jump list appears

Don't forget

Click the program name on the Start menu or on the Jump list on the Taskbar, to start a new instance of the program, with an empty document.

4 Select an entry to open the application with that file

5 Right-click the Task button, and the Jump list is displayed

6 The application name, and the option to pin/unpin the program is included on the taskbar version of the Jump list

Hot tip

The selected file is at the top of the list, being the most recently opened.

73

...cont'd

You can open files from the Jump list on the Taskbar.

1 Select an entry to open that file in the application, and that entry becomes the top item on the Jump list

2 To fix an entry in position, right-click it and select Pin to this list, and it is added to the Pinned section at the top

3 You can view, add and remove pinned items on the Jump lists on the Start menu as well as the Taskbar

Automatic logon

You may want Windows to start up immediately, without the need to select your user account and enter your password. You can do this by enabling auto-logon. Sign on with your account and:

1 Press the Windows logo key + R to display the Run box

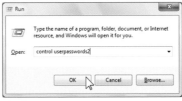

2 Type the command control userpasswords2 (see page 374) and press Enter

3 User Accounts displays, with your account selected

4 Clear the box Users must enter a user name and password to use this computer, then click OK

5 Type your password, then enter it again to confirm

When you power on the computer, it starts up fully, without any need for user interaction.

Automated shutdown

You can also automate the shutdown process, for example to end Windows after a certain time has elapsed.

1 Display the Run box (press WinLogo + R)

2 Type the command e.g. shutdown.exe /s /t 600 where /t nnn is the timeout period, and then press Enter

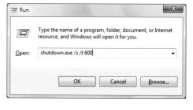

3 A message is displayed and Shutdown is initiated, to complete after the specified timeout period (ten minutes in this example,

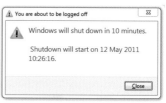

4 For any delay greater than 600 seconds, the message is displayed briefly in the notification area, then removed

Note that the /f (force) option is implied when a timeout value greater than 0 is specified for the /t option. This will force all running applications to close without forewarning users.

If necessary, you can cancel the shutdown, at any time during the timeout period.

1 Display the Run box, and type the command: shutdown.exe /a then click OK

2 A message is shown in the notification area and the pending shutdown will be cancelled

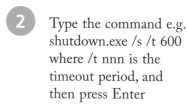
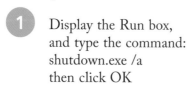

You can create shortcuts on the desktop for Shutdown and Abort commands. First however, you must show the desktop icons.

1 Right-click the desktop and select View, then click Show desktop icons

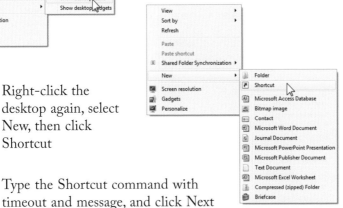

2 Right-click the desktop again, select New, then click Shortcut

3 Type the Shortcut command with timeout and message, and click Next

4 Accept the suggested name for the shortcut, or type a name that you prefer and click Finish

5 The shortcut is added to the desktop

6 Add a similar shortcut for the Abort command needed to cancel a scheduled shutdown

77

Change shortcut icon

When you have created a shortcut on the desktop, you can change the shortcut icon to make it easier to spot.

1 Right-click the shortcut and select Properties

2 Ensure the Shortcut tab is selected, and click the Change Icon button

3 Since there are no icons stored in the Shutdown program, click OK

4 Windows lists the icons stored in Shell32.dll, which has icons for actions such as Shutdown, Abort and Logoff

5 Choose a suitable icon for the shortcut and click OK

6 Repeat the process for any other shortcuts you have created

7 The shortcuts are shown on the desktop with their new icon images

78

Add keyboard shortcut

You can assign a combination of keys to your desktop shortcut, then you can run the shortcut by pressing the appropriate key combination.

1 Right-click the shortcut, and then select Properties

2 Click the Shortcut tab

3 Click in the Shortcut key box, which initially says None

4 Press the key on your keyboard that you want to use, for example Z

5 Windows assumes the additional keys Ctrl+Alt, giving a key combination, e.g. Ctrl+Alt+Z

6 Click OK to apply this key combination to your shortcut

You can press a key combination, for example Ctrl+Shift+Z, and Windows will apply this. However, make sure to avoid combinations that are already in use.

To find comprehensive lists of existing keyboard shortcuts:

1 Select Start and click Help and Support

2 Search for Keyboard shortcuts

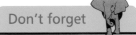

Don't forget

If you're prompted for an administrator password or confirmation, type the password or provide the confirmation as requested.

Beware

You can't use the Esc, Enter, Tab, Spacebar, PrtScn, Shift, or Backspace keys to create a keyboard shortcut.

Mouse settings

You can tailor the mouse settings to meet your needs.

1 Click Start, type Mouse and select Change mouse settings

2 From the Buttons tab, you can switch the functions of the right and left buttons

3 Move the slider to adjust the speed of the double-click action

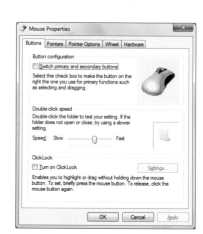

4 From the Pointers tab, click the Scheme bar to choose the style of mouse pointer you prefer

5 The various pointers in the selected set are displayed

6 From the Pointer Options tab, adjust the pointer speed

7 Select Snap To to move the pointer to the default button when you open a dialog box

8 Click OK to apply any changes, or click Cancel to keep existing settings

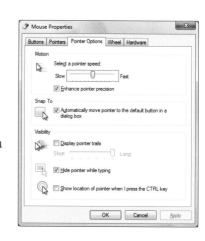

Don't forget

Double-click the folder to test the speed, and make it faster or slower as it suits you.

Hot tip

Pointer schemes include large, extra large and high contrast types.

Don't forget

Display pointer trails, or show the location of the pointer when you press Ctrl, to make the pointer easier to spot.

5 Manage files and folders

Use Windows Explorer to manage your files, folders and libraries, sorting and organizing the contents and linking to the locations that hold the required data. Windows provides libraries for documents, music, pictures and videos but you can define your own libraries for your projects or to manage information such as family history.

82 Files, folders and libraries

83 Windows Explorer

85 Windows Explorer layout

86 Windows Explorer toolbar

87 Folder contents

88 Change your view

89 Sort contents

91 Windows 7 libraries

92 Add a location

94 Location unavailable

95 Arrange library contents

96 Create a library

97 Adjust properties

98 Customize folders

Files, folders and libraries

Data storage devices are defined as blocks of fixed-size sectors. These are managed by the file system, which defines a root folder with lists of file names and folder names. Each folder can contain further file and folder names. This gives a hierarchical structure.

Files of the same or related types will usually be stored in the same folder. For example, your main hard drive will be organized along the following lines:

The root folder includes the Program Files folder which contains applications installed on your system, and the Users folder which contains the folders and files associated with each user account. In your user account folder, you will see a number of folders including your Music folder. The example shows the files and folders associated with a particular artist.

Windows 7 goes a stage further and associates folders with similar content into Libraries. The folders included in the library may actually be stored separately on the disk, or may be on a different disk on the computer or elsewhere on the network.

To manage the file, folders and libraries, Windows uses the Windows Explorer application.

Windows Explorer

There are many different ways to start Windows Explorer or change the particular files and folders being displayed.

1 Click the Windows Explorer shortcut icon on the Taskbar, or right-click the Start button and select Open Windows Explorer

Don't forget

You can select Start, All Programs, Accessories to select Windows Explorer from the Start menu and display Libraries. Press the Windows Logo key + E, to open Windows Explorer with Computer.

2 The Libraries folder is displayed, and the taskbar shortcut becomes an active task button

3 Click an entry on the Navigation pane to display those contents instead, for example select Computer

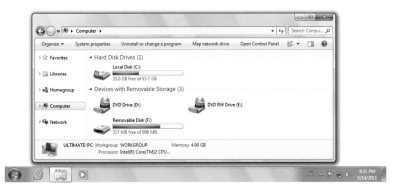

Hot tip

Click Start and select the desired folder from the Start menu, to open it in a new window.

4 To retain the current entry, and open another, right-click the newly required entry and choose Open in new window

...cont'd

The task bar button for the program initially shows a single icon. When you open a second window, another icon is stacked. When you open three or more windows, a third icon added.

1 Move the mouse pointer over the task button, and thumbnails for the open windows are displayed

2 Click on a thumbnail to switch to that window

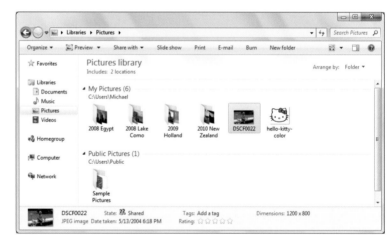

84

3 To change the elements displayed for Windows Explorer, click Organize button and select Layout

4 Select an unticked entry to add it, or select a ticked entry to remove it from the window

Windows Explorer layout

This shows all the elements for Windows Explorer, including those normally hidden.

Back and Forward   Menu bar   Address bar   Toolbar   Library pane   Search box   Resize or close

Don't forget

The Menu bar was featured in previous versions of Windows, but is not normally used in Windows 7.

Navigation pane   Contents pane   Details pane   Preview pane

Windows Explorer preview

The type of preview displayed depends on the file type. For documents and PDFs, you will see part of the first page. For music files, you'll get a Play link.

Beware

For file types Windows does not recognize, or when a folder is selected, you will see a message saying: No preview available.

85

Windows Explorer toolbar

The toolbar always includes the Organize button on the left and three buttons on the right, for the commands Change your view, Show (or Hide) the preview pane, and Get help.

For Favorites, no other commands are offered.

Libraries has an extra command, New library.

Documents has the Share with, Burn and New folder commands.

Music has the Play all command (as does the Videos library).

Pictures adds the Slide show command.

If the window size is too narrow to contain all the items, a side arrow is added. You click this to display the additional items.

In these examples, Computer has additional commands to Map network drive and Open Control Panel. Network has an additional command to Add a wireless device.

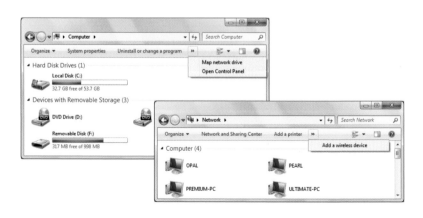

Folder contents

You'll also find that the way in which the contents of folders are displayed varies depending on the type of file involved.

In these example views, the Navigation, Details and Library panes have been hidden, to put the emphasis on the Contents pane.

Documents
Details view:
- Name
- Date modified
- Type
- Size

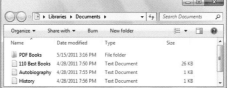

Music
Details view:
- Name
- Contributing artists
- Album
- Track number
- Title

Pictures
Large Icons view

Data Folders
Medium Icons view

Libraries
Tiles view

Since views can easily be varied, you may find the setup for some of the folders on your system may be different.

87

Don't forget

Documents and Music both use the Details view, but the fields displayed are appropriate to the particular file type.

Hot tip

The Videos library also uses the Large Icons view, while Network and Computers use the Tiles view, the same as Libraries.

Change your view

1 Open the folder whose view you want to change, and click the arrow next to the Change your view button

2 Click the slider, then drag while holding down the mouse button, with changes being applied as the slider moves

3 Release the pointer at the desired view, and the changes are applied to the folder and any subfolders it contains

4 Alternatively click any view, for example Tiles or the new Content view, to display that view immediately

Sort contents

You can sort the contents of any folder by name, date, size or other attributes, using the Details view. You can also group or filter the contents.

1 Open the folder and select the Details view

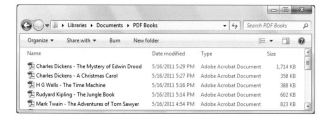

2 Click on a header such as Size and the entries are sorted

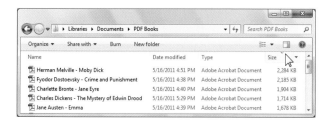

3 Click the header again, and the sequence is reversed

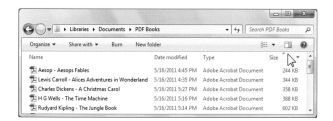

4 Change the view, and the sequencing that you have set up will be retained for the new view

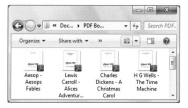

...cont'd

You can reorganize the contents from views other than Details.

1 Open the folder, and right-click an empty part of the Contents, being sure to avoid the icon borders

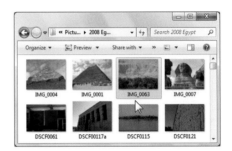

2 Select Sort by, to change the sort field or sequence

3 Select Group by, and select the field (for example Size) by which you want to arrange the entries in ranges

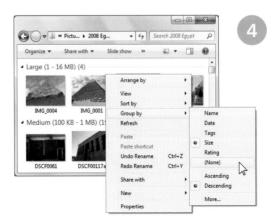

4 To remove the grouping, select Group by and then (None)

Windows 7 libraries

At install, Windows 7 has four libraries each with two locations:

Documents	My Documents, Public Documents
Music	My Music, Public Music
Pictures	My Pictures, Public Pictures
Videos	My Videos, Public Videos

1 Open Windows Explorer to show libraries

2 Double-click a library, for example Pictures, to open it

3 The Library pane indicates there are two locations, and the folders contained in each of these locations are listed

Don't forget

You can include other locations in the existing libraries, and you can also create your own libraries (see page 96).

Hot tip

You can also open the Pictures library from the Navigation pane, or from the Pictures button on the Start menu.

Add a location

1 Select the Locations link in the Libraries pane, then click the Add button

Pictures library
Includes: 2 locations

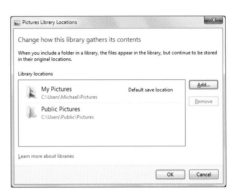

2 Double-click the drive containing the required folder

3 Select the folder and then click Include Folder

4 The selected folder becomes a new location in the library

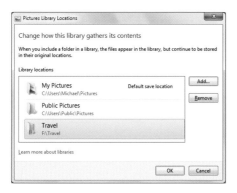

5 Click OK and the contents of the location are displayed

Removable drives

1 Select a folder on a DVD or on a USB flash drive, then click Include Folder

2 You are warned this folder cannot be included

Location unavailable

If you've added folders from a removable hard disk or from a network drive, there may be times when they are not available.

1 Right-click the Safely Remove Hardware icon, and select the external hard disk

2 The drive is prepared for removal and a message is then displayed

3 The library now shows folders from this drive as Empty

4 Select the Locations link, and the folder from the detached drive is shown as unavailable

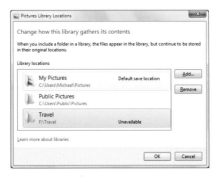

Arrange library contents

Library contents are usually organized by location and folder, but you can change this if you wish.

1 Click the Arrange by box, initially Folder, and select an alternative e.g. Month

2 The contents of all the folders are gathered together in groups by month and displayed as stacks

3 Select a stack and press Enter (or double-click) and the contents of that stack are displayed, grouped by Day

Don't forget

There is an option to Clear Changes which removes any sorting or grouping and reverts to the default display.

Hot tip

The Details pane shows the number of pictures in the selected stack. If no stack is selected, it shows the total number of stacks.

Beware

When you've selected an arrangement, there's no Clear changes, but you can select Folders and that option will be restored.

95

Create a library

You can create a library of your own to manage other collections, for example project plans, or family history.

1 Open the Libraries folder and click the button marked New Library

2 Type the library name, e.g. Projects and press Enter

The first folder that you add will be assigned as the save location, but you can change this later if you wish.

3 Double-click the new library to open it, and you'll be invited to add folders

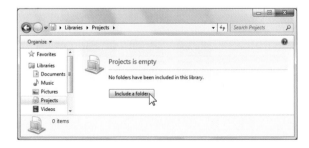

Adjust properties

When you've added folders, your library appears on the navigation pane and shows locations and folders, just like default libraries.

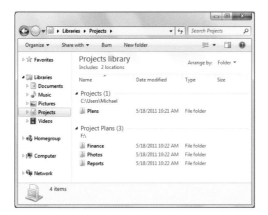

Don't forget

From the right-click menu you can open the library in a new window, share it with other users, and hide or show it in the navigation pane, as well as displaying properties.

1 Right-click the library name in the Navigation pane or in the Libraries folder and select Properties

From here you can:

- Select a location and click Set save location

- Include a new folder or location

- Remove an existing location

- Hide or show in Navigation pane

- Check Sharing status

- Restore defaults after making changes

- Apply the changes you make

Hot tip

By default, the library will be optimized for the type of file it contains, or for general items if the file types are mixed. However, you can choose a particular file type if you prefer.

2 Click OK to save your changes, or click Cancel to abandon your changes

Customize folders

1 Right-click the folder and select Properties

2 Click the Customize tab on the Properties panel

3 To specify a folder picture, click the Choose File button

4 Find and select the picture image and click Open

5 Click OK on the Properties panel to add the image

6 The folder image is inserted and displayed

6 Searching techniques

Windows provides many ways to help you find the programs, utilities and information that you need. There's a search box on the Start menu, and in each folder window. The Address bar helps identify locations. Indexing speeds up searches, favorites and saved searches let you revisit places.

100	Computer search
101	Start menu search
102	Address bar
104	Navigation pane
106	Folder and search options
108	Indexing options
110	Enhanced search
112	Using search filters
113	Favorites
114	Save searches
115	Move and copy

Computer search

When you are looking for a file on your system and you know the name, you might decide to use the Computer folder, since that's where you find all the drives.

1 Select Start, Computer (or press WinLogo + E)

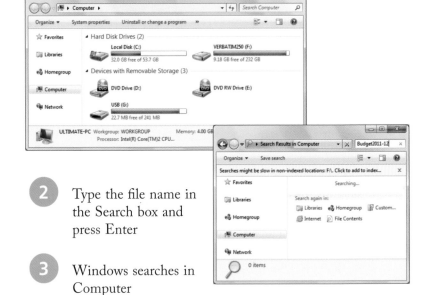

2 Type the file name in the Search box and press Enter

3 Windows searches in Computer

4 The green bar shows the progress of the search

5 As each matching result is found, they are displayed, with file paths, in this case Documents library and a USB drive

Start menu search

You can also use the Start menu quick search box. This is excellent when you are looking for a file to open or a program to run.

1 Click the Start button

2 Begin typing the program or file name - no need to click the search box

3 As you type, matching files are listed in groups

4 Press Enter to open or run the top entry

5 Click any other entry to open or run it

6 To see where the file is stored, without opening or running, right-click and select Open file location

7 The appropriate folder will be opened, in this case the user's Documents folder

8 You can now work with the file, e.g. send to another user

Don't forget

The search results are based on the text in the file name, file tags and other file properties. Only files that have been indexed are included in the results.

Hot tip

As you continue to type the file name, the search results are refined more closely until the one you want becomes evident.

101

Beware

Note that the Start menu search doesn't find files on the USB flash drive, since these drive types cannot be indexed.

Address bar

The address bar at the top of the folder contains the location path of the folder or library, and you can use this to check the actual folder path and to switch to other libraries and folders.

1 Click the space in the address bar to the right of the location names (and left of the down-arrow)

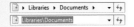
2 The current location is shown in the standard drive and folder path format

3 Click anywhere in the folder to revert to the location path

4 Click a location name, for example the user name, to switch to that location

5 Click the arrow to the right of a location name, for example Users, to display all the folders in that location

6 When the folders are displayed, you can select any folder to switch to that location

Don't forget

The current folder location, in this case the active user, is shown highlighted in the list.

7 Click the back arrow to redisplay the previous folder

8 If the address bar entry is truncated to the left (indicated by a double bracket, you'll need to widen the window to see the missing portion

9 Click the arrow at the left to see the top level locations

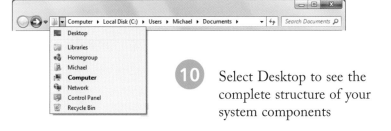

10 Select Desktop to see the complete structure of your system components

Hot tip

As this illustrates, the libraries, user folders, network folders etc are included as special folders in Desktop, along with Computer and the desktop icons. Note that Windows Explorer is also used to display the Control Panel.

103

Navigation pane

Don't forget

If the Navigation folder isn't displayed, click the Organize button on the toolbar and select Layout, Navigation pane.

The Navigation pane allows you to explore and select folders in your libraries or on the drives in your Computer folder.

1 Open Windows Explorer at any folder and you'll see the Navigation pane with its five sections, on the left side

2 Move the mouse pointer over the Navigation pane and triangles appear alongside the section names

3 Click a white triangle(▷) to expand a list or a black triangle (◢) to collapse a list

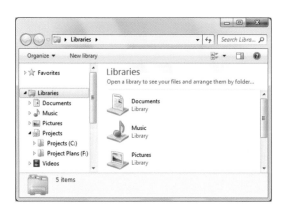

Hot tip

Double-click any name to expand that folder and display its contents with the one action.

4 Select a folder name to display its contents and find files

...cont'd

5 Similarly, you can explore the drives, folders and files in your Computer folder

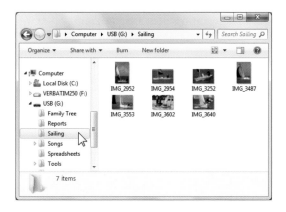

You can explore all of the sections of your system in one list.

1 Right-click an empty section of the Navigation pane and select Show all folders

You'll see the whole contents of your system, starting at Desktop.

If the entries in the Navigation pane are collapsed, you can select Expand to current folder, to automatically expand the navigation pane to the folder that's selected in the folder window.

Don't forget

Again, you click the triangles or double-click the names to expand and collapse the entries.

Hot tip

Alternatively, you can select Organize and click Folder and search options then click the box to Show all folders.

105

Folder and search options

You can change the way files and folders function and how items are displayed on your computer using Folder and search options.

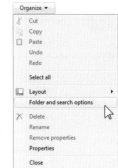

1 Open a folder and select Organize, then click Folder and search options

2 When Folder Options displays, select the General tab

From this panel you can:

- Choose to open each folder in the same window, or in its own window

- Use double-click to open an item, or use the browser style single click to point and select items

- Control the operation of the Navigation pane

- Restore defaults after previous changes

3 Select the View tab

From here you can:

- Apply the View for the current folder to all folders of the same type

- Reset folders

- Apply advanced settings to files and folders.

- Restore defaults after making changes

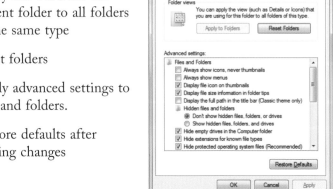

4 Scroll down to reveal the remaining settings

Among these settings are options to:

- Automatically open the folders that you were using when you last shut down Windows whenever you start your computer, thus restoring your work session

- Hide or show file tips that display when you point to files

- Disable the use of the preview pane, to improve performance

5 Select the Search tab

The Search settings let you manage what to search and how to search.

- Choose whether to search contents of files when you are looking in non-indexed locations

- Include or exclude subfolders in search results

- Accept or reject partial matches

- Use natural language search

- Include system directories and compressed files

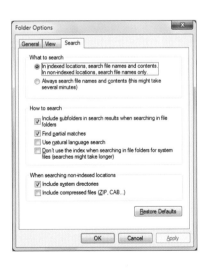

Again, you can click the Restore Defaults button to undo any changes that might previously have been applied.

Indexing options

When you add a folder to one of the libraries, that folder will automatically be indexed. You can also add locations to the index without using libraries.

1   Select Start, type Indexing Options and press Enter

2   Click Modify then expand the folder lists and select new locations to index, for example Books, and click OK

3 The contents of the new locations are added to the index

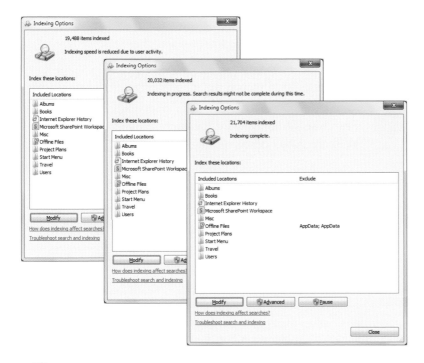

Don't forget

Indexing proceeds in the background, and may slow down during periods of user activity.

Beware

If required, you can press Pause to suspend indexing, but you are recommended to do this for no more that 15 minutes at a time.

4 To make changes to the settings for indexing, click the Advanced button and select the Index Settings or File Types tab

Hot tip

You can choose to index encrypted files, ignore accents on characters for matching, change the index location, or delete and rebuild the index. You can also specify file types that are indexed by properties only or contents plus properties.

Enhanced search

The file name search, as discussed on page 100, can be enhanced to help with files that appear difficult to locate. There are several facilities which can be helpful depending on where you're searching and what you're searching for.

Add operators

Refine your search using the operators AND, OR, and NOT, to specify file properties or text, for example:

1 Search in all libraries for file containing the text values William AND Shakespeare

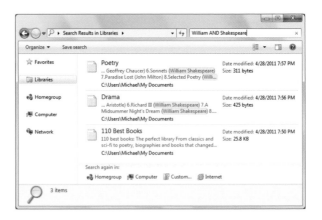

2 Reduce the number of matches by adding a restriction William AND Shakespeare NOT Wordsworth

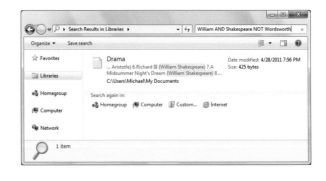

Add search filters

Search filters are a new feature in Windows 7 that make it easy to search for files by properties such as Author or Size or Type.

...cont'd

To add a search filter:

1 Open the folder, library, or drive that you want to search

2 Click in the search box, and then select a search filter

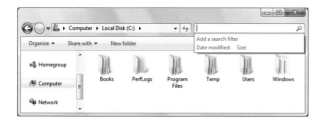

The libraries have numerous additional search filters based on the type of file the library is optimized for.

The search filters displayed for the libraries are:

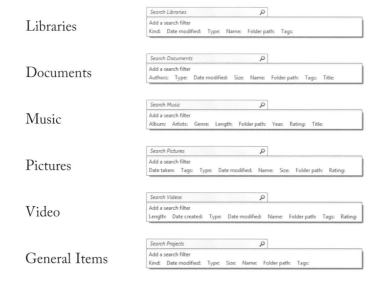

Libraries

Documents

Music

Pictures

Video

General Items

Hot tip

Just a few search filters are offered for drives and folders, but you can specify additional filters in the search expression.

Don't forget

You can't specify which search filters you'll see, but you can change the type of file that a library is optimized for (see page 97), and this will change the search filters offered.

Using search filters

1 Select the folder to search, and specify your search text if you know part of the name or contents

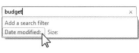

2 To refine the results, click an available filter, for example Date modified

3 Select one of the date ranges specified, choose a specific date, or choose a range of dates (select the first, press Shift, then press the second date to define the range)

4 If there are still too many matches, you can select a second filter, such as Size

5 Choose one of the size ranges specified, such as Small (10-100 KB)

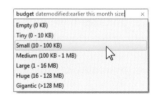

6 Each time you make a change, you get a list of files that satisfy all of the criteria specified at that time

Using keywords to refine a search

If you want to filter on a property that doesn't appear when you click in the search box, you can use special keywords. These are made up of a property name followed by a colon, sometimes an operator, and then a value. The keywords are not case sensitive. For example:

1 Search for a file with file name beginning Budget

System.FileName:~<"Budget" ×

Don't forget

You can use the AND, OR and NOT operators in combination with the search filters and the system keywords.

112

Hot tip

The operators include:
- ~< Begins with
- = Matches exactly
- ~= Contains
- ~! Doesn't contain

Other keywords include:
- System.Author
- System.DateModified
- System.Kind
- System.Size

Favorites

The Navigation pane includes a section where you keep shortcuts to the locations on your system that you may often need to review. To view your Windows Explorer favorites:

1 Open any folder and select the Favorites section which initially has three default shortcuts - Desktop, Downloads and Recent Places

Don't forget

Favorites can also be used to save searches that you may want to use again.

2 Use any of the methods discussed to go to folders that you would like to add to Favorites

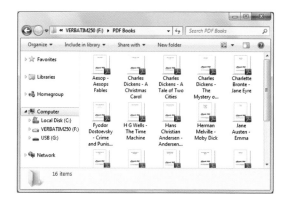

3 For each folder, right-click Favorites in the Navigation pane and select Add current location to Favorites

Hot tip

You can use this menu to sort the Favorites, or to restore the defaults if you have removed any of them. To remove a Favorite, default or new, you right-click the name and select Remove.

4 Select Favorites to see the changes

Save searches

If you regularly search for a certain group of files, it might be
useful to save your search. To save a search:

1 Carry out a search as previously described

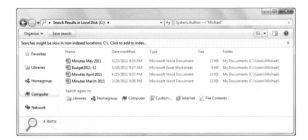

2 When the search is complete, click the Save search button

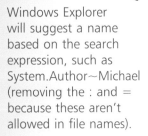
3 Type a name for the search, and then click Save

A shortcut to the saved search will be added to the Favorites
section of the navigation pane.

The search itself will be saved in the Searches folder, which you
will find in your personal folder.

Move and copy

You can use the Search results and the Navigation pane to help move or copy files and folders from their original locations.

1 Use Search to display the items you wish to copy or move (in this case all Word files in Users named Minutes)

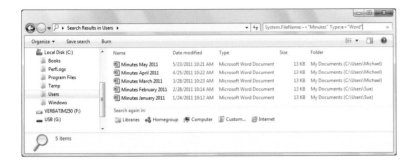

Hot tip

Select the first item, then press Shift and select the last in a range, or press Ctrl and add individual items to the selection.

2 Select the items to copy, using Shift or Ctrl as necessary

3 Expand the Navigation pane (clicking the triangles, not the folder names) to show the target folder

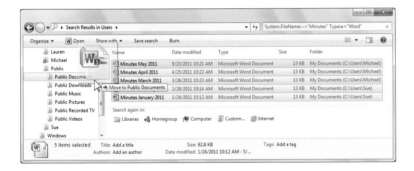

Don't forget

If the destination is on the same drive as the selected items, the default is Move, otherwise the default becomes Copy. However, you can still make your preferred selection.

4 Right-click part of the selection and drag the items onto the Navigation pane, over the name of the target folder

5 Release the mouse and click Move here or Copy here as appropriate, and the files are added to the destination

...cont'd

Don't forget

You don't have to use Search, you can Move or Copy from the original location using the same techniques.

6 As soon as the move takes place, Windows Search adjusts the search results, in this case showing Public documents

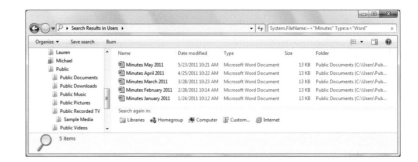

7 Select the target folder, and you'll see all the items added

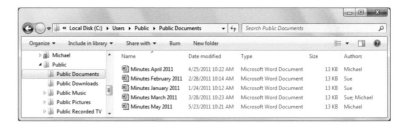

Hot tip

In this case, documents that are being prepared by more than one author have been moved to the Public area.

Drag with left mouse button

1 Left-click and drag, then release the mouse button over the destination, and Windows will Move or Copy immediately, with no menu

Force move or copy

With either left-click or right-click, you can force the action you want, whether the same or different drives are involved.

Beware

Don't use the left-click option unless you are very familiar with it, since there's no opportunity to confirm the action.

1 Press Shift as you drag and Move becomes the default

→ Move to Public Documents

2 Press Ctrl as you drag and Copy becomes the default

+ Copy to Public Documents

7 Built-in programs

There are programs built into Windows to help you in many areas, including text processing, scan, fax, and image management, and calculations. There are tools to write information to CD/DVD, and record sound and images. There are also special tools available when you need to work in depth with your computer.

118 Windows applications

119 Text management

121 Other text applications

123 Image management

126 Computations

128 Disc Writers

130 Utilities

132 Command Prompt

133 Windows PowerShell

134 System Tools

135 Administrative Tools

136 Desktop Gadgets

Windows applications

The main purpose of Windows is to manage the hardware and devices on your computer and to provide the operating environment to run Windows applications such as Microsoft Office and Adobe Creative Suite. However, there are numerous applications already included in Windows. To see what is on offer:

1 Select Start and click All Programs

Separately supplied
Desktop Gadgets
Disc Writer
Image management
Text management
Administrative Tools

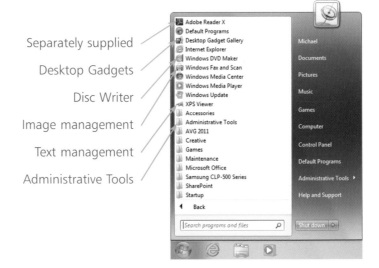

2 Click Accessories to expand this folder

Computation
Text management
Image management
Utilities
Text management
System Tools
Administrative Tools

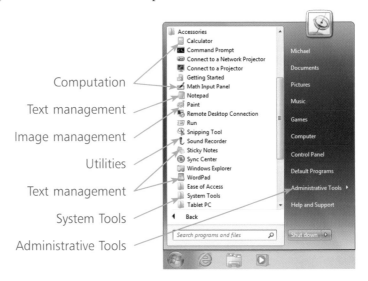

Text management

There are several applications that provide various levels of text management capabilities.

Notepad

Notepad is a basic text-editing program and it's most commonly used to view or edit text files, usually with the .txt file name extension, but any text file can be handled.

1 Select Start, All Programs, Accessories, Notepad, then type some text, pressing Enter to start a new line

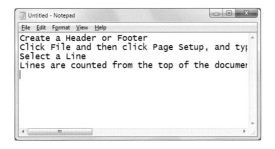

2 Parts of the lines may be hidden, if lines are longer than the width of the window

3 Select Format, Word Wrap to fit the text within the window width

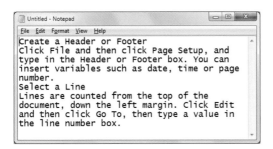

4 Select Edit to cut, copy and paste text, or to insert a Time/Date stamp into the document

5 Select File to save or print the document

119

Hot tip

Select Format, Font to choose the Font, Font Style and Size. This will apply to all the text in the whole document.

Don't forget

When you print a document, the lines are wrapped between the margins, whatever the Word Wrap setting.

...cont'd

WordPad

WordPad is a text-editing program you can use to create and edit documents which can include rich formatting and graphics. You can also link to or embed pictures and other documents.

1 Select Start, All Programs, Accessories, WordPad to create a new document, and type in some lines of text

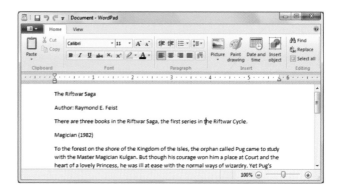

The text automatically wraps as you type, and the Enter key starts a new paragraph.

2 Select text and use the formatting bar to change font etc

Hot tip

Saving as Rich Text Format (.rtf), Open Office XML (.docx) or OpenDocument Text (.odt) will retain the text styling. However, the other three text formats save as plain text, and remove images or links.

```
Rich Text Format (RTF)
Office Open XML Document
OpenDocument Text
Text Document
Text Document - MS-DOS Format
Unicode Text Document
```

3 Click the Save button on the Quick Access toolbar, type the file name and confirm the file type, then click Save

Other text applications

XPS Viewer

To protect the content as well as the formatting of a document, use the XML Paper Specification (XPS) format and XPS Viewer to view, save, share, digitally sign, and protect your documents.

You can create an XPS document in any program where you can print, for example:

1 Open a document in WordPad, click the WordPad button and select Print

2 Select Microsoft XPS Document Writer as the printer, then click Print

3 Confirm the save location and provide a name for the document, then click Save

4 Double-click the icon for the saved file, and it will be opened by XPS Viewer, where you set permissions and add digital signatures

The Riftwar Saga

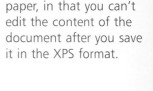

Don't forget

An XPS document is like an electronic sheet of paper, in that you can't edit the content of the document after you save it in the XPS format.

121

Hot tip

You can apply permission restrictions for your XPS document so that no one can view, copy, print, or digitally sign your document without your authority.

...cont'd

Sticky Notes

You can keep track of small pieces of information such as phone numbers, addresses or meeting schedules using Sticky Notes. You can use Sticky Notes with a tablet pen or a standard keyboard.

To create a new Sticky Note:

1 Select Start, All Programs, Accessories, Sticky Notes

2 The new note appears on the desktop with the typing cursor active

3 Type the text of the reminder that you want to record

4 Text wraps as you type, and you can press Enter to start a new line

5 The note is extended in length to accommodate text

6 Drag a corner or edge to resize or reshape the note

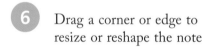

You can format text, add bullets to make a list, or change the text size using keyboard shortcuts.

1 Select the text that you want to change

2 Use the appropriate keyboard shortcut to format the text

Ctrl+B	Bold text	Ctrl+Shift+L	Bulleted list
Ctrl+I	Italic text	Ctrl+Shift+L (repeated)	Numbered list
Ctrl+U	Underlined text	Ctrl+Shift+>	Increase text size
Ctrl+T	Strikethrough	Ctrl+Shift+<	Decrease text size

Hot tip

Sticky Notes don't have to be yellow. Right-click the note and choose one of the six colors offered.

Don't forget

To create another note, click the New Note button (+). To remove a note press the Delete Note button (×).

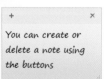

You can create or delete a note using the buttons

Image management

Paint

Paint allows you to create drawings on a blank drawing area or in existing pictures, photographs or web graphics. To open Paint:

1 Select Start, All Programs, Accessories, Paint, and the program opens with a blank canvas

Paint button   Quick Access Toolbar   Home tab   Ribbon   Drawing area   Color palette

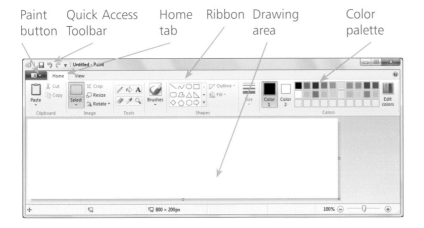

2 Right-click an image file and select Open with, Paint

Zoom tools   View tab   Scroll bars

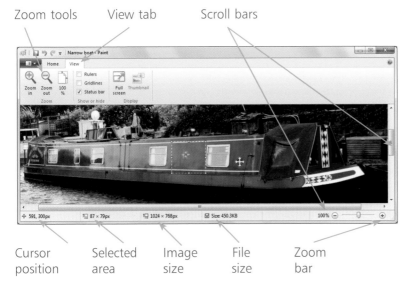

Cursor position   Selected area   Image size   File size   Zoom bar

You can zoom in on a certain part of the picture or zoom out if the picture is too large, and show rulers and gridlines as you work.

Don't forget

You may have other image programs on your system, in addition to the ones reviewed here, depending on the products installed and the hardware connected.

Hot tip

When you paste an image onto the Paint drawing area, it will be automatically resized if necessary to fit the whole image.

Don't forget

Paint can open and save as a number of image formats including .bmp, .jpg, .gif, .tif and .png.

Monochrome Bitmap (*.bmp;*.dib)
16 Color Bitmap (*.bmp;*.dib)
256 Color Bitmap (*.bmp;*.dib)
24-bit Bitmap (*.bmp;*.dib)
JPEG (*.jpg;*.jpeg;*.jpe;*.jfif)
GIF (*.gif)
TIFF (*.tif;*.tiff)
PNG (*.png)

...cont'd

Windows Photo Viewer

You can use Photo Viewer to view your pictures and photos, individually or as a slide show. You won't find Photo Viewer on the Start menu or via Search. Instead, you use Preview.

1 Open the folder containing the picture you want to view

2 Select the picture file, and the toolbar is revised to show associated functions, including Preview

3 Click the arrow next to preview and select Windows Photo Viewer

Here you can rotate images clockwise or counterclockwise, zoom in or out, and view other pictures in the folder as a slideshow. You can also email or print images, or burn them to CD/DVD.

Windows Fax and Scan

Windows provides software to support sending and receiving faxes, but you need a fax modem installed or attached to your computer, plus connection to a telephone line.

There's also support for scanning documents and pictures, but you need a scanner (or all-in-one printer) attached to your computer.

To start Windows Fax and Scan:

1 Select Start, All Programs and Windows Fax and Scan

25%	
50%	
100%	
200%	
Fit to Page	
✓ Fit to Width	

2 An example document is displayed, and this provides guidance for getting started with faxes and scanning

3 To scan a document or picture, click the Scan button then click New Scan on the toolbar, and follow the prompts

125

Computations

While there's no spreadsheet capability built in to Windows, it does offer some facilities for computations.

Calculator

1 Select Start, All Programs, Accessories and then Calculator

Click calculator buttons or press equivalent keyboard keys, to enter numbers and operations such as Add, Subtract, Multiply, Divide, Square Root, Percent and Inverse.

2 To complete the calculation, select or press the Enter key

You can also store and recall numbers from memory, and the History capability keeps track of stages in the calculations.

This is just the Standard calculator. You can also choose to use Scientific, Programmer and Statistics versions of the calculator.

1 Open Calculator, select View and choose for example Scientific

The Scientific calculator includes many functions and inverse functions, including logarithms and factorials.

You can use Calculator to convert between different units of measure. It will subtract dates or add and subtract days from a date. There are also worksheets to calculate fuel economy or lease and mortgage payments.

Math Input Panel

Math Input Panel uses the math recognizer built into Windows 7 to recognize handwritten math expressions. You can then insert the recognized math into a word-processing program.

1 Select Start, All Programs, Accessories, Math Input Panel

2 Enter the equations, which are interpreted as you write

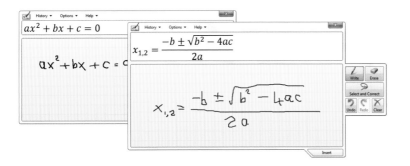

3 When each equation is complete, press Insert to add it to the active word processing document

4 The equations appear in the word processing document

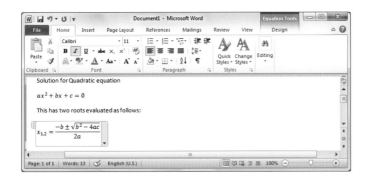

Disc Writers

There are several applications in Windows that can create CDs or DVDs, assuming you have a drive with writer capability.

DVD Maker

With this program you can make DVDs that you can watch on a computer or on a TV using a regular DVD player.

1. Select Start, All Programs and Windows DVD Maker

2. If the Overview displays, click Choose Photos and Videos

3. Click Add items

4. Navigate to the folder containing the videos or photos you want

5. Select the items, using Shift or Ctrl to select multiple files, and then click Add

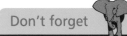

If you change your mind about any items, select them and click the Remove items button.

6 Click Add items to add videos or photos from other folders, or click Next if you've finished collecting

Hot tip

If you'd like to continue later, select File, Save and save the show definition as a DVD Maker Project.

Double-click the Project icon to load the project and continue editing.

7 Preview the contents, make changes as needed, then select Burn to write the film show to DVD

Disc Image Burner

This program takes an ISO file, which is a single file that is a copy of an entire data CD or DVD. You may encounter ISO files when you download software from websites.

To run the program:

1 Right-click the ISO file icon, and select Burn disc image

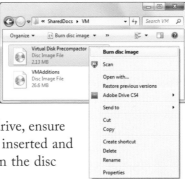

2 Select your DVD writer drive, ensure a writable DVD has been inserted and follow the prompts to burn the disc

Don't forget

When you burn the CD or DVD from the ISO file, the new disc has the same folders, files, and properties as were on the original disc.

Utilities

Other applications in Windows include various utilities such as the following two programs which illustrate the wide range of functions offered.

Sound Recorder

You can use Sound Recorder to record sounds from a microphone or other audio device plugged into your sound card. You save the sounds as audio files and use them for example to customize one of the Windows sound schemes.

To start recording:

1 Select Start, All Programs, Accessories, Sound Recorder

2 Start your audio device and click Start Recording

3 Click Stop Recording, type the file name and click Save

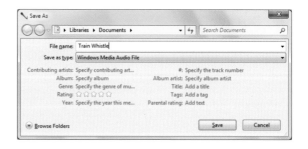

Snipping Tool

This will capture a screen shot, or snip, of any object on your screen, and you can then annotate, save, or share the image. For example, if there's a window open with information to be copied:

1 Select Start, All Programs, Accessories, Snipping Tool

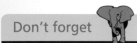

Don't forget

You can connect an audio or video device, such as a VCR, video camera, cassette player or CD/DVD player, to the Line In jack on your sound card.

Hot tip

If appropriate you can add descriptive details such as artist, album, track number and title. The audio file is saved as type Windows Media Audio (.wma).

Train Whistle   Length: 00:01:14
                 Size: 886 KB

2 Select the arrow next to New to pick the snip type e.g. rectangular

3 Click a corner and drag to mark out the area you wish to capture

4 Release the mouse, and the snip is copied to the Clipboard and the mark-up window

5 Highlight or annotate the snip if desired then click the Save Snip button, adjust the name and location, then click Save

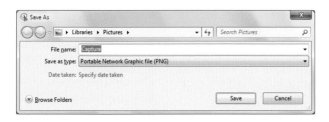

Command Prompt

All versions of Windows have included a command line feature for typing MS-DOS commands and other computer commands.

1 Click Start, All Programs, Accessories, Command Prompt

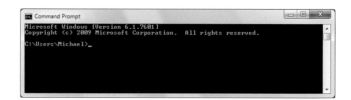

2 To display a list of commands with a brief description of each, type Help and press Enter

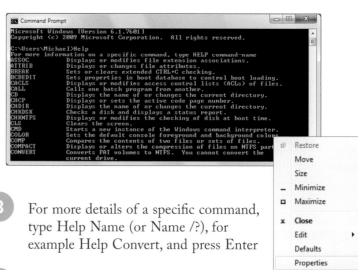

3 For more details of a specific command, type Help Name (or Name /?), for example Help Convert, and press Enter

132

4 To adjust command prompt options, right-click the title bar and select Defaults (for all command prompts) or Properties (current command prompt only)

5 To close the command prompt, type Exit and press Enter

Windows PowerShell

To support systems administrators and advanced users, Windows 7 introduces a new command-line and scripting environment, far more powerful than the old MS-DOS batch file system.

1 Select Start, All Programs, Accessories, Windows PowerShell

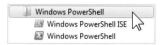

2 Select Windows PowerShell for the command-line

Don't forget

Windows PowerShell can execute Cmdlets (which are .NET programs), PowerShell scripts (file type .ps1), PowerShell functions and executable programs.

133

3 Enter Get-Command for a list of PowerShell commands

4 Select Windows PowerShell ISE for the Integrated Scripting Environment, and enter the same command

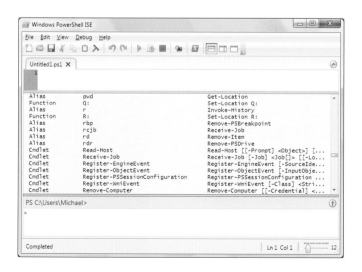

Hot tip

You'll find more help in the MSDN library at http://msdn.microsoft.com/library in the PowerShell section under Windows Development, and Administration and Management.

5 For help, go to http://technet.microsoft.com/powershell

System Tools

134

1 Select Start, All Programs, Accessories and click the System Tools folder to show the list of tools

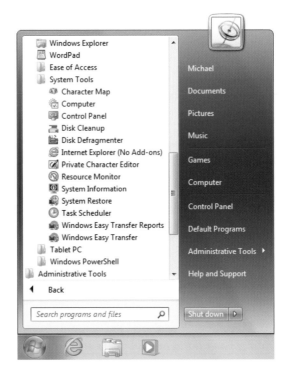

2 Scroll down the Start menu past the System Tools to the Maintenance folder where you'll find more tools

Administrative Tools

Administrative Tools are intended for system administrators and advanced users. To see the list available on your system:

1 Select Start and click the Administrative Tools button on the right of the Start menu, or select All Programs and click the Administrative Tools folder

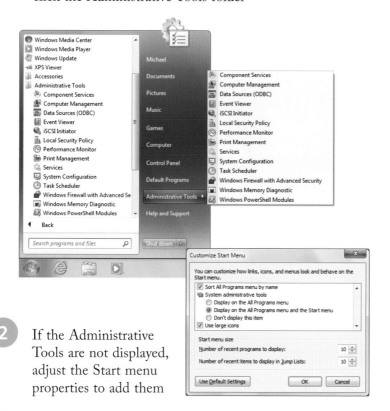

2 If the Administrative Tools are not displayed, adjust the Start menu properties to add them

3 Alternatively, you can always access the Administrative tools from within the Control Panel

135

Beware

Using default settings, the Administrative tools are hidden on the Start menu and All Programs, but they will be found in the Control Panel.

Don't forget

Select Start, Control Panel, click System and Security and then select Administrative Tools.

Desktop Gadgets

There are two ways to show the Desktop Gadgets on your system:

1 Select Start, All Programs, then click Desktop Gadget Gallery

2 Right-click a clear area on the desktop (avoiding icons) and select Gadgets

3 Click the link at the bottom of the panel Show Details or Hide Details for the selected gadget

4 Double-click any gadget to add it to the right hand side of the desktop, with subsequent gadgets aligned beneath

5 If the gadgets don't display on the desktop, right-click the desktop and select View, Show desktop gadgets

8 Windows Live Essentials

Microsoft provides
Windows Live Essentials,
a set of free applications
that supplement and extend
Windows, with email,
messaging, photos and
movie support and security
features. Other sources
offer free programs such as
a PDF Reader, Antivirus
support and text and image
management applications.

138 Getting started

139 Windows Live Essentials

140 Select and download

142 Completing installation

144 Other Windows Essentials

145 Adobe Reader

146 AVG Antivirus Free Edition

148 Irfanview

149 Notepad++

150 OpenOffice.org

152 Paint.NET

154 μTorrent

Getting started

Windows Live Essentials is a suite of freeware applications from Microsoft which offers email, instant messaging, photo-sharing, blog publishing, security services and other facilities. The programs are designed to integrate with Windows, with one another and with other Windows Live web-based services such as Windows Live Photos and Windows Live Hotmail.

Previous versions of Windows would have included many of these items as part of the base system. Microsoft has separated off these components, to make updating easier (and perhaps to avoid potential anti-trust issues).

To download and install Windows Live Essentials:

Don't forget

You will usually find Getting Started on the top level Start menu. It is also found in Accessories and in Control Panel (when you choose View by, Large icons).

1 Select Start, Getting Started

2 Click the item Go online to get Windows Live Essentials to display a description and a link to the website

Beware

Your system may not have the Windows Live Essentials in Getting Started. In this case, you'd go to web page http://download.live.com.

3 Click the website link (or double-click the item)

Alternatively, you can click the arrow next to Getting Started and select Get Windows Live Essentials to go straight to the website.

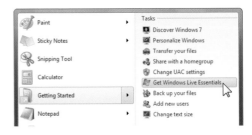

Windows Live Essentials

Whichever method you use to visit the website, the Live.com website is displayed, with Essentials selected.

Don't forget

The Live.com detects that you are running a compatible operating system, and so offers the download option.

1 Scroll down to see details of the main components that are included in Windows Live Essential

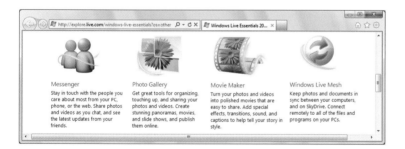

Hot tip

The details may change over time, since the Windows Live Essentials are expected to be more frequently updated than Windows itself.

2 Scroll further to see descriptions of the other components that are included in Windows Live Essentials

Select and download

1 At the Live.com website, with Essentials selected, click the Download now button

2 Choose to Run the Windows Live setup program

3 The setup program is installed and run, and you are prompted to choose the programs that you want to install

140

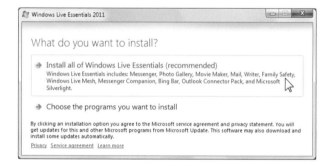

4 Select to install all the Windows Live Essential programs, as recommended

5 The programs are installed in turn

6 Click Restart Now to complete the install (see page 142)

To install a selection of the programs, run the Setup program and:

1 Click Choose the programs you want to install

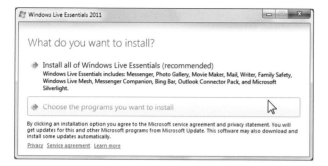

2 Clear the box for programs you want to avoid installing

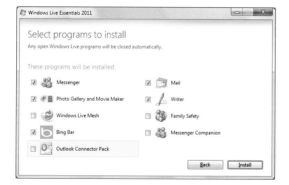

3 The next time, Setup shows which programs are installed

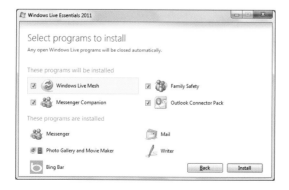

Completing installation

When the restart completes, Internet Explorer is automatically opened with the Live.com website displayed. New add-ons will have been added to support the installed programs.

1. If the notification panel displays, click Choose add-ons to decide which to enable, or click Don't enable

2. To choose add-ons later, click the Tools button and select Manage add-ons

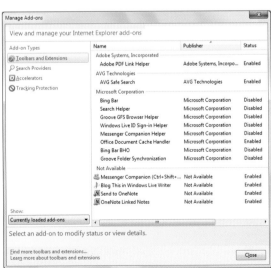

The Windows Live programs will be added to the Start menu, and highlighted as new entries. They may appear towards the top of the All Programs menu, or in folders i.e. Microsoft Silverlight and Windows Live.

When you choose to download all the programs, you'll have installed the following programs on your system:

Bing Bar	Family Safety
Mail	Messenger
Messenger Companion	Movie Maker
Outlook Connector Pack	Photo Gallery
Windows Live Mesh	Writer

Not all these programs appear on the Start menu. Bing Bar and Messenger Companion are installed as Internet Explorer add-ons, while the Outlook Connector Pack is installed as an extension to Microsoft Office Outlook. You'll also find an extra program Microsoft Silverlight, a requirement of Windows Live programs.

Hot tip

Microsoft Silverlight is a programmable web browser plugin that enables developers to include features such as animation, vector graphics and audio-video playback in their Internet applications.

Other Windows Essentials

There are a number of applications, not included with Windows and not supplied by Microsoft, that could well be considered Windows essentials. They supplement the existing Windows applications or they fill in the gaps.

There are numerous programs that you could choose from, to meet any particular need, and you'll find many lists of favorite Windows applications on the Internet. However, the following programs are considered generally well-behaved and suitable for Windows 7 and, like Windows Live Essentials, they are available free of charge.

Category	Program
PDF Viewer	Adobe Reader
Antivirus	AVG Antivirus Free Edition
Photo Viewer	Irfanview
Text Editor	Notepad++
Office Apps	OpenOffice
Photo Editor	Paint.net
File sharing	uTorrent

All of these programs are available over the Internet, ready for download and installation.

In the following pages you'll find the details needed to get started with each of the programs, including:

Website address
Brief description
Installation notes
Screenshot of application

Each program will be added to the Start menu in the location suggested by the product supplier during the installation, usually an entry at the top of All Programs, or a separate folder.

Adobe Reader

http://www.adobe.com/products/reader.html

Adobe Reader is the worldwide standard for viewing, printing, and commenting on PDF documents of all types.

To install the application:

1 Go to the website and select the Download link

2 Clear the Google Toolbar box, then follow the prompts to download and install Adobe Reader

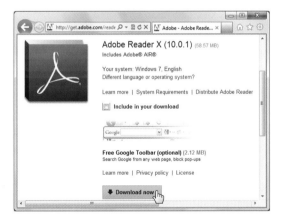

3 Double-click any PDF file to open it in Adobe Reader

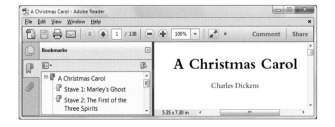

Don't forget

Adobe may use the Adobe Download Manager to install the Adobe Reader and manage updates in the future.

Beware

You may find extras such as the Google Toolbar being offered. You can usually ignore these unless you are sure they will be needed.

145

Hot tip

Adobe Reader is not just for viewing documents. Select View, Read Out Loud to set the Reader in narrative mode.

Read Out Loud ▶

AVG Antivirus Free Edition

http://free.avg.com/

A product like this is definitely essential since Windows has no built in virus protection. The free edition of AVG Antivirus provides excellent protection for the home environment, though you might need a more advanced edition for business use.

To install AVG Antivirus on your system:

1   At the website, select Download Now for the free edition

Don't forget

AVG does offer a very useful free edition, but will remind you at every opportunity that there are more advanced trial and chargeable versions, so be sure you select the option you require.

2   Follow the prompts to download and run the installation software

3   When installation starts, you must again confirm you want the free edition

Hot tip

The AVG 2011 Gadget will be installed on the desktop, unless you clear the box before selecting Quick Install.

4   Select Quick Install for the standard configuration

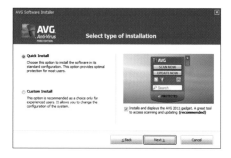

5 AVG will suggest its Security Toolbar and Secure Search, but you can clear these boxes to avoid adding these

Don't forget

AVG will automatically configure itself to work with the email and browser programs installed on your PC.

6 When the installation completes, you can register your name and email address to receive AVG product news

147

7 Click Finish and the AVG User Interface is displayed, and you are prompted to run an initial scan

Hot tip

After installation, AVG will download the latest updates, and will continue to update itself every day, to ensure full protection against the latest threats.

Irfanview

http://www.irfanview.com/

IrfanView is a very fast and compact graphic viewer for Windows that is freeware (for non-commercial use). It supports many graphics file formats, including multiple (animated) GIF, multipage TIF and videos.

1 Visit the website and select the Irfanview download link

2 Follow the prompts to download and install Irfanview

3 On completion, the FAQ web page is displayed and Irfanview starts up

4 In this example, image 15 of 198 is showing

5 Click forward or back buttons to scroll all the images

Notepad++

http://www.notepad-plus-plus.org/

Notepad++ is a free text editor and Notepad replacement that is particularly designed for source code editing and supports over 50 languages, ranging from Ada to XML and YAML.

1 Go to the website and select the Download tab

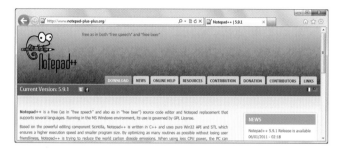

2 Choose to download the current version

3 Select to download and run the Installer version

4 Follow the prompts to run the Setup Wizard and install Notepad++

5 The program opens with the Change Log, showing new features and fixes

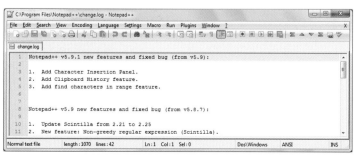

Don't forget

In addition to language support, the main advantage over the built-in Notepad is tabbed editing, which allows you to work with multiple open files.

149

Hot tip

If you are interested in programming, you can download the actual source code for this application.

OpenOffice.org

http://www.openoffice.org/

OpenOffice.org is an open-source suite with a powerful set of applications that are very similar to the Microsoft Office, and include techniques such as macros and templates, but have the advantage of being free to use.

 Visit the website and select Download from the options

 Select Download now to get the version for your system

3 Follow the prompts to unpack and save the installation files ready for the actual installation

4 Provide your name and optionally your organization, as they are to be used in OpenOffice documents

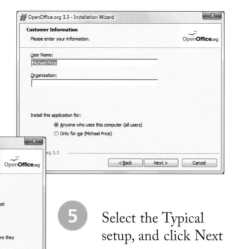

Don't forget

You will also be asked to register your details, the first time you run OpenOffice.org.

5 Select the Typical setup, and click Next

6 Upon completion, click Finish to end the Wizard

7 Select the shortcut on the desktop or in All Programs, to start OpenOffice.org 3.3

Hot tip

OpenOffice.org consists of six components: Writer (word processor) Calc (spreadsheet) Impress (presentations) Draw (vector graphics) Base (database) and Math (formula editor).

Paint.NET

http://www.getpaint.net/

Where the built-in Windows Paint doesn't have the power you need, Paint.NET gives you facilities to crop, cut, or edit an image.

1 Click Download or click the Paint.NET v3.5.8 link

Don't forget

It's not equivalent to the full Adobe Photoshop, but it is just what's needed for casual graphic design tasks.

Beware

There are many links to lots of programs, such as Facemoods, WhiteSmoke and FLV Player, so make sure that the link you choose does download Paint.NET itself.

2 Click the Download Now button for Paint.NET

3 Choose to Open the compressed file Paint.NET.3.5.8.Install.zip

4 This expands to the executable file Paint.NET.3.5.8.Install

5 Choose Quick for the install method and click Next

6 Agree terms and conditions and continue

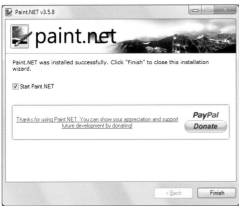

7 Follow the prompts to complete the installation

8 Click Finish, to start Paint.NET

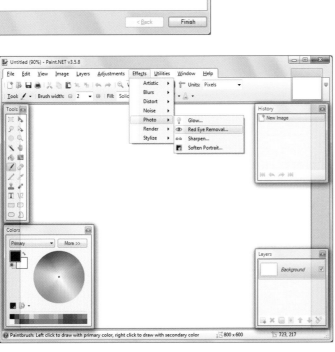

Don't forget

During the installation, Paint.NET will be optimized for best performance on your particular system.

Beware

Paint.NET is free, and you are reminded not to accept any requests for payment. However, you are encouraged to contribute to future development.

153

Hot tip

Select Effects to see the range offered, Photo for example with Glow, Sharpen and Soften as well as Red Eye Removal. Adjustments also applies various changes to the appearance.

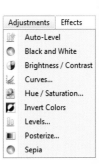

μTorrent

http://www.utorrent.com/

μTorrent (also referred to as uTorrent) is a freeware, but closed source BitTorrent client. The μ in its name implies the prefix micro, in deference to the program's small size: the program is only 391KB, but it can handle very large downloads, very rapidly.

1 At the μTorrent website click the Free Download button

2 Follow prompts to download and run the Setup Wizard

3 When the installation completes, μTorrent is launched

Don't forget

A BitTorrent client is a computer program that manages downloads and uploads using the BitTorrent protocol. This is used for peer-to-peer file sharing for distributing large amounts of data.

Hot tip

Note that μTorrent is added to Windows Startup and to the Firewall exceptions.

Beware

Make sure that files you select for downloading via μTorrent are in the public domain and not subject to copyright.

9 Enhance your email

You can use the communications tools built in or added to Windows to communicate with others, sending messages and attachments, to individuals or groups of contacts. The Calendar facility helps you manage appointments and tasks. You can also receive more general communications, in the form of newsletters and information feeds.

156   Email (electronic mail)

157   Windows Live Mail

158   Create Windows Live ID

159   Add email accounts

160   Add another email account

162   Windows Live Mail window

164   View messages

166   Attachments

168   Adding contacts

169   Junk email

170   Mail Calendar

171   Windows Live Calendar

172   Instant messaging

174   Newsgroups

176   RSS feeds

Email (electronic mail)

You can use email (electronic mail) to receive and send messages and files, to individuals or groups of people. You can send messages at any time of day or night. The recipients don't have to be at their computers, since they find the messages waiting the next time they check their email. However, if they are at their computer (or using their smartphone) they'd get the messages immediately and could respond straightaway.

This is much more efficient than regular mail or telephone services, and it is free, no matter how far away the recipients might be. The only cost is for your Internet connection, though you also need an email program or web-based email service.

Web mail

You can register for a free web-based email service, such as Gmail, Windows Live Hotmail, or Yahoo! Mail. These services allow you to check your email using a web browser, on your own computer, or on any computer connected to the Internet, for example a friend's computer, or a computer in a public location such as a library or hotel.

Email programs

On your own computer you can also check your email using an email program, from Microsoft or another supplier. Email programs often have more features and are faster to search mail than most web-based email services.

In previous versions of Windows, Microsoft supplied an email program as an integral component, either Outlook Express or Windows Mail. There's no built-in email program for Windows 7, but you can download Windows Live Mail as part of the Windows Live Essentials (see page 138). We will use this as the example product for Windows email.

Microsoft Outlook

Microsoft also provides an email program Outlook, which is part of the Microsoft Office system. This provides similar functions to Windows Live Mail, but it must be purchased as a separate product or as part of the Microsoft Office Suite.

Don't forget

To connect your computer to the Internet, you must sign up with an Internet service provider (ISP), who provides a modem or router that gives access over phone line or cable.

Hot tip

To set up your email program, you must obtain details from your ISP, such as your email address, password, names of your incoming and outgoing email servers.

Don't forget

An email address consists of a user name (or a nickname), the @ sign, and the name of your ISP or web-based email provider, for example: sue29@gmail.com.

Windows Live Mail

Windows Live Mail may already be installed as part of the Windows Live Essentials (see page 138), or it can be installed as an extra program if not originally selected.

To start Windows Live Mail:

1 Select Start, All Programs, Windows Live Mail

2 The first time you may be asked to select Windows Live settings, included your browser home page

3 Clear the box if you want to retain your existing home page then click OK

4 You'll be asked to add your email accounts

5 If you want to obtain a Windows Live ID at this time, click the link Get a Windows Live email address

Don't forget

Since you can expect to use Windows Live Mail frequently, right-click the entry in the All Programs menu and select Pin to Taskbar or Pin to Start Menu (see page 71), to make it easier to access.

Hot tip

If you have a Hotmail or MSN email address, this acts as a Windows Live ID. Otherwise, use an existing email address, e.g. Gmail, Yahoo or an ISP email.

Hot tip

You can also choose to create a Windows Live ID immediately, and use this in Windows Live Mail.

Create Windows Live ID

Don't forget

You can create the Windows Live ID when you first start Windows Live Mail or go to website www.live.com and click Sign up.

Sign up

Hot tip

Windows Live will check to see if your proposed Windows Live ID has already been used, and suggest alternatives if necessary.

Don't forget

As you select each field, Windows Live gives you advice and information, for example it assesses your password and it explains what is needed.

Strong
Strong passwords contain 7-16 characters, do not include common words or names, and combine uppercase letters, lowercase letters, numbers, and symbols.

1 At the Windows Live sign up web page, enter the details requested, starting with your proposed Windows Live ID

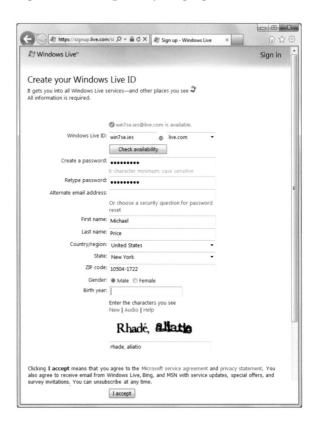

2 Enter your password, alternative email address (or choose a security question), name and other details requested

3 Type the security phrase and click I accept, and you'll be signed in to Windows Live (with one message waiting)

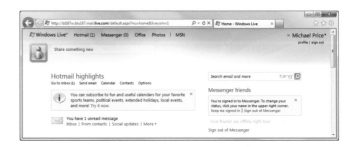

Add email accounts

1 In Windows Mail, enter the email address and password
you want to use and type the display name for messages

Don't forget

If you do not sign in to
Windows Live, you may
get an error message
saying Unable to send
or receive messages for
that ID.

2 If this is a Windows
Live ID, you should sign
in to Windows Live

3 Your email
account will
be added to
Windows Live
Mail

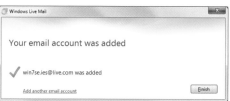

Hot tip

Click the link to Add
another email account,
if you have others you
want to define.

4 Available messages will be downloaded from the server

Hot tip

By default, the message
in the Inbox is opened
and displayed in the
reading pane. However,
this can be switched off
(see page 163).

Add another email account

1 Select the link to Add another email account or select Accounts, Email in Windows Mail

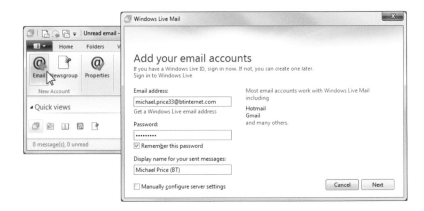

2 Type the email address and other details, and click Next

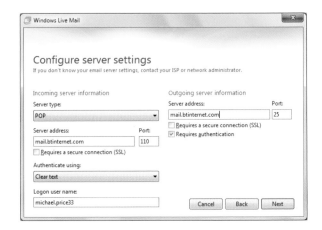

3 Select the Server type, and enter Server addresses and other details (as provided by your ISP) then click Next

4 This email account is also added to Windows Live Mail

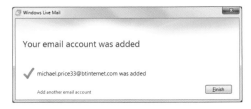

5 The messages for the specified email are downloaded from the server to the Inbox for the account

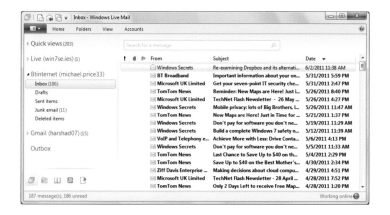

Don't forget

The layout of Windows Live in these examples has been adjusted (see page 163) to allow more room to display the list of messages.

6 You may find that some messages are identified as junk email and automatically moved to the Junk email folder

 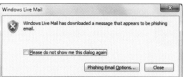

Beware

Not all of the messages identified as junk email are necessarily invalid. One phishing message for example is a genuine communication that happens to be addressed to Dear Customer, which raised the warning.

7 Some messages may be identified as phishing email, trying to deceive you into giving up personal information, and these are also moved to the Junk email folder

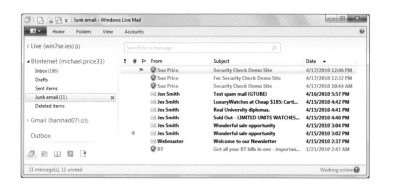

161

Windows Live Mail window

1 Open Windows Live Mail, and it typically has Mail selected, with folders, Inbox, preview and calendar

Windows Live Mail button

Quick Access Toolbar

Title bar

Ribbon

Tabs

Folder list

Email accounts

Inbox message list

Attachment icon

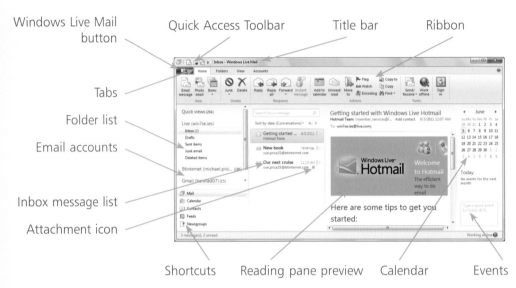

Shortcuts   Reading pane preview   Calendar   Events

The Home tab displays the commands on the ribbon that you require for working with messages you send and receive.

Don't forget

When you switch to Calendar, Contacts, Feeds or Newsgroups, the Home tab displays a different set of commands appropriate to the chosen function.

2 Click the Folders tab to create, copy or move folders

3 Click the View tab to change the window view and layout

4 Click the Accounts tab to add accounts or view properties

To change the view and layout of the Mail window:

1 Open Windows Live Mail, select the Mail function and click the View tab

2 Click Reading pane, and select Off to avoid showing a preview of the selected message

3 Click Calendar pane, which operates as a toggle to hide or show the calendar

4 Click Compact shortcuts, to show the functions as a set of icons

5 Right-click the ribbon and select Minimize the Ribbon, to hide it

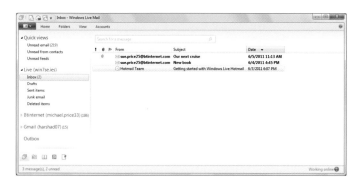

6 To redisplay the ribbon temporarily, so you can select a command, simply click the appropriate tab

Don't forget

Click the toggles Quick views or Status bar, to hide or show the respective items.

Hot tip

Click Add to Quick Access Toolbar to add the command that's currently selected on the ribbon.

163

Hot tip

Right-click the Tab bar and select Minimize the Ribbon to redisplay it permanently.

View messages

To see the messages that are available for any of your accounts:

1 In Windows Live Mail, select Mail and click the account

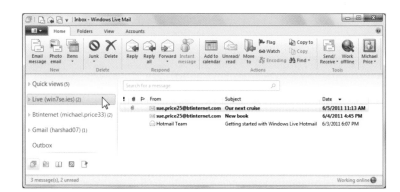

2 To see mail for all the accounts defined, click Quick views

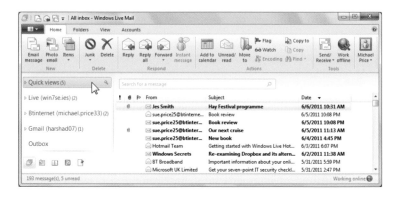

By default, Windows Live Mail will check on the server for new email messages, at startup and then every 10 minutes.

1 To change the delay time, click the Windows Live Mail button and select Options, Mail, then click the General tab

2 Enter the new time required and click OK

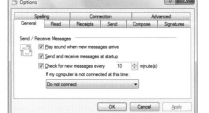

To read an individual message in the account or Quick views list:

1 Double-click an entry in the list (or select the entry and press Enter) to open the message

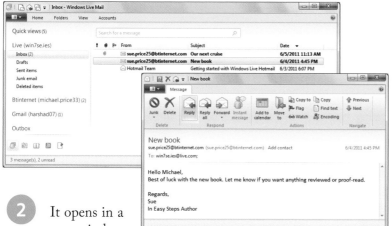

2 It opens in a new window

3 Click Reply and type the response

4 Click the Send button

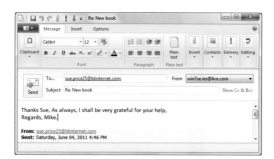

5 The reply is moved to your Outbox, from where it is sent to your mail server

6 A copy of the reply is saved in your Sent items folder

Don't forget

Click the white triangle next to the account name to display the folders - Inbox, Drafts, Sent items etc.

Hot tip

You can reply to the sender, reply to all addressees, or forward the message to one or more other users.

Beware

You may receive a message requesting confirmation. Click the Verify link, or type the characters and select OK.

165

Attachments

1 Select and open a message with an attachment

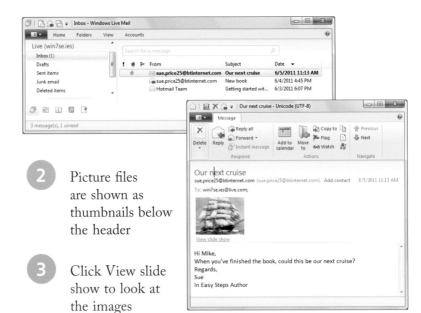

2 Picture files are shown as thumbnails below the header

3 Click View slide show to look at the images

4 Right-click the thumbnail or file icon and select Save as (for just that attachment) or Save all

5 Confirm the folder location and click Save to write the attachments to disk

To add an attachment to your messages or replies:

1 Type the message then click Insert, Attach file

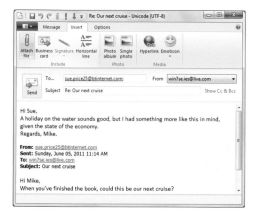

2 Locate the required folder, select the file and click Open

3 The file is added as an icon below the message header

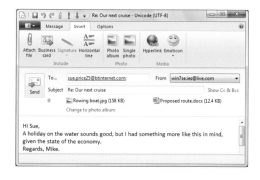

Adding contacts

1 When you receive an email from a new contact, right-click the Inbox entry and select Add sender to contacts

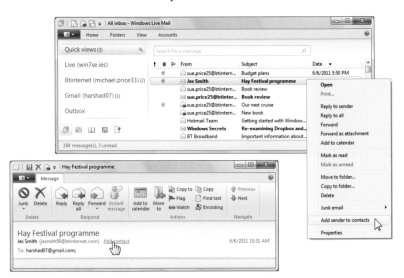

2 Alternatively, open the message and click the Add contact link next to the sender name (unless already in Contacts)

3 In either case, the available details are displayed

4 Add any further information and click Add contact

Junk email

Junk email, or spam, is unsolicited mail that is sent to lists of email addresses. Your ISP will provide filters to filter spam so that it doesn't actually reach your computer. Your antivirus program may redirect suspect mail. For spam that gets past these checks, Windows Live Mail lets you set up rules to block suspect senders and redirect junk mail.

1 Click the Windows Live Mail button application icon, select Options and then choose the Safety options

2 Click the Options tab

3 Review the option selected and adjust if appropriate

4 You can permanently delete junk mail, but this risks deleting valid mail inadvertently redirected

5 Decide if you want to notify Microsoft of junk mail detected

6 Click the Safe Senders and the Blocked Senders tabs, to add particular email addresses or domain names

7 Click the Phishing tab to enable or disable the protection against phishing attacks

8 Click the International tab to block messages from specific countries or in a particular language group

Hot tip

The default is High, but you can try a lower setting if you are the only user on the computer.

169

Beware

You may find that your email is filtered before it gets downloaded, so sign on to your account at the appropriate website and check the junk mail folder there, in case valid messages have been trapped by error.

Mail Calendar

There's full Calendar capability included in Windows Live Mail.

1. Open Windows Live Mail and select the Calendar icon

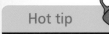

2. Select a date, double-click a time period and define an
event start time, end time and reminder time

3. Click Save and close, to add the event to the calendar

Windows Live Calendar

1 Sign in at www.live.com and the events are copied online

2 Check the event times, and you may find that they are out by several hours

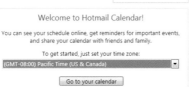

3 Select Hotmail, Calendar and you will be prompted to select your time zone

4 Select the time zone used in Mail calendar, and the event times will be corrected

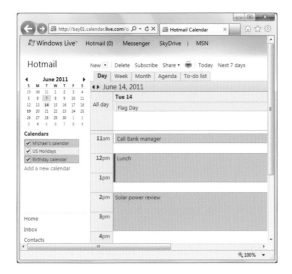

Don't forget

If your email account is a Windows Live ID, your local Mail calendar will be synchronized with your online calendar at www.live.com.

Beware

If there's a mismatch between Mail and online Calendar time zones, events may be mistimed.

171

Hot tip

A holiday calendar for your country, and a birthday calendar based on your contacts list are also created. These will be accessible from the Mail calendar.

Instant messaging

The ID you set up for Windows Live Mail can also be used to communicate live with others, using the instant messaging application Windows Live Messenger. You will have downloaded this as part of Windows Live Essentials (see page 138).

Hot tip

You'll be prompted to connect to services such as Facebook, and to provide your cellphone number, but you can skip these steps initially.

1 Select Start, All Programs, Windows Live Messenger and sign in using your Windows Live ID (see page 158)

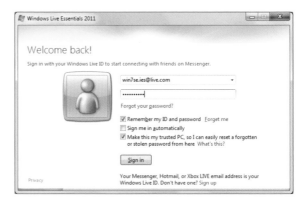

Don't forget

Choose Private to avoid everyone having access to the information in your profile, which could include date of birth or other personal information.

2 You can choose settings such as Remember my ID and password and Sign me in automatically at start up

3 Choose your privacy setting - Public, Limited or Private - to control who has access to your details and activities

4 Windows Live Messenger completes setup and starts up

5 Click Add a contact (or add people you know from other instant messaging services or social networks)

6 Specify the email address then click Next and follow the prompts to send an invitation

7 When the invitation is accepted, Messenger detects whether your contact is online

8 Press Enter to start a conversation with the selected contact (or double-click any name)

Newsgroups

To take part in a discussion, you need to access the appropriate newsgroup server and subscribe to the particular newsgroup.

To specify the newsgroup server in Windows Live Mail:

1 Choose the Newsgroup shortcut icon, then select the Accounts tab and click Newsgroup in New Account

2 Supply the display name or nickname that you want others to see and click Next

3 Provide your email address for personal replies

You could make a deliberate error in the email address, such as putting "at" rather than @. This will be obvious to a human reader, but would help avoid your email address being detected by robots that search the Internet for email addresses to use for spam.

4. Name the newsgroup server you have decided to use, for example: freenews.netfront.net

5. Click Next then click Finish to add the account

6. The names of the newsgroups will be downloaded - there are over 40,000 in the list for the example newsgroup server

7. Type keywords related to your interest, e.g. Bridge, to list only those newsgroups that are relevant

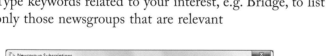

8. Select a particular newsgroup, click Subscribe and Go to

RSS feeds

Windows Live Mail includes support for RSS feeds (updates to contents of frequently changing websites such as news services). You would normally use Internet Explorer to find and subscribe to RSS feeds as you browse websites online, but an email client such as Windows Live Mail is useful for reading the RSS feeds.

1 Open Windows Live Mail and click the Feeds shortcut, then select Quick Views to see updates from all the feeds

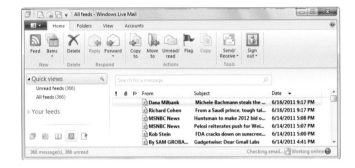

2 Expand Your feeds to select an individual feed e.g. CNN

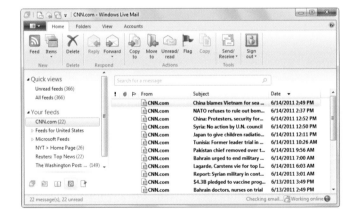

3 If you know the URL, you can click Feed and subscribe

Don't forget

Windows Live Mail picks up all the RSS feeds for which subscriptions have been defined in Internet Explorer (see page 192).

Hot tip

Internet Explorer has some predefined feeds from Microsoft and from Government sources.

▲ Feeds for United States
    Popular Government Ques... (9)
    USA.gov Updates: News an... (9)
▲ Microsoft Feeds
    Microsoft at Home (37)
    Microsoft at Work (37)
    MSNBC News (55)

176

Hot tip

If you have the URL, you can subscribe to a feed from Windows Live Mail. Internet Explorer will automatically add these to its list of feeds.

10 Internet Explorer

Windows includes Microsoft
Internet Explorer as the
default browser. Version
9, the latest release, takes
advantage of hardware
acceleration on graphics
adapters, manages the effects
of add-on applications
and includes improved
tabbed browsing facilities.
It also integrates well with
Windows to make use of
jump lists and pinning
to make it easy to get to
frequently used websites.

178 Internet Explorer version 9

180 Internet Explorer window

182 Page back and forward

183 Search for web page

184 Change search provider

185 Open in new window

186 Tabbed browsing

188 Home page

189 Favorites

190 Pinned sites

191 Browsing history

192 RSS feeds and web slices

194 Managing add-ons

195 InPrivate Browsing

196 Zoom and Print

198 Compatibility View

Internet Explorer version 9

You can also download Internet Explorer 9.0 to Windows Vista. However, for Windows XP, the last available version is Internet Explorer 8.

As discussed earlier, the version of Internet Explorer originally shipped with Windows 7 was Internet Explorer 8. This was superseded in April 2011 by Internet Explorer 9, which was shipped as an upgrade to be applied via Windows Update (see page 404).

You can quickly check if your version of Internet Explorer has been upgraded by looking at the forward and back arrows at the top left - they are the same size in IE8, but the back arrow is noticeably larger in IE9.

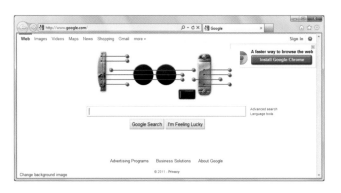

There's a simplified interface, with no titlebar text and with the command, favorites and other bars hidden by default. You should also be aware of improved performance and function, since the new features of Internet Explorer 9 include:

- Full hardware acceleration for text, graphics and video

- Notification when add-ons slow browser performance

- Jump Lists and pinned sites, with thumbnails and controls

- Accelerators for quick access to web services from the page

- One Box - for navigating to websites and for searching

- Visual search suggestions shown as you type

- Tab recovery messages and prompts when websites time out

- H.264-encoded HTML5 video support

- Compatibility mode to view websites with older designs

Hot tip

This screenshot illustrates the Google Doodle that celebrated the birth of Les Paul, the jazz and country guitarist.

There are several ways to start Internet Explorer:

1 Click the Internet Explorer icon on the taskbar

2 Select Start, All Programs and then Internet Explorer

3 If you've pinned the entry to the Start menu, just select Start, Internet Explorer

4 Select Start, then start typing Internet Explorer and click the entry that appears

Whichever way you open Internet Explorer, the first time it appears you'll get the Home page displayed, plus a second tab with a Welcome message and information on the new version.

5 Click the **x** on the second tab to close it, leaving the Home page open

Don't forget

Search reveals a second entry Internet Explorer (no Add-ons). This is in Start, All Programs, Accessories, System Tools, and it is a special, troubleshooting version.

Hot tip

If you are running 64-bit Windows, there's a third Internet Explorer (64-bit), but the default (and recommended) is the standard 32-bit, which is much faster than the 64-bit version.

Hot tip

Closing the second tab gives you the same display you get when you start Internet Explorer on subsequent occasions.

Internet Explorer window

When you open Internet Explorer it displays the Home web page in a simplified view with these components included:

One bar
address and search

Tab
bar

Mini
toolbar

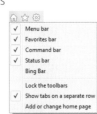

Web page   Page title   Scroll bars

To show the other bars, hidden by default:

1 Right-click alongside the Tab bar and select Favorites bar. Right-click again for the Command, Status or Menu bar

| Menu bar |
| Favorites bar |
| Command bar |
| Status bar |
| Bing Bar |
| Lock the toolbars |
| Show tabs on a separate row |
| Add or change home page |

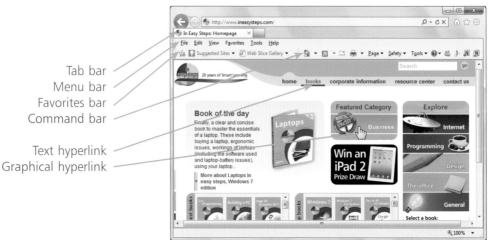

Tab bar
Menu bar
Favorites bar
Command bar

Text hyperlink
Graphical hyperlink

2 Click the One box to highlight the website address

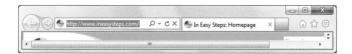

3 Start typing, to delete the old address and enter the new

4 Press Enter to display the website required

5 Select a hyperlink to display another web page

Don't forget

Click in the address box to display the typing cursor and make adjustments to the existing address.

Hot tip

Hyperlinks to other pages may be text or graphics. When you move the mouse over a link, the pointer changes to a hand, and the link is often underlined or otherwise highlighted.

Page back and forward

When you have visited several pages, you can move back and forward between them.

1 Click the large Back arrow to view the previous web page

2 Click the Back arrow for the previously visited web page or the Forward arrow for the more recent web page

3 You can also right-click the Arrows and select a web page

4 Your old visits are remembered for future browser sessions

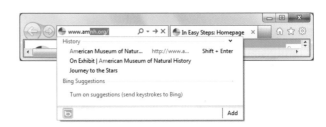

Search for web page

1 Select the One box and type keywords for your search, for example New York art gallery

2 Press Enter to search using the default search engine

3 Move the pointer over an entry to see more info

4 You can Turn on suggestions, to get a list of possible marches from the default search engine, as you type

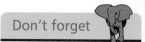
Don't forget

By default, Internet Explorer uses the Microsoft Bing search engine, but you can choose one yourself (see page 184).

Hot tip

You can switch from Web pages to lists of Images, Videos, Shopping, News and Maps, based on the same search words.

Change search provider

1 Click the One box and start typing an address

2 Click the Add button to add a search provider

3 The Internet Explorer Gallery displays on a separate tab. Select the search provider you want and click Install

4 Choose to make this your default if desired, and click Add

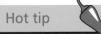

5 Select the One box and start typing

6 You could add further search providers e.g. Yahoo, and your preferred choice will remain as the default

Open in new window

To follow a series of links without discarding an existing sequence of pages, you can open a new browser window. There are several ways to do this.

1 Select Start, All Programs, Internet Explorer (or click Internet Explorer pinned to the Start menu)

2 Right-click the Internet Explorer shortcut on the taskbar, and select Internet Explorer on the Jump list

3 Press Ctrl+N to open a new window with the same web page, then select the web link required

4 Right-click the required link and select Open link in new window to display that web page in its own browser window

Don't forget

Each time you select Internet Explorer from Start menu or taskbar Jumplist, it opens a new browser window at the Home page.

Hot tip

You can switch between the separate Internet Explorer windows by clicking the Internet Explorer shortcut on the taskbar and selecting the appropriate thumbnail.

Tabbed browsing

Tabbed browsing enables you to open multiple web pages in a single browser window and switch between them by clicking the appropriate tab. To open a new tab:

1 Click the New Tab button on the tab row or press Ctrl+T

On the new tab page, you can type a web address into the Address bar, open previously closed tabs or browsing sessions, or select one of your regular sites.

2 Press Ctrl as you click a link to open it on a new tab, or right-click the link and then click Open in New Tab

When you open links on a web page in new tabs, these tabs are grouped, in the same color as the page they were linked from.

If you open many tabs, the title areas become narrower with scroll buttons when some tabs move off screen. To make larger numbers of tabs easier to work with, you can enable Quick Tabs.

 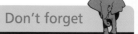
1 Click the Tools icon then select Internet options, then Tabs Settings on the General options panel

2 The Tabbed Browsing Settings panel displays

3 Click the box to Enable Quick Tabs and click OK, then close and reopen Internet Explorer

4 With multiple tabs active, press Ctrl+Q to show them all

Home page

You can choose which page gets displayed as your Home page when you open Internet Explorer.

1 With the required web page already displayed, right-click the Home button and select add or change home page

2 Use the web page as the home page, or add it to the current home page

3 If there's more than one tab open, you can use the tab set as your home page

Alternatively, you can display the Internet options (see page 187) to change the home page.

1 On the General options you can choose to:

- Type web page addresses
- Use the current tab set
- Use the default web page
- Use a blank page

2 Click OK to apply the changes specified

Internet Explorer will open the selected home page or pages when it opens, or when you click the Home icon on the tool bar, or when you use the keyboard shortcut Alt+Home.

Favorites

You can ask Internet Explorer to remember web page addresses.

1 With the required web page open, click the Favorites button, select Favorites and click Add to Favorites

Don't forget

The Favorites button opens the Favorites Center, which contains the Favorites, Feeds and History lists.

2 The name is the page title, but you can revise this as needed

3 Use the Favorites folder, or create a new folder

4 The favorites you create are added to the list displayed when you click the Favorites button

5 Click the green arrow to fix the list, so you can explore the folders

Hot tip

The list will continue to be displayed, even with Internet Explorer restarts, until you click the X at the top right to close the Favorites Center.

Pinned sites

Internet Explorer 9 has a new way to help you access frequently used websites - you can pin them to the taskbar.

1 Drag the icon from the address bar

2 Release the mouse button to drop the icon on the taskbar,

3 Click the Pinned Site icon to display the web page

The window is different from the normal Internet Explorer window. The Home button has been removed from the toolbar, and the Pinned site icon added next to the Back and Forward arrows, which are colored to match the icon. Clicking the icon returns to the Pinned site web page, which acts as a custom Home page for this instance of Internet Explorer.

Some websites are specifically designed for Pinned site operation.

Browsing history

You can review the websites and web pages that you have visited previously.

① Click the Favorites button and select History from the tabs in the Favorites Center

② Click a period (day or week) to display the websites viewed

③ Click the website name to display the list of web pages viewed at that site

④ Select a web page to view its contents (and remove the History list from view)

⑤ To change how the History gets displayed, click the arrow next to the View By Date button and select for example View By Most Visited and the list contents (and the button name) are changed

⑥ You can also View By Site, or View By Order Visited Today

⑦ Choose Search History and type appropriate keywords, then click Search Now

⑧ Previously visited web pages with those keywords included in their titles are listed

Don't forget

You can select Add to Favorites to add any of the History web pages that you select. You do not have to select the Favorites tab.

Hot tip

To keep the History list in view while you select web pages, click the green arrow . Click the Close button ✖ to remove the list.

Beware

Sometimes, when sharing a computer or using a public machine, you may not want to leave details of your browsing activity. See page 195 for InPrivate browsing.

RSS feeds and web slices

You may be able to keep up to date with frequently changing websites, without having to visit the sites to check for updates. Many sites offer RSS feeds or web slices to notify you of changes.

Internet Explorer can detect when RSS feeds or web slices are available, and will draw your attention to these with an icon. This is on the Command bar, so you'll need to make this available.

1 Right-click the toolbar and select Command bar

2 When you visit a website, Internet Explorer automatically searches for RSS feeds and web slices

3 An orange RSS icon means feeds have been detected

4 Click the arrow next to the icon to display the feeds available

5 A green RSS icon means that web slices (with or without feeds) have been detected on that web page

6 Click the arrow next to the RSS icon, to show the feeds

7 Select the name of an RSS feed to view the current items

Don't forget

You see an invitation to subscribe, plus a list of current items. You can sort these by date or alphabetically.

8 Click Subscribe to this Feed, and click the Subscribe button, to add the feed to the set of feeds being managed by your browser

Hot tip

As when you add your Favorites, you can create a folder, to organize your various RSS feeds.

9 Click the Favorites button and select the Feeds tab, to see the list of feeds in your browser

10 Select a feed to see the list of updates available

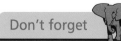

Don't forget

The names of feeds that have new entries available will be highlighted.

193

Managing add-ons

1 To run the Add-on Performance Advisor and review your add-ons, click the Choose add-ons button

2 Disable any add-ons that are not needed but are causing delays

3 To review all the add-ons, click Tools and select Manage Add-ons

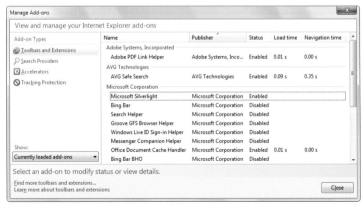

InPrivate Browsing

There are several ways to select InPrivate Browsing from an existing Internet Explorer session:

1 Select the Tools button and then click Safety

2 Click New Tab and scroll down to the links

3 Press the key combination Ctrl+Shift+P

In each case, Internet Explorer will launch a new browser session that doesn't keep any information about the web pages you visit or the searches you perform. Closing the browser window ends the InPrivate Browsing session.

4 You can also right-click the taskbar button for Internet Explorer or for a Pinned site to display the jump list Tasks

Don't forget

InPrivate Browsing helps prevent the browser retaining details such as temporary Internet files, form data, cookies, user names and passwords.

195

Hot tip

When you select InPrivate Browsing from a Pinned site, it opens with that web page, but with InPrivate turned on.

Zoom and Print

When you have a web page displayed, you can zoom in to see the finer details, or zoom out to get an overall view.

1 Click the Tools button and select Zoom then choose the zoom level you want

2 The web page is displayed with text and graphics resized

3 Right-click the Toolbar and select Status bar, and the Zoom level is shown on right hand side

4 Click the arrow next to the Zoom level to select a new level

5 Click the Zoom level button to return to 100%

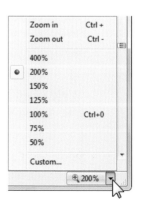

When you are ready to print a web page:

1 Click the Tools button and select Print, Print preview

2 By default, the Change Print Size option is set to Shrink To Fit, so the web page prints on a single sheet of paper

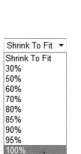

3 Click the down-arrow and select the 100% Print Size option, and the width is truncated

4 Select the Page Setup button to change print margins, headers and footers, and the Printer button to send the output to the printer

Don't forget

If you display the Command bar, you can select the Print and the Print Preview options from there.

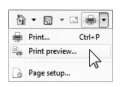

197

Hot tip

If you select Custom immediately after Shrink To Fit, you'll see the Zoom level applied, in this case 67%.

Compatibility View

The address box contains a number of buttons - Search, Autocomplete, Refresh and Stop. For some web pages however, an additional button appears. For example:

1 View www.nasa.gov, then view www.nga.org

2 Look more closely at the address box for each

The Nga.gov website has the Compatibility View button added. Internet Explorer has examined the website and recognized that it was designed for an earlier version of Internet Explorer, and so offers the option to enable Compatibility view.

3 Click the Compatibility View button, and it turns blue to show that it is now in effect for all web pages in the site

Compatibility View will remain enabled for that website on subsequent visits, until you click the Compatibility View button again to disable it.

11 Manage digital images

The computer is the ideal way to manage and organize the digital images you capture with your still camera, camcorder or cellphone. You can edit and print photos or create slide shows, or turn your photos and videos into movies that can be displayed on the TV or published to the Internet, to share with your family and friends.

200 Digital images

201 Image file formats

202 Digital camera

203 Install the software

205 Transfer the Photos

207 View the imported images

208 Transfer more images

209 Create panoramic image

211 Import with Windows

212 Windows Live Photo Gallery

213 Edit photos

215 Print your photos

216 Video clips

217 Edit your video clip

218 Create a movie from photos

220 Save and publish your movie

Digital images

Digital images may be created in a graphical application (see page 123), using a scanner or with digital still and movie cameras. The images are defined in terms of picture elements or pixels. The location, color and intensity of each pixel is stored in the image file. The images can then be displayed, enhanced, printed and shared using software on your computer or on specialised websites.

The size of the file depends on the image resolution (the number of pixels used to represent the image) and the color depth (the number of color variations defined). For example:

Pixel size	Bytes	Colors	Name
8-bit	1	256	
16-bit	2	65,536	hicolor
24-bit	3	16,777,216	trucolor

Another factor that influences the image size is the degree of zoom that the camera utilizes. Cameras use the capabilities of the camera lens to bring the subject closer, enlarging the image before it is stored as pixels. This is known as Optical zoom.

High resolution cameras can take images of say 4000 x 3000 pixels in trucolor. This works out at 36 million bytes per picture. Various image file formats have been developed to store such large images. These incorporate image compression algorithms to decrease the size of the file. The algorithms used are of two types: lossless and lossy.

Lossless compression algorithms reduce the file size without losing image quality, though they will not be compressed into as small a file as a lossy compression file.

Lossy compression algorithms take advantage of the inherent limitations of the human eye and discard information that does not contribute to the visible effect. Most lossy compression algorithms allow for variable quality levels (compression) and as these levels are increased, the file size is reduced. At the highest compression levels, the deterioration in the image may become noticeable, and give undesirable effects.

Image file formats

BMP (Windows bitmap)
This handles graphics files within Windows. The files are uncompressed, and therefore large, but they are widely accepted in Windows applications so simple to use.

GIF (Graphics Interchange Format)
This is limited to 256 colors. It is useful for graphics with relatively few colors such as diagrams, shapes, logos and cartoon style images. The GIF format supports animation. It also uses a lossless compression that is effective when large areas have a single color, but ineffective for detailed images or dithered images.

JPEG (Joint Photographic Experts Group)
The JPEG/JFIF filename extension is JPG or JPEG, and it uses lossy compression. Nearly every digital camera can save images in the JPEG format, which supports 24-bit color depth and produces relatively small files. JPEG files suffer generational degradation when repeatedly edited and saved.

PNG (Portable Network Graphics)
This was created as the successor to GIF, supporting trucolor and providing a lossless format that is best suited for editing pictures, where lossy formats like JPG are best for final distribution of photographic images, since JPG files are usually smaller than PNG. PNG works with well with web browsers.

RAW image format
This is used on some digital cameras to provide lossless or nearly-lossless compression, with much smaller file sizes than the TIFF formats from the same cameras. Raw formats used by most cameras are not standardized or documented, and differ among camera manufacturers. Graphic programs and image editors may not accept some or all of them, so you should use the software supplied with the camera to convert the images for edit, and retain the raw files as originals and backup.

TIFF (Tagged Image File Format)
This is a flexible format that saves 24-bit and 48-bit color, and uses the TIFF or TIF filename extension. TIFFs can be lossy and lossless, with some digital cameras using the LZW compression algorithm for lossless storage. TIFF is not well supported by browsers but is a photograph file standard for printing.

Don't forget

These are the main image file format types you will encounter in dealing with digital photographs and website images.

Don't forget

You should save originals in the least lossy format, and use formats such as PNG or TIFF to edit the images. JPEG is good for sending images or posting them on the Internet.

Digital camera

The Canon IXUS 107 digital camera is used to illustrate the ways you can manage your digital images in Windows 7.

This is a 12 megapixel camera with 4x optical zoom, and a 2.7 ins TFT LCD color monitor (approx 230,000 dots). It can take movies (at 30 frames per sec) as well as still images.

The image sizes supported are as follows:

Large	4000 x 3000 pixels
Medium 1	3264 x 2448 pixels
Medium 2	2592 x 1944 pixels
Medium 3	1600 x 1200 pixels
Small	640 x 480 pixels
Widescreen	4000 x 2248 pixels
Movie 1	640 x 480 pixels
Movie 2	320 x 240 pixels

To store these images, the camera supports a number of different types of memory cards, including:

SD	2 GB
SDHC	Above 2 GB up to 32 GB
SDXC	More than 32 GB

Other memory card types supported include MultiMediaCard, MMCplus and HC MMCplus.

Image files are recorded as JPEG for still images and AVI for movie images. Audio is recorded as a Wave file. The camera incorporates two levels of compression, Fine and Normal. These reduce the images to approximately 25% or 12.5% respectively.

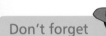

Install the software

1 Insert the supplied CD and select Run Setup.exe from the AutoPlay panel

2 Select you country and language when prompted then choose Easy Installation

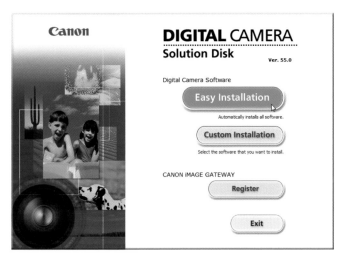

3 Click Install to begin installation of the two applications

...cont'd

4 Follow the prompts to allow the installation of each of the programs to proceed in turn

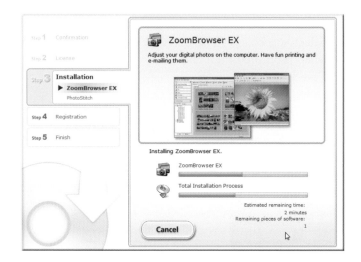

5 You will be offered the opportunity to register with the Canon Image Gateway online service

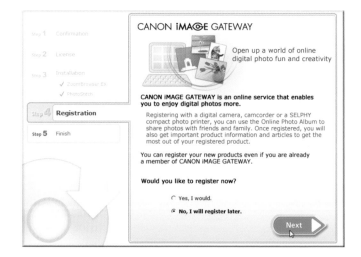

6 Finally, you are recommended to restart the computer, to make the software available

Restart

Transfer the Photos

1 Connect the camera to the computer using the USB cable provided and turn on the camera

Don't forget

Connect the camera to the mains power, or ensure that the battery is fully charged, before you start uploading images to your computer.

2 The first time, Windows recognizes that new hardware is attached and installs the drivers for the camera

3 The camera is added to the Devices and Printers folder, and the device program displays the options available

Hot tip

You can select Change Program to use Windows or Windows Live Photo Gallery in place of Canon CameraWindow to download images from the camera.

4 Select Browse files to view the camera contents from Windows, or double-click the device in Computer

5 Choose the option to Download images from Canon Camera using the Canon CameraWindow utility to transfer images from the camera

...cont'd

Don't forget

With CameraWindow you can import images to the computer, organize the images on the camera, or upload images to YouTube or Canon Image Gateway. `

Hot tip

Normally you'd select untransferred images, but you might want to re-import images if you have made changes and need the original image for backup purposes.

Beware

There's no Safely Remove option for the device, so make sure all activity involving the camera has ceased, then turn off the camera and disconnect.

6 Select the option to Import images from camera

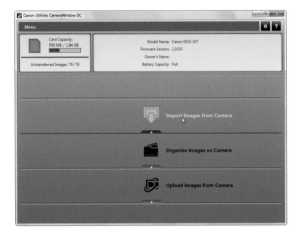

7 Choose Import untransferred images, Select images to import, or Import all images, as desired

8 The images are copied

9 When transfer completes, close CameraWindow, switch off the camera and detach it from the computer

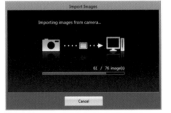

View the imported images

When you close the CameraWindow utility, the ZoomBrowser Ex application automatically starts up.

1 It displays Last acquired images, arranged by the date taken (yyyy_mm_dd), and retaining the image number

2 There are three modes for browsing images - Zoom, Scroll and Preview, or you can select Slide Show

3 There are a number of functions offered, including import, view and classify, edit, export, backup to CD, print and email, and connection to the Canon Image Gateway

4 Select File, Exit (or press the Close button) to finish

On the camera, the images are numbered in sequence starting from IMG_0001 (with gaps for deleted images). They are stored on the memory card in folders by month taken, e.g. 100__06.

On the computer the images retain their numbers and are stored in folders by day taken, e.g. 2011_06_27.

Transfer more images

Don't forget

As before, connect the camera with the USB cable and switch it on then select the Download images option (see page 205).

1 Connect the camera to the computer to download images

2 Select Import untransferred images and only the latest images (in this case 5 out of 81) will be copied over

Hot tip

Close CameraWindows after the transfer ends, then turn off the camera and disconnect it.

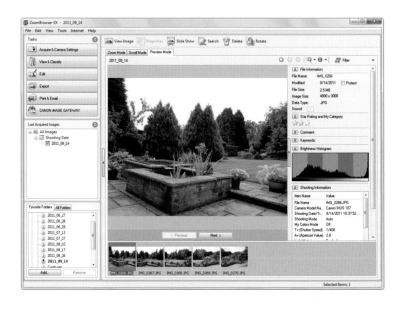

3 The Last acquired images are displayed in ZoomBrowser

4 These images are a set of overlapping views of a scene

Create panoramic image

If you have a set of overlapping images that you want to join together to create a wide panoramic view:

1 Select Start, All Programs, Canon Utilities, open the PhotoStitch folder then select the PhotoStitch application

Don't forget

You can preselect images in ZoomBrowser then click the Edit task and choose Stitch Photos, to open PhotoStitch with the photos ready to be arranged and merged.

2 Select PhotoStitch to merge images, then click Open and select the image files you want to join together

3 Drag images to change their sequence, then click Merge

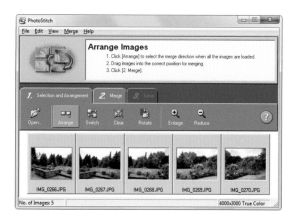

...cont'd

4 Select Start to merge, then select the Display Seams button to view the joins

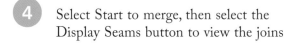

5 Select Save to write the merged file to your hard disk

6 Display the full merged image to see the effect produced

Import with Windows

1 Attach the camera or memory card, and Windows identifies the device and installs drivers

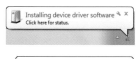

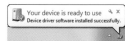

2 From the AutoPlay panel, select the option to Import pictures and videos using Windows

3 Specify a descriptive tag to be used for folder and file names, in this case the camera used

4 Click Import Settings to view or change the folder naming and location

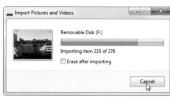

5 Click Import to transfer the pictures and videos and display them in Windows Explorer

Photos and videos imported with the camera software, rather than Windows (or Photo Live Gallery), will not be designated as Imported, and you must select the Pictures folder to display them.

Hot tip

You may not wish to use software supplied with your camera, if it is not Windows 7 compliant, or if you have several photo devices and want a standard solution.

Don't forget

The next time that you import from this device, Windows will only select new items and tells you when there is nothing to transfer.

Windows Live Photo Gallery

Hot tip

If you have Windows Live Essentials (see page 138) installed on your system, you can use Windows Live Photo Gallery.

Hot tip

If the pictures cover a variety of events, you can choose Review, organize and group items prior to import.

Don't forget

Windows Live Photo Gallery offers to become the default for a range of image file types. Click the box and choose No if you use other graphics editors for the file types.

1 From Autoplay, select Import pictures and videos using Windows Live Photo Gallery

2 The first time, you must accept the license terms

3 Specify a folder name for the new items

4 Add tags if desired, then click Import

5 The image files are transferred to the folder specified

6 Windows Live Photo Gallery displays the contents of the folder, grouped by month and year taken

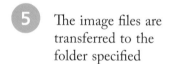

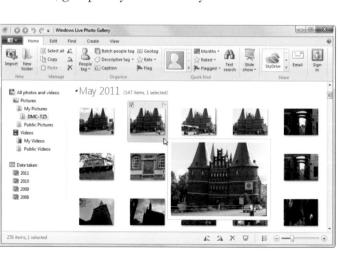

Edit photos

1 Double-click the image in Windows Live Photo Gallery and check that the Edit tab is selected

Hot tip

The software provided with your camera gives similar facilities to Live Photo Gallery. For more powerful and professional editing, use a program such as Adobe Photoshop.

2 Select Fine Tune, and click Adjust Exposure

3 Slide pointers either way until you get the desired effect

Don't forget

Successive changes may degrade the image, so you might want to click Revert to original to undo changes that proved unhelpful, and start over.

4 To keep the revised image, select Close File and changes are automatically saved back into the folder

...cont'd

At any time, even after saving the changed image and closing the file, you can still retrieve the original picture.

5   From Windows Live Photo Gallery, Edit the picture and select Revert to original

6   Click Revert, and the original is recovered, and all changes are nullified

You can check the contents of the Original Images folder where the initial copies of images are stored:

1   Click the Application button for Windows Live Photo Gallery and select Options then click the Originals tab

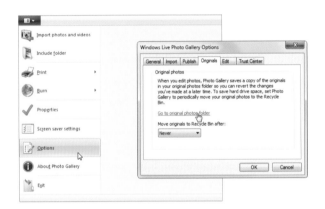

2   Click Go to original photos folder, and click the Address bar to show the file path for the folder

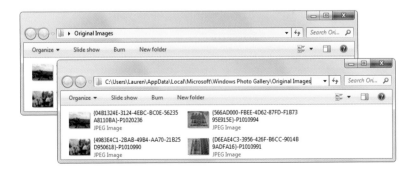

Print your photos

1 Open Windows Live Photo Gallery and select pictures to print, using Ctrl or Shift to select multiple files

2 Click the Application icon, select Print and Print again

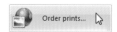

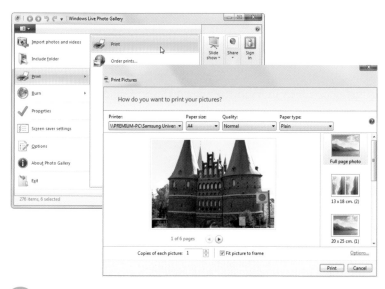

3 The default is to print one picture per page. Scroll down to view the variety of layouts offered

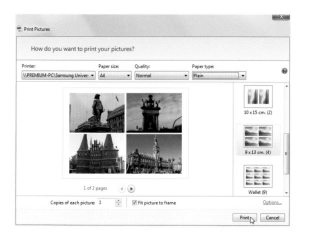

Hot tip

You can access the same Print function in the Pictures Library folder. The only difference is that Live Photo Gallery has the option to Order prints over the Internet.

4 Check the print quality and the paper size and type, then confirm the printer selection and click Print

215

Video clips

Hot tip

The Panasonic DMC-TZ5 creates video clips as .MOV files. The Canon IXUS-107 creates .AVI files, and there's a .THM thumbnail file with the same filename for each video file.

As well as still photos, digital cameras can take video clips, just like those taken by a digital camcorder. The video clips have a different file format from still photos. There are many formats in use. Those that you are most likely to encounter include:

.AVI   Audio Video Interleave File
.MOV   Apple QuickTime Movie
.MPG   MPEG Video File
.WVM   Windows Media Video File

Video clips are imported along with your photo images, and you can list the videos in Windows Live Photo Gallery.

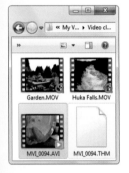

1 Double-click a video clip, and it will open and play

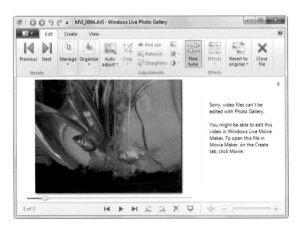

2 Click Fine Tune, and you find video files can't be edited in Photo Gallery. Movie Maker is suggested instead

Edit your video clip

1 Select the video clip, click Create tab and then Movie

2 In Windows Live Movie Maker, click Video Tools, Edit

Don't forget

You can choose to speed up or slow down the video clip, if you want to create a special effect.

From here you can set a new start point or finish point, split the video or trim sections out of the video. When you've finished:

3 Click the application button and select Save project as

4 Amend the name and click Save

Hot tip

You can add music and captions and make other changes. These only affect the project movie. The original video clip is unchanged.

Create a movie from photos

Windows Live Movie Maker can be used to give a professional appearance to your photos by adding transitions and effects, music and voice-over, titles and credits. When finished, you can save the photos as a movie, and write it to DVD to watch it on the TV, or email it to friends and family, or share it on the web.

You start with your imported collections of photos.

1 Open Windows Live Photo Gallery, select the folder and choose the items you want to include in your movie

2 Select the Create tab and click the Movie button

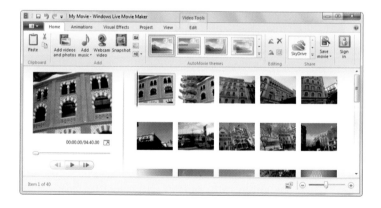

3 A new project, again called My Movie is generated as a slideshow, with a delay of 7 seconds between slides, and initially with no transition between slides or other effects

P1020012.JPG
Duration: 00:07.00
Transition: None
Pan and zoom: None
Effects: None

4 Move the mouse pointer over one of the AutoMovie themes, and you'll see the effects immediately displayed

There are seven themes - Default, Contemporary, Cinematic, Fade, Pan and Zoom, Black and White, and Sepia. Review each in turn to decide which is most effective.

5 Click the desired theme, to apply it to your movie

6 Click the Play button to run the movie

7 Click Preview full screen (or press F11) to see the movie full size

8 Drag the slider to move ahead, or click the Pause button to stop playing

9 Select Video Tools, Edit to adjust the time delay between slides

Duration: 7.00

Save and publish your movie

1 Press the Application button and select Save movie, then choose a setting e.g. high definition (1440 x 1080)

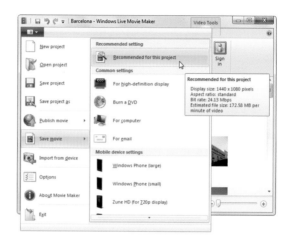

2 The project is saved in .wma video format, and includes copies of all the pictures, video clips and audio files

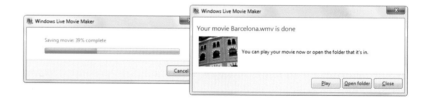

3 Select Publish Movie to prepare the movie for the Internet

4 You can save the movie on your Windows Live SkyDrive or select a service e.g. Facebook, YouTube or Flickr

5 Click Exit to end Windows Live Movie Maker

12 Music and media

The soundcard in your computer lets you play music from audio CDs or digital files, listen to radio broadcast over the Internet, or play videos with audio tracks. You can also share your media files with others on your network. With a microphone, you can even dictate to your computer.

222 Audio connections

223 Play CDs

224 Copy CD tracks

225 Media Player Library

226 Download media files

228 Internet radio

230 Home media streaming

231 Play to device or computer

232 Windows Media Center

234 Dictate to your computer

236 Text to speech

Audio connections

Digital out

Microphone in

Analog line in

Front/
Headphones

Center/
Subwoofer

Surround

Surround/
Back

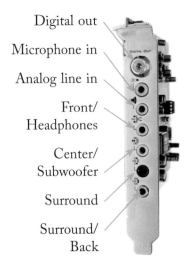

Desktop and laptop computers are equipped with audio facilities that can produce high fidelity audio playback. On desktop machines, the soundcard can provide the connections for various types of speakers ranging from simple stereo speakers to multiple speaker sets with surround sound.

For a laptop or notebook, the options are often limited to microphone and headset sockets, though some laptops include more sophisticated connections such as the SPDIF (Sony Philips Digital Interface) used for home theater connections.

You may have speakers attached to your computer, or built into the casing of portable computers. To check the configuration:

1 Select Start, Control Panel, then Hardware and Sound, and then Manage audio devices (from the Sound section)

2 Select Speakers and click Configure, then select your configuration, click Next and follow the prompts to Finish and save the speaker specification

Play CDs

Assuming you have a DVD/CD drive on your computer, you can use your soundcard and speakers to play an audio CD.

1 Insert the CD in the drive, and AutoPlay is displayed

2 Choose the action Play audio CD using Windows Media Player

The CD begins to play, as an unknown album and showing no details other than the track numbers and their durations.

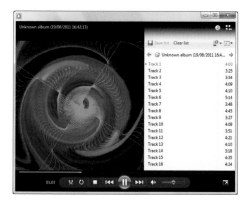

If you are connected to the Internet, Windows Media Player will locate and download information about the CD, and display the album and track titles. You can also change the Visualization to display the album cover image.

Hot tip

Click the box Always do this for audio CDs, and the selected option is carried out automatically in future, whenever an audio CD is identified.

Hot tip

Right-click the window and select Visualization to choose the effects to display, for example the Album art (cover image).

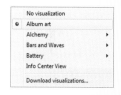

Don't forget

Drag the window to its minimum size, especially if you select to always show the player on top of other applications.

223

Copy CD tracks

You can copy songs from the audio CD, an action known as Ripping the CD, where Media Player makes file copies that get added to your library. To specify the type of copy:

1 Right-click the Media Player windows and select More options

2 Click the Rip Music tab

3 Set Format as one of the Windows Media Audio (WMA) file formats, or select the MP3 format for greater flexibility

4 Select the bit rate - higher bit rates will give much better quality but will use up more disk space

5 Click the Rip CD button to extract and compress the tracks

6 The tracks are added to your Music library, and stored with a folder for each artist, and a subfolder for each of their albums

Media Player Library

1 When the CD has been copied, select Go to Library (or click the Switch to Library button)

2 Select Music to display the Music library, by artist and track

3 Select Artist or Genre to group all the associated albums

4 Select Album to display the albums alphabetically by title

Don't forget

The Windows Media Player library displays the contents of the Music, Videos and Pictures libraries for the current user, with links to the libraries of users who are online and members of the HomeGroup.

Hot tip

Click Organize and select Customize navigation pane, to group music by other properties, such as year, rating or composer.

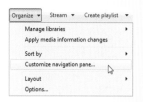

Hot tip

Double-click a group to display the individual tracks that it contains, arranged by album.

Download media files

You can add items to your media library from online.

1 Click the arrow on the Online Stores tab and select Browse all Online Stores

2 You can download audio books from Audible, videos from Mixplay, and music from Emusic or Farolatino

3 For example, pick eMusic and click Yes to connect online to that store

4 Provide your email address, password and country and click Get started

5 You can choose from plans that offer various numbers of downloads for a monthly fee

If you'd rather not commit to a regular plan, you can select an online store such as Farolatino and download media files on-demand, with no set requirement.

1 Select the Farolatino online store and switch to that store

2 Provide a user name and password, and your name, email address, date of birth and country

3 Respond to the Confirmation of Registration email and sign in using your user name and password

4 Select a category or search for an artist to find an album

5 Play an extract, view the video or download the MP3

227

Internet radio

If you just want to listen to music without saving it on your computer, Media Player can link you to Internet radio stations.

1 Click the arrow on the Online Stores tab and select Media Guide

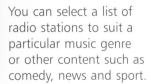
2 Select the Internet Radio option

3 Search by keyword, scroll the list of stations or select a category, for example Oldies music

4 Review the Editor's Picks or scroll the whole list to select a station you'd like to try, then click Listen

5 The selected radio station Boomer Radio begins to play

6 Select Visit to open the website for the station

Hot tip

The radio channels are in effect playlists of related songs that are stored at the station's website and broadcast specifically for you when you visit that radio station.

7 You can review details of the channels or choose channels directly from the website and play them in the browser

8 Close the browser to return to the Media Player

If you want to return to a radio station that you played earlier, select Media Guide and Internet Radio, and you'll find a list of recently played stations. Click Listen for the one you want.

Don't forget

The Pause button is disabled for radio, so click the Stop button, and you can select Go to Library, or Play again to resume that channel.

1 Click Switch to Now Playing, to display the Player mode and see the artist and song title

2 To return to the channel list, click Switch to Library

Home media streaming

Anything that you can play in Windows Media Player, you can share with other computers and devices on your home network.

1 Open Windows Media Player, select the Library view and click the Stream button

2 This should show Allow remote control, Automatically allow devices to play, and More streaming options

With these settings, your Windows Media Player will have access to Other Libraries, in particular the media libraries that were shared when the computers on your network joined the HomeGroup (see page 261).

3 Select one of the computer/user combinations to see what's available - in this example Music, Videos, Pictures and other items

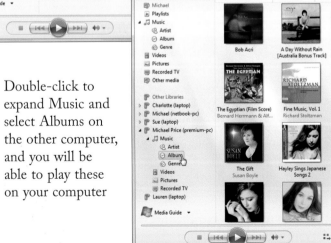

4 Double-click to expand Music and select Albums on the other computer, and you will be able to play these on your computer

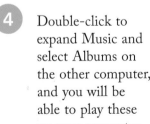

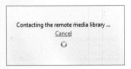

Play to device or computer

You can also use media streaming to play items from your computer on another computer or device on the network.

1 Start by turning on the networked device (a networked TV for example) or start Windows Media Player on the target computer

2 Open Windows Media Player on your computer and ready the items for playing but press the Pause button

3 Click the Play to button and select the device or computer you want to use

4 Windows Media Player contacts the device and initiates playing the selected media files. You can the control the operation from either computer

Hot tip

The Play to function is also supported by the example Windows Phone (see page 293), which can also stream media files to networked devices or computers running Windows Media Player.

231

Don't forget

You don't have to use Windows Media Player to initiate Play to. You can simply highlight a group of files in one of the library folders, then right-click the files, select Play to and click the target device.

Windows Media Center

If you use your computer as a home entertainment system, the Windows Media Center provides another way to manage your media files and functions.

1 Click Start, All Programs and Windows Media Center

2 The Media Center includes pictures & videos, music, movies and TV (live, recorded and Internet)

3 Click Search for details of the free streaming Internet TV video service, with TV shows, movies, trailers and clips

4 View pictures, slide shows and videos from your libraries, and view or input media files from a removable device

5 You can play music, create playlists, watch slide shows while playing music, or copy music from CDs and DVDs

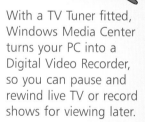
6 The Extras library provides access to Windows games, including Chess, Mahjong and FreeCell, and also showcases various news, sport and lifestyle websites

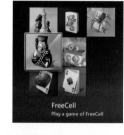

7 From Tasks, you can burn to CD/DVD, sync your devices and even Shutdown your computer when you've finished the session

Dictate to your computer

One way to interact with your computer is to simply tell it what you want, with Windows Speech Recognition.

1 Click Start, Control Panel, Ease of Access, then Start Speech Recognition

2 Select the type of microphone that you'll be using, a headset microphone being best for speech recognition

3 Follow the advice to position the microphone effectively then read text aloud so the microphone volume can be set

4 Follow the prompts to choose Manual or Voice activation mode, and run Speech Recognition when Windows starts

5 Click Start Tutorial to learn about the basic features and to Train your computer to better understand you

When you start Windows, Speech Recognition will start up and switch itself into Sleeping mode, or Turn listening off (depending on the activation mode you have set).

1 If it is Off, right-click the Speech Recognition bar and select Sleep

2 Say "Start listening" (or click the button on the bar)

3 Say "What can I say?" to view the Speech Reference Card

Text to speech

You can let the computer talk to you, using the text to speech facilities of the Narrator application.

Hot tip

You can select Start, All Programs, Accessories, Ease of Access and then click Narrator.

1 Press Windows Logo key + U to open the Ease of Access Center and select Narrator (or press Spacebar when Narrator is highlighted)

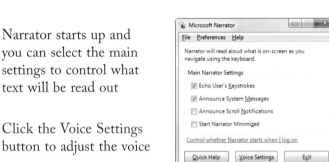

Don't forget

From the Ease of Access Center select Use the computer without a display and choose Turn on Narrator, to have the program start automatically when you start Windows.

2 Narrator starts up and you can select the main settings to control what text will be read out

3 Click the Voice Settings button to adjust the voice

There is only one voice currently available, but it does sound very natural. Adjust the speed, volume and pitch to suit your preferences. Narrator will read the contents of the screen, including the text content of programs such as Notepad, WordPad, and Windows Help and Support.

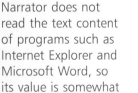
Beware

Narrator does not read the text content of programs such as Internet Explorer and Microsoft Word, so its value is somewhat limited, in comparison to Speech Recognition.

4 Click the Help command to see a list of keyboard shortcuts such as:
Insert+F8 (read current document)
Insert+F6 (read current paragraph)
Insert+F4 (read current word)
Ctrl (stop Narrator from reading text)

13 Devices and printers

You can add various types of printers and scanners to your computer, and Windows will normally provide the software device drivers needed to manage the devices. Windows can also help when you regularly print from your laptop at multiple locations.

238   Add a printer

240   Updating device drivers

242   Sharing the printer

244   Share printer with XP

246   Wireless printer

249   Virtual printers

251   Generic / text only printer

253   Location aware printing

254   Add a scanner

256   Using the scanner

Add a printer

To see what devices and printers are defined on your system:

1 Select Start, Control Panel, then pick Hardware and Sound and finally click Devices and Printers

2 Alternatively, click the View devices and printers entry, in the Hardware and Sound category

3 The Devices and Printers panel is displayed with, in this example, six devices associated with the computer

Memory card readers   Display screens   Keyboard   Mouse   System devices

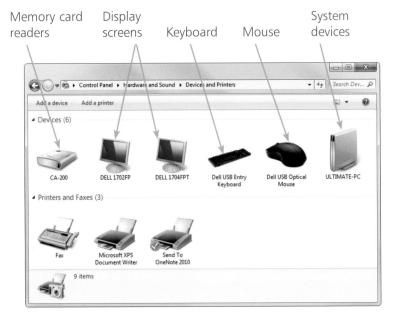

4 There are three items under Printers and Faxes, but these are virtual printers or software devices (see page 249)

As initially installed, there are no physical printers or scanners defined in the Windows 7 system. However, for a printer that attaches via the USB ports, adding the device is simply a matter of plugging it in and letting Windows complete the definition on your behalf.

Don't forget

You can customize the Start menu (see page 64) to display Devices, and then select the option indirectly from the Start menu.

Hot tip

There's an option to Add a printer, for devices that are not recognized automatically, and you can select Add device, to add a wireless or network device.

To add a USB printer to the computer

1 Switch on the printer, and plug its USB cable into a port

2 Windows immediately detects the new device and begins to install the necessary device driver software

Don't forget

If you select Add printer, to add a local printer, you are told this option is not for USB printers.

→ Add a local printer
Use this option only if you don't have a USB printer.

3 Windows adds USB printing support and driver software, and lets you know when the installation has completed

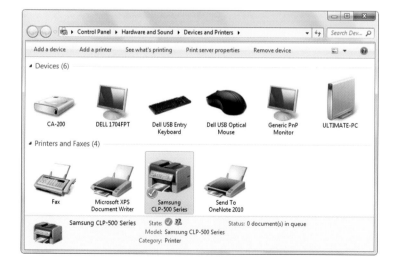

Hot tip

You can make the printer available for sharing (see page 242), as indicated by the People flag shown in the Details pane for the printer.

4 Open Devices and Printers, and you'll see the new printer has been added and assigned as the default printer

Updating device drivers

To check the date for your printer driver:

1 From Devices and Printers, right-click the printer, then select Printer properties and click About

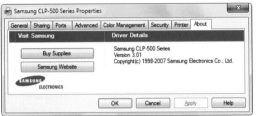

2 The driver in this case is copyright 1998-2007, which could be considered somewhat dated

3 To check for the latest driver visit the manufacturer's website, e.g. www.samsung.com, and select Support

4 Provide the model number and select Find Product

5 The support site has a Windows 7 driver that supports this printer, with a November 2010 release date

6 Click the Download button and follow the prompts to save the driver installation file on your system

Don't forget

You can run the program immediately, but if you save it to disk and then run the program, you can retain a copy for backup purposes.

7 Run the installation program to start Setup

Samsung_Universal_
Print_Driver.exe

8 Follow the prompts to configure the printer

Hot tip

You may be required to accept terms and conditions, and you may be asked to specify if this is to become the default printer.

241

9 The new driver will be added to Devices and Printers

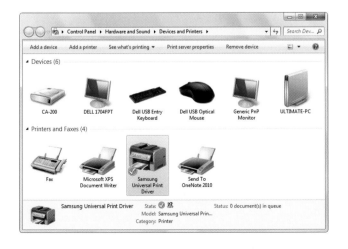

Hot tip

The printer will now be managed by the up-to-date driver software.

Sharing the printer

When you have attached a printer to your computer and installed the driver needed, you can allow other users to use it.

If you've set up or joined a HomeGroup (see page 260) you may have allowed sharing already. To check the settings:

1 Select Start, Control Panel and then click Choose HomeGroup and sharing options, in Network and Internet

2 This shows that your printers are being shared with other members of the HomeGroup

3 Scroll down and select Change advanced sharing settings

4 You may need to turn on file and printer sharing

To access the shared printer from another Windows 7 computer:

1 Open Windows Explorer, select Network and open the computer with the printer to be shared

2 Right-click the printer and select Connect

3 Windows searches for a printer driver

4 Agree to use the driver from the computer

243

5 Windows copies the files

6 The printer is added to Devices and Printers, and is made the default printer

Share printer with XP

Computers running with systems other than Windows 7 can also share the printer. For example, to access from Windows XP:

1 Select Start and then click My Network Places

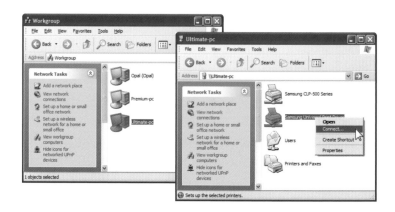

2 Click View workgroup computers, open the computer then right-click the printer and select Connect

3 Confirm you'd like to install the driver for the printer

4 Windows connects to the computer with the required printer and copies the driver software

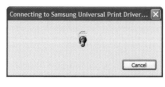

5 The printer is added to the Printers and Faxes folder, and you can right-click to Set as Default Printer

You can also add network printers via Printers and Faxes.

1 Select Start, Printers and Faxes
   and click Add a printer

You can add printers
that are attached locally
to your computer, to
another computer on
the network, or directly
attached to the network.

2 The Add Printer wizard starts, and
   you can seek a printer on your network

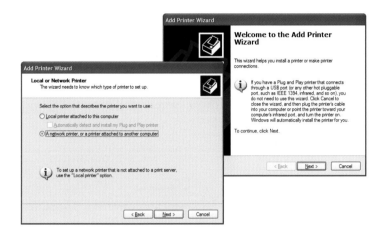

3 Choose to Browse for Printer, and you see a list of
   printers available in the workgroup on your network

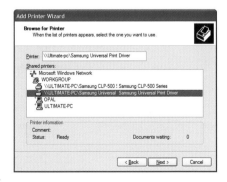

You will be asked to
confirm that you want to
copy the driver from the
computer hosting the
printer.

4 Select the printer, specifying it as the default if desired,
   and complete the wizard

5 The printer is added to the folder

Wireless printer

Don't forget

If you have a wireless printer set up on your network, you can add it to your Windows 7 computer.

1 Open Devices and Printers, and select Add a printer

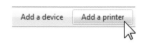

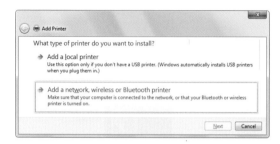

2 Choose to Add a network, wireless or Bluetooth printer

3 Select the wireless printer from the list offered

Hot tip

Windows may already have the driver, but even when it doesn't, it will still try to help you obtain the driver.

4 Usually, Windows will be able to install the printer

5 In this case, the driver required isn't available

The Action Center detects the problem and offers a solution.

Don't forget

You are connected to the printer manufacturer's website, to download the relevant installation program.

1 Download and run the driver installation program

Hot tip

During the install, you'll be asked to agree terms and conditions, and to confirm the specific printer you want to add.

2 Follow prompts to install printer software

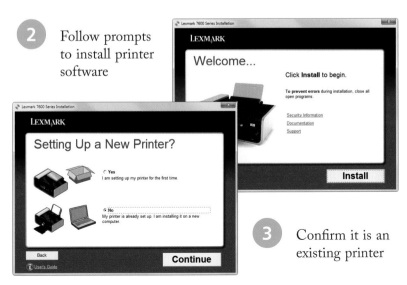

3 Confirm it is an existing printer

4 Indicate that the connection to be defined is wireless

5 Confirm that the printer is powered up and online

6 Press Continue and follow the prompts

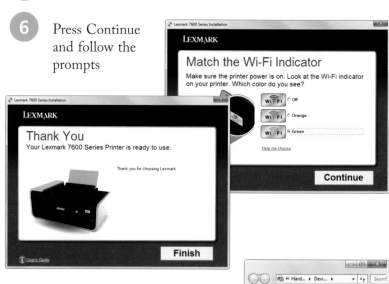

7 When the installation completes, the printer is added to Devices and Printers, and flagged as the default

8 You should reset the default printer if appropriate

Virtual printers

You may have some items in Devices and Printers that are not physical devices but are software programs that act as virtual printers. To see how these could be used:

1 Open a document with text and graphics in WordPad

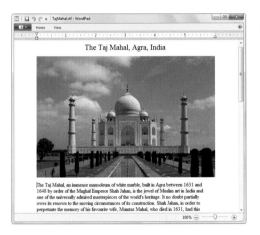

2 Click the WordPad button and select Print

Don't forget

WordPad is chosen since it supports text and graphics, but you could use any Windows program.

3 Choose one of the virtual printers, for example Adobe PDF

4 You'll be asked to confirm the location and file name, and a PDF version of the document is saved

Alternatively:

1 Select Microsoft XPS Document Writer as the printer

2 Provide a name, and the document will be saved in XPS format

Hot tip

These printer drivers both create files and operate similarly, but there are differences, e.g. one suggests a file name while the other does not.

...cont'd

Some printer drivers pass control on to other programs:

1 Select Fax as the printer and Fax Setup is started

2 Choose your setup, then complete the cover page, and send your document as a .tif image file

If you have Office 2010 installed, you may have the option to send documents and other prints to OneNote.

1 Select Send to OneNote 2010 as the printer

2 Choose where in OneNote to insert the printout

Generic/text only printer

To create a generic/text only printer:

1 Open Devices and Printers, click Add a printer and select Add a local printer then click Next

Don't forget

You can install a generic/ text only printer driver in Windows 7 as a way to capture text information in a file, or for use with an application that requires this type of printer driver.

2 Select Use an existing port and choose FILE: (Print to File) and click Next.

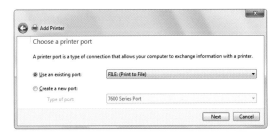

Hot tip

If you are creating support for an old printer, you'd choose the port it uses, COM1: for example.

3 In the Manufacturer field select Generic and in the Printers field select Generic/Text Only then click Next

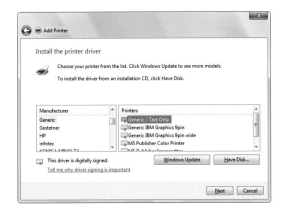

...cont'd

④ Accept or amend the suggested name and click Next

⑤ Select Do not share this printer and click Next, then clear the box Set as default printer, and click Finish

⑥ The printer is added to Devices and Printers

To check out the operation of this printer:

① Create a simple document using Notepad - it is helpful to use plain text for the initial testing

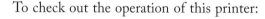

② Select Print and choose the Generic/ Text Only printer

③ Provide the file name (type .prn is usual for printouts) and click OK

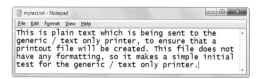

Location aware printing

If you print from your laptop at several places - home, office and college for example - you'll need to switch printers when you change location. Windows 7 can do this for you automatically. Wherever you print, Windows 7 remembers which network and printer you use. When you return to that place, Windows switches the default printer to match the one last used. To manage the location-aware printing settings that are recorded:

1 Open Devices and Printers, and select a printer then click Manage default printers on the toolbar

2 Make sure that the option to Change my default printer when I change networks has been selected

3 Click Select network and choose a network, click Select printer and then the printer, then click Add

4 Repeat steps 3 and 4 for each network, then click OK

Beware

This feature is available in the Professional, Ultimate and Enterprise editions of Windows 7, and only on laptops and other portable devices that use a battery.

Don't forget

For a wireless network to appear in the list, you must have previously connected successfully to that wireless network.

Hot tip

Select an existing entry to Remove it, or select a different printer and then Add changes to Update.

Add a scanner

You can install a scanner to the Devices and Printers folder.

1 To install a USB connected scanner such as the Epson Perfection 1260, insert the USB cable and switch on

2 If the driver is available, the scanner will be installed

3 If the driver is missing, an error message displays

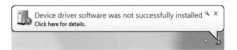

4 An Action Center message gives the solution - download and install the driver from the Seiko Epson Corporation

5 Select the link and at the manufacturer's website, select your operating system e.g. Windows 32-bit

Don't forget

Windows 7 will have the drivers for many scanners, but may not include older devices.

Hot tip

Windows checks its compatibility database and identifies where to find the missing driver.

Beware

The driver for this scanner is available in a Windows 32-bit version. If your system is 64-bit, Epson cannot provide a suitable driver.

Windows 32-bit
Macintosh
Other Operating Systems
All Operating Systems

6 Installation instructions for the selected system are shown

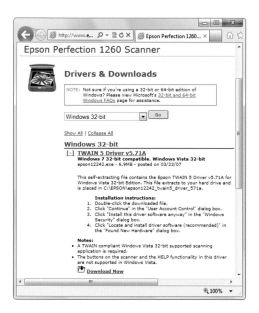

Don't forget

The downloaded file is self-extracting and contains the drivers for a number of Epson scanners, including the Perfection 1260.

7 Click Download Now, and choose to Run or Save the file

Hot tip

You may find it best to unplug the scanner before installing the software. When you reconnect the scanner, Windows will now recognize and add it.

255

8 When you do run the downloaded file, it will start the installation process, and the scanner will be added

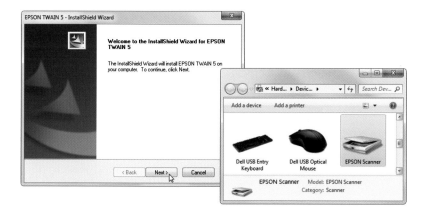

Using the scanner

1 Open Devices and Printers, right-click the scanner device and select Scan Properties

Beware

There are four buttons on the scanner, but only the Start button is supported in the Windows 7 driver.

Start Button
Copy Button
Scan to E-mail Button
Scan to Web Button

2 Click the Events tab, and select the Start button

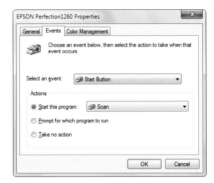

Hot tip

You can invoke the Scan program when you want to import an image, or the Windows Fax and Scan Application.

Scan
Windows Fax and Scan Application

3 Choose Start this program and select Scan

4 Insert a document and press the Start button

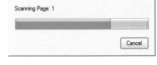

5 The document is scanned and the image is imported

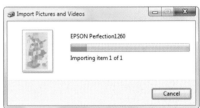

Don't forget

The images are stored in a folder with the name set to the date that they were scanned.

6 View the image in the Pictures library

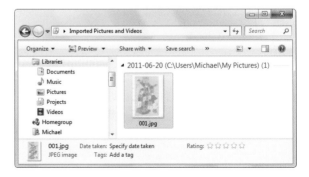

14 Networking Windows

If you have more than one computer, even just a laptop and a desktop machine, you can connect them with cables or wireless, and share information between the computers. Windows makes it easy to set up and manage the network that you create.

258   Create a network

260   Create a HomeGroup

262   Network and sharing center

264   Connect to wireless network

266   Dual network access

267   Manage wireless networks

268   Network versus HomeGroup

269   Network map

270   Sharing folders

272   Monitor network

Create a network

A network consists of several devices that exchange information over a cable or via radio waves. A computer plus Internet router forms a small network. If you have other computers, they can be added to share the Internet connection and perhaps share data information with each other, creating a larger network.

To be able to connect to the network, each computer requires an Ethernet (wired) network adapter plus cable, or a wireless network adapter. The flow of data between the computers and the router is managed by Windows.

To start a new network using a wired network adapter

1 Install a network adapter in the computer (if required)

2 Start up the computer and Windows recognizes there is a network adapter with no connection

3 Connect the adapter to the router using a network cable

4 Windows will automatically detect a new network and ask you the network location type

258

Select Public network for locations such as libraries, Internet cafes, hotels or airports. HomeGroup is not available, and Network discovery is turned off.

Select Work network for the office, college or other workplace where you generally know who will be connecting. Network discovery is turned on, but you can't participate in a HomeGroup.

Select Home network for the home or other known and trusted environment. You can create or join a HomeGroup, and Network discovery is turned on.

5 Select your network location e.g. Home network

Don't forget

Network discovery lets you find other computers on the network, and lets other network users find your computer. Turning Network discovery off hides your computer.

259

Hot tip

The network adapter settings will now show the connection to the network.

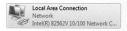

6 Windows completes the network definition

7 Your computer is now linked to any other computers on the network

8 If the router includes Internet access, you will also be able to connect to the Internet

Create a HomeGroup

When you select Home network, and no HomeGroup has been set up, you are invited to create a HomeGroup.

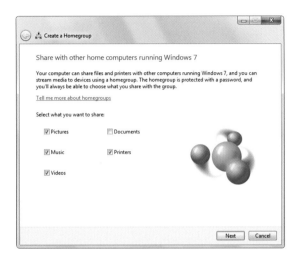

Don't forget

When there is already a HomeGroup on the network, you will be invited to participate.

1 Choose what to share with other users on the network, the default being media files and printers, then click Next

Hot tip

You can view or change the password from the Network and Sharing Center (see page 262), or from the Control Panel.

2 Windows provides the password needed for other computers to join the HomeGroup

3 Record the password and click Finish

When you connect to a Home network which already has a HomeGroup, you are invited to join.

You will only be invited to join the HomeGroup if you specify your network location as Home when you connect to the network.

If the HomeGroup was created by another user on the network, you must be given the password to be able to participate.

1 Click Join now

2 Select what you want to share and click Next

3 Type the password and click Next

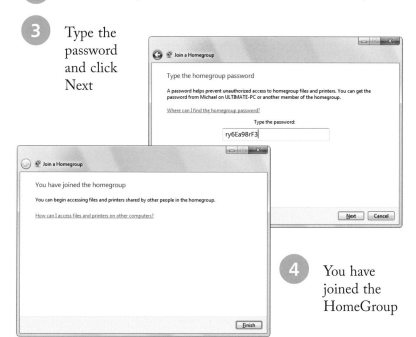

Everyone on the network who joins the HomeGroup will be able to share everything that you make available.

4 You have joined the HomeGroup

Network and sharing center

Don't forget

You can also select Start, Control Panel and click View Network status and tasks, to open the Network center.

Hot tip

Select the Network location, in this case Home network, if you need to switch to an alternative network location.

Hot tip

Select View or print the HomeGroup password, if you need a reminder or if you want to share it with another user on the network.

1 Select the Network icon in the Notification area and click the option to Open Network and Sharing Center

2 Your basic network information is displayed

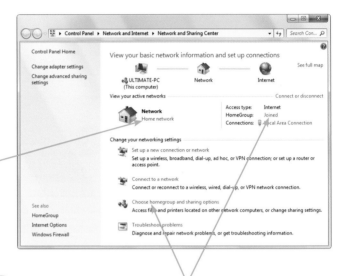

3 Click the HomeGroup status, or select the link to Choose HomeGroup and sharing options

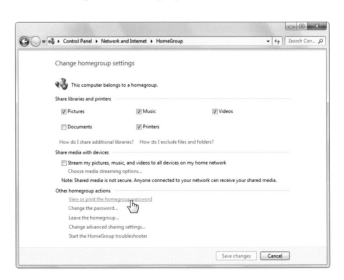

1 For detailed information, click Local Area Connection

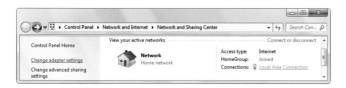

2 The connection status is displayed. Click the Details button for network connection details, including addresses

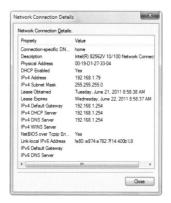

3 Click Close then Close again to return to the Center

4 Click Change adapter settings, on the left hand menu to view the adapter status and make changes to the settings

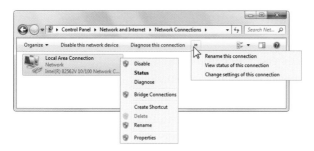

5 Click the toolbar buttons, or right-click the adapter icon to select one of the options or to view the properties

Connect to wireless network

1 Click the Network icon in the Notification area

2 Windows will detect available wireless networks

3 Click the network you want to join, and the Connect button appears

4 Click to Connect automatically whenever your computer is in range of the network

5 Select the Connect button, and you are prompted for the security key

6 Click the box to hide the characters that you type

7 Click OK to connect

8 Windows connects to the network and validates the security key

9 The computer is shown as connected to the network

10 Internet access will be indicated if it is available on the network

11 Click the network icon and select Open Network and Sharing Center

12 Network information for the wireless network is displayed

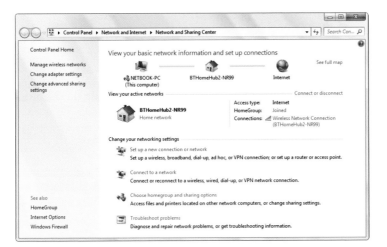

13 Click Wireless Network Connection to display the status

14 Click the Details button for the wireless network connection details

15 Click Close then Close again to return to the center

Dual network access

One network
connection

Two network
connections

1 Open the Network and Sharing Center for the Laptop

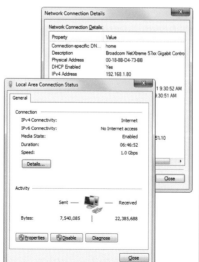

2 View the details for the two connections

Manage wireless networks

1 Open the Network and Sharing Center and select the link to Manage wireless networks

Don't forget

The last wireless network you connect to may become the default if there are several wireless networks to choose from. However, you can change the sequence.

2 To change the priority given to a network, right click the network entry and select Move up or Move down

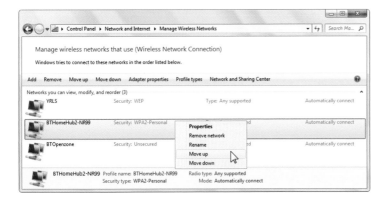

3 Select Properties if you want to change from Connect automatically to Connect to a preferred network

4 Click OK to apply the change

Hot tip

If you move around in a location with more than one wireless network, you may find your computer switching between the networks, if you've set each for automatic connection.

Network versus HomeGroup

When you have network discovery on, Windows will find all devices on the network that are not specifically hidden. To see what devices are visible to your computer:

1 Select Start, Computer and click Network

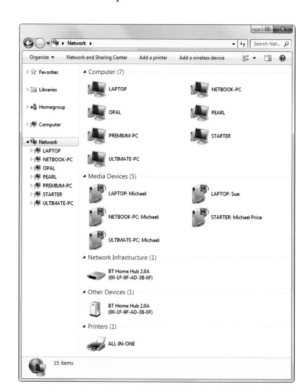

268

2 Select HomeGroup to see the computers that belong

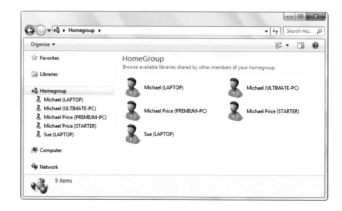

Network map

1 From the Network and Sharing Center, click See full map

2 Windows creates and then displays the network map

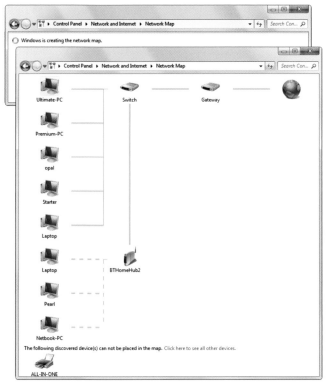

Don't forget

Only computers that have discovery turned on will appear on the map. So you'll see Home and Work computers, but not Public computers.

Hot tip

The information that is displayed depends on the device type. For example, the XP computer supports IPv4 addresses but not IPv6.

3 Move the mouse pointer over an icon to display details, as here with the Ethernet and wireless connections for the Laptop

Sharing folders

If you want to share a folder that is not in a library, or if you want to share with computers running other operating systems, you need the file sharing wizard.

1 Open Windows Explorer and locate the required folder

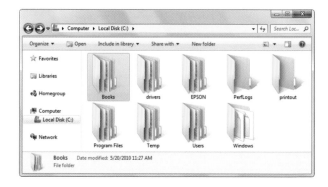

2 Click the Share with button and select HomeGroup with all members, or Specific people to share with individuals

3 Type a user name and click Add to include that user

4 Click the user names to change the permission from the default Read to Read/Write (or Remove)

5 Click the Share button to assign the folder permissions granted

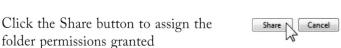

The folder is shared, and you are given the options to email the links for the shared item, or to copy the link into a program.

1 Click the link to Show me all the network shares on this computer

Another way to apply share options to a folder is to use Properties:

1 Right-click the folder icon and select Properties

2 Select the Sharing tab

3 Click the Share button to run the Sharing Wizard

4 Click Advanced Sharing to apply further controls, for example to limit the number of simultaneous users

The default is 20 users, but you can choose a lower value if required to improve performance.

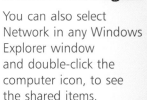

Monitor network

Windows provides several tools to monitor the activities on your network.

Don't forget

Network monitors can help you identify the causes of unexpected or excessive network activity on your system.

1 Right-click the taskbar and select Start Task Manager

2 Select the Networking tab, to see activity charts for the network adapter or adapters (wireless and wired)

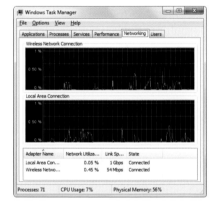

3 Select Start, type Resource then click Resource Monitor

Hot tip

You can also download some of the Gadgets from the Online Gallery to keep an eye on your network activity, for example, the System Monitor and the Network Meter.

4 Comprehensive tables and charts are displayed, giving a real-time view of all of the networking activity

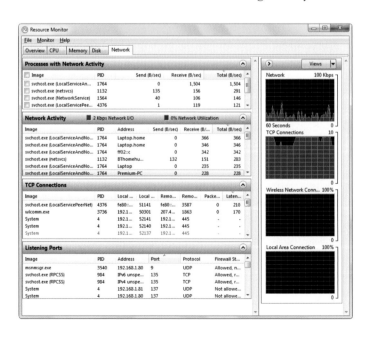

15 Laptops and Multitouch

Windows supports portable computers, with power management facilities, the Mobility Center and tools such as handwriting recognition. There's also Multitouch support for touchscreen monitors on all-in-one and desktop computers.

274 Portable computers

275 Power management

276 Portable power management

278 Battery meter

280 User interface for portables

282 Windows Mobility Center

284 Mobility Center functions

286 Netbook computers

288 Touch and Tablet PCs

290 Taking advantage of Touch

Portable computers

Portable computers are machines that run from battery power, and are usually designed with space-saving and weight reduction in mind. There are various categories of portable computer, differentiated by the extent to which one or other of these design targets has been implemented.

- **Laptop** - Larger and heavier, typically with 17" screen and seven to ten pounds in weight, and usually higher processing capabilities, to form a desktop replacement

- **Notebook** - A smaller Laptop, typically 12" to 17" screen and three to six pounds, but of similar power to laptops

- **Netbook** - Smaller, lighter and lower powered mini laptop, with no internal optical drive, but very portable, with 10" or 11" screen, weight of one to two pounds, and a long battery life

- **Tablet PC** - A notebook or netbook with a touch screen in place of (or as an alternative to) a keyboard, but still running a full PC operating system

- **Convertible** - A notebook with keyboard, where the screen can be rotated or flipped to give the Tablet PC configuration

- **All-in-One Computer** - Space-saving machine, with a 21" to 23" monitor that will often be touch sensitive, that accommodates the processor, memory, adapters and drives, with a wireless keyboard and wireless mouse

You can set up Windows 7 to take into account the specific characteristics of your portable computer. Certain features can have a major impact on performance and battery life. Some features are specific to portable computers and not available for desktops. Then there is the Windows 7 Starter edition which in many ways is appropriate for mini or netbook computers. We'll look at some of these features to see how they affect your use of portable computers.

Power management

This feature is provided for all types of computer, though it takes on particular significance for battery powered PCs.

On a mains powered computer such as the HP TouchSmart 610:

1 Select Start, Control Panel, Hardware and Sound then select Power Options

2 You can select one of the power plans offered, or create a power plan (based on an existing power plan)

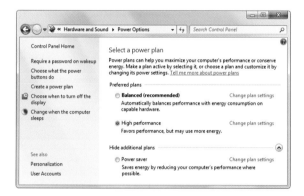

3 Select the action Choose what the power buttons do, to specify Do Nothing, Hibernate, Sleep or Shutdown when you press the power button on your computer

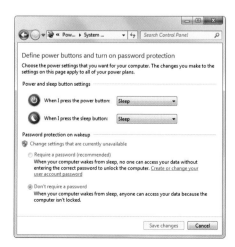

4 On some keyboards there is a Sleep button, for which you can specify Do Nothing, Hibernate or Sleep

Not all computers support Hibernation, so this option does not always appear.

Hot tip

Power plans set the idle time after which the display is turned off or the computer put to sleep. For High performance, the setting is Never.

Don't forget

Power Options defines the computer Power button, not the Start menu Power button, which is controlled via Start menu properties (see page 64).

Portable power management

On a battery powered computer:

1 Select Power Options

Don't forget

The subtasks for Power Options now include Change battery settings, and Adjust screen brightness, though you won't find the latter on all portables.

Power Options
Change battery settings
Change what the power buttons do
Require a password when the computer wakes
Change when the computer sleeps
Choose a power plan

2 The power plans are listed, and in addition there's Choose what closing the lid does, and a screen brightness slider

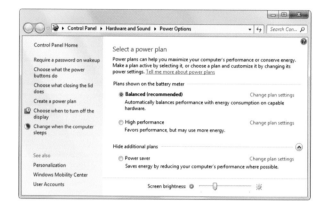

3 When you select Change plan settings (to view the details of an existing plan), you'll see the plans are more complex

Hot tip

A Netbook computer, without adjustment for screen brightness, has just two options, display and computer, but still with separate settings for battery and mains.

You can choose the idle period before the system will Dim the display, Turn off the display and Put the computer to sleep, and there are separate settings for On battery and Plugged in. There are also two sliders to Adjust plan brightness for the two situations.

4 Select either Choose what the power buttons do, or Choose what closing the lid does, to get the same panel

277

5 On portable computers there will be three settings, for Power button, Sleep button and Closing the lid, again with separate values for On battery and Plugged in

6 To make changes to Password protection on wakeup, click Change settings that are currently unavailable

7 Make the desired amendments, then click Save changes to apply them and return to Power Options

Battery meter

You'll find an icon in the notification area that is specific to battery powered computers. This is the Battery meter, which gives you a snapshot of the battery status.

1 The icon changes to show if the computer is plugged in or is on battery

2 In either case, the icon can be partially filled to show the level of charge

3 Move the mouse pointer over the icon, and the battery status is displayed as a tool tip

4 Left-click the icon to see the battery status, choose from the power plans offered, or select More Power Options

5 Right-click the icon for links to Power Options, Windows Mobility Center (see page 282) and Turn system icons on or off

6 When the computer is plugged in to the mains, the battery status shows that charging is taking place

7 When charging finishes, the battery status shows Fully charged (100%) and the icon is filled

Sometimes there's no battery meter icon displayed in the notification area. Assuming that the computer is battery powered:

1 Select Show hidden icons, to look for the icon in the overflow area

2 To make sure that the icon will always appear in the notification area, click Customize

3 Locate the Power icon and select the option to Show icon and notification

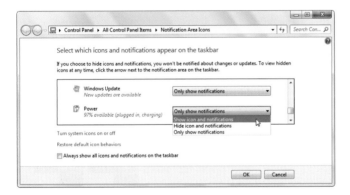

4 If the icon was not found in overflow, select Customize as above then click Turn system icons on or off

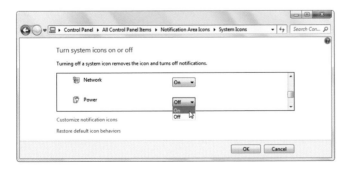

5 Locate the Power icon, turn it on and click Customize notification icons to make sure it will be displayed

User interface for portables

The user interface places considerable demands on the power reserves, especially if your portable computer is configured to use Windows Aero.

If performance or battery life is a problem you can switch to a less demanding interface.

1 Right-click the desktop and select Personalize, then choose a theme such as Windows 7 Basic

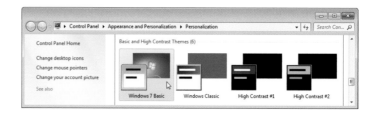

2 This removes all Aero features

If you'd like to stay with Aero, but want to reduce the overhead, you can turn off some of the features that might be considered decorative rather than functional.

3 Open Personalize, select the Windows 7 theme and click Windows Color at the bottom of the window

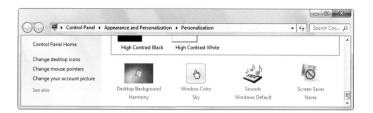

Don't forget

Try varying user interface settings to see if they affect battery life or performance. If possible, stay with Aero, albeit with some features disabled, since it is better suited to Windows 7 applications.

4 Clear the box for Enable Transparency to turn this off

5 You now have Aero features but no transparency

Hot tip

Here you see taskbar active thumbnails, but no transparency effects.

6 You can also use the Visual Effects panel (see page 428) to change transparency and other settings, to improve the performance

281

Windows Mobility Center

You'll find Windows Mobility Center (WMC) on any portable computer, though not usually on a desktop or all-in-one computer. There are several ways to open Windows Mobility Center:

Don't forget

Select Start, All Programs and you'll find Windows Mobility Center in the Accessories.

There is also a keyboard shortcut WinLogo+X which opens Windows Mobility Center.

1. Select Start, type mobility center and select the program from the top of the Start menu

2. Select Start, Control Panel, Hardware and Sound, and then Windows Mobility Center

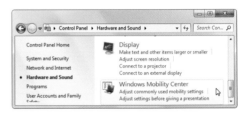

3. You get a link to Windows Mobility Center when you right-click the battery icon (see page 278)

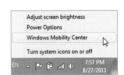

4. WMC for Dell XPS M1710 laptop (Ultimate)

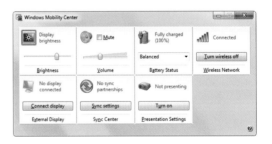

5. WMC for Asus Eee PC 1000HE netbook (Ultimate)

Hot tip

The entries depend on the facilities on the particular computer, so the laptop shows Display brightness, but this is not supported on the example netbook.

1 Select Start, type mblctr. exe and select the program

2 You are told Windows Mobility Center is available only on laptops

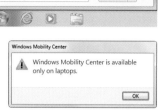

You can bypass this message if you update the Registry (see page 448) to say you have a mobile PC, by adding the keys and values shown.

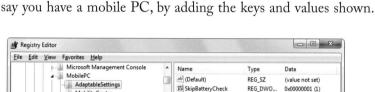

3 WMC for Dell E520 desktop (Home Premium)

4 WMC for HP TouchSmart 610 all-in-one (Home Prem)

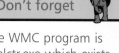
Don't forget

The WMC program is Mblctr.exe which exists on desktop and all-in-one machines, but normally does not run.

Hot tip

Add key MobilePC to HKCU\Software\Microsoft and add these keys to it
    AdaptableSettings
    MobilityCenter
Insert these entries
    SkipBatteryCheck
    RunOnDesktop
into the respective key, as a Dword value 1.

Delete the MobilePC key when you want to remove access to WMC.

Hot tip

Since these computers are both Windows 7 Home Premium, there's no Presentation Settings (see page 284) on either.

Mobility Center functions

The entries shown in Windows Mobility Center offer functions and display properties concerned with Battery status, External Display, Presentation Settings, Screen brightness, Screen Orientation, Volume, Sync Center relationships and Wireless Network, selected as appropriate to your computer configuration.

Presentation Settings

This is available only on computers with Windows 7 Professional, Enterprise or Ultimate editions. It provides a way to set up your computer in the appropriate state for running a presentation.

Don't forget

There are other places where you can access most of these functions, but the Mobility Center brings them together in a convenient group.

Hot tip

When it is enabled for presentations, your computer stays awake, system notifications are turned off and your additional choices of settings are applied, so your presentations do not get interrupted.

1. Open Windows Mobility Center and click the Projector icon on the Presentation Settings tile

2. Click the box for I am currently giving a presentation

3. If desired, Turn off screen saver, Set the volume for presentation purposes, and Show a selected background

4. Click OK to apply and save the settings

5. Click Turn off to restore normal setup, re-enabling notifications and allowing the computer to hibernate

In future, you'll turn Presentation Settings on or off, with a click of the button on the tile.

6 Attach the display, then open Windows Mobility Center and select Connect display, on the External Display tile

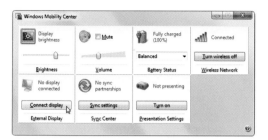

Don't forget

You can connect to a second display for presentations using Presentation mode, a function available on all computer types, and all editions of Windows 7.

7 On the Presentation mode panel, choose to Duplicate or Extend the primary display or use the External display

Don't forget

You can go straight to Presentation mode by pressing the shortcut keys WinLogo+P.

8 Open Windows Mobility Center and click the Display connected icon to change the resolutions on the monitors

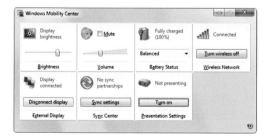

Hot tip

The external display could be a second monitor, or a projector and screen, but in either case is simply referenced as Projector.

9 To return to a single monitor, select Disconnect display and then select Disconnect Projector

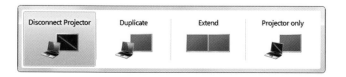

Netbook computers

Don't forget

The hardware specs for netbooks are continually being improved, so in the future you may find more memory and higher power processors, perhaps including 64-bit.

To achieve the high level of portability inherent in the netbook computer, its specifications are constrained. On the Asus 1000HE for example, there's a small screen (10.1", 1024x600), a low powered 1.6 GHz processor, only 1 GB RAM and no CD/DVD.

On the plus side, there's long battery life (9.5 hours), 160 GB HDD, 1.3M Pixel web camera, and wireless, ethernet and bluetooth connectivity.

The Windows 7 Starter edition with its reduced requirements may seem designed for such machines, and some netbooks are shipped with this as standard. However, there are limitations with this edition, in particular there's no support for Aero, Mobility Center, Touch, HomeGroup creation (you can join), Encrypting File System and BitLocker, and you can't customize the desktop.

Hot tip

Windows Anytime Upgrade is supported in Starter, so it is easy to upgrade to a higher edition on your netbook.

1. Use the Windows Experience Index to assess the options

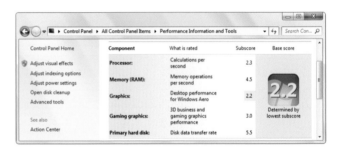

Graphics is an area of weakness, so you wouldn't expect to play 3D games or edit video, and you'll want to keep sensible limits on numbers of concurrent tasks. You might also want to apply some of the suggestions for reducing the power demands of the user interface. With such precautions, you'll find that any edition of Windows 7 can run successfully on a netbook computer.

There are other ways you can enhance a netbook. You can use Taskbar Properties (see page 66) to reduce the size of icons, and hence the size of the taskbar. You can also choose to autohide the taskbar. This will help maximize the space that's available on the screen.

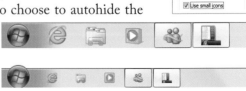

You can add a Flash Drive such as the Verbatim Netbook USB Drive and use ReadyBoost to improve the overall performance of the system (see page 439). This helps compensate for the limited memory in your netbook.

Another way Verbatim can help improve your netbook or any laptop is with their Portable Audio Bar. This is a small, lightweight audio speaker that clips on the top edge of the display and plugs into the USB port. It can be very helpful if you give a presentation with a soundtrack or if you need to contribute music to an event.

1 Attach the Audio Bar and plug it into the USB port

2 The first time you connect, device software is installed

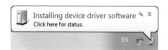

3 You can now use the audio bar in place of the netbook's internal speakers, and control it from the Speaker icon in the Notification area

Hot tip

The Audio Bar is added to the Start menu Devices and Printers folder, as an Unspecified USB audio device.

287

Don't forget

You can also select Start, Control Panel, Hardware and Sound, Sound and change the default speaker selection.

4 When the presentation is finished, unplug the audio bar to restore the normal operation of the internal speaker

Touch and Tablet PCs

Windows 7 incorporates multitouch capability, but this of course requires that your device has a touch sensitive panel. These are incorporated into Tablet, Convertible and some All-in-one computers, and also as a separate touch monitor that could be attached to any type of computer, desktop or portable.

There are several technologies in use for touch panel, including capacitive, surface wave, infrared and resistive. These all detect the location of a touch with a finger. For capacitive, it must be an ungloved finger. For the other methods, a pointer can be used.

Multitouch panels will detect two simultaneous points of contact, thus making it possible to detect gestures. such as pan, press and tap, rotate, zoom in and zoom out. To check your system:

 Open System Properties and scroll to System, you'll see the Asus 1000HE netbook has No Pen or Touch Input

Hot tip

Computers with no Touch facilities will have the note that No Pen or Touch Input is available for this Display.

Don't forget

In addition, the normal Windows applications will be touch-enabled, and will accept touch gestures in place of mouse actions or certain keystrokes.

 The HP 610 has Touch Input with 2 Touch Points

Open the Start menu, and you'll see there are sets of touch-specific applications from Microsoft and from the computer manufacturer, HP in this case

4 Select Start, All Programs, Accessories, Tablet PC, Tablet PC Input Panel (or type input panel and press Enter)

5 The on-screen keyboard appears ready for "touch-typing" or you can click the Handwriting tab

6 Press the input area and write words with your finger

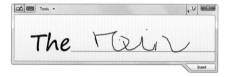

7 Words are recognized as you write, and you can correct or delete as required. Click the Help button for guidance

8 There's also a Math Input Panel, for entering formulas

Taking advantage of Touch

The Microsoft Touch Pack for Windows 7 is a collection of games and programs that you interact with using your fingers. To use them, you need multitouch support on your computer.

Some of the applications supplied are particularly designed to show the advantages of Touch, so may offer useful practise.

1 Select Start, All Programs, Microsoft Touch Pack for Windows 7, Microsoft Surface Globe

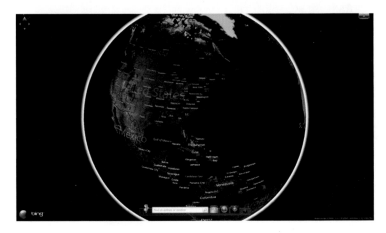

You can explore the Earth, as a flat map or in immersive 3-D.

2 On the HP 610, select Start, All programs, HP, HP TouchSmart to display the Carousel

Hot tip

The HP TouchSmart computers support the Windows Media Center which you can also navigate using taps and gestures.

You can spin the carousel, select and open applications, add notes and images to the desktop, and find the files you need, all using nothing but your fingers!

16 Sync with smartphone

You can connect your

smartphone to your

Windows computer, directly

using a cable or via your

wireless network, and

synchronize content such as

messages, appointments and

photographs. The Windows

Phone uses Zune software

and can also connect to the

Windows Live website.

292   Smartphones

293   Windows Phone 7

294   Set up Windows Phone

286   Windows Phone software

298   Set up software and phone

300   Choose what to sync

302   Enable Wi-Fi

304   Networked Windows Phone

395   Play To TV or Computer

306   Outlook Hotmail Connector

308   Copy Contacts and Calendar

310   Update Windows Phone

Smartphones

If you are travelling about, you may sometimes find that even the tablet PC or netbook is too much equipment to carry around with you just to access your email or keep in touch with your friends and contacts via Facebook or Twitter. The answer to this is the ultimate portable PC, the smartphone.

Smartphones combine the functions of a personal digital assistant (PDA) and a cell phone. They also serve as portable media players and camera phones, and feature high-resolution touchscreen, GPS navigation, Wi-Fi and mobile broadband.

Smartphones have a complete mobile operating system. There are several different systems, including:

- Google Android
  The Android platform has over 150,000 apps, most of which are free, and access to Google services. It is ideal for gaming, comics, eBooks and social networking

- Apple iOS
  The iPhone was the first major smartphone platform, and now has 350,000 apps available. It is constantly evolving and supports a variety of options, from Facetime to news feeds

- Nokia Symbian
  The most popular smartphone operating system, it supports features such as multi touch input for touchscreens, HDMI ports, and is good for services, wallpapers, themes and widgets

- Research In Motion BlackBerry OS
  Mainly for business users, with access to exclusive services from BlackBerry, e.g. Messenger, push email and App World

- Microsoft Windows Phone 7
  The newest system, with a multitouch interface and services such as Xbox LIVE integration, Zune content streaming and Microsoft Office Hub, where you can edit documents

All these smartphone systems can be linked in one way or another to Windows 7. In this book, we'll look at Windows Phone 7.

Note: Above figures true at the time of printing.

Hot tip

Smartphone operating systems each have their own style and character. They can be on many different models, and they allow you to download and run a variety of applications.

Don't forget

The use of the Windows Phone 7 system is low but is expected to grow, since Nokia will be using this system rather than Symbian for its future smartphones.

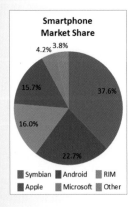

Smartphone Market Share

- Symbian
- Android
- RIM
- Apple
- Microsoft
- Other

37.6%
22.7%
16.0%
15.7%
4.2%
3.8%

Windows Phone 7

Windows Phone 7 is a replacement for the Windows Mobile operating system. It is designed to control Windows Phones from suppliers such as Acer, Dell, Fujitsu, HTC, LG, Nokia, Samsung and ZTE. Windows Phone devices must meet the minimum standard as follows:

- Capacitive, 4-point multi-touch screen (480x800) resolution

- DirectX9 rendering-capable GPU

- 256 MB of RAM with at least 8 GB of Flash memory

- Accelerometer with compass, ambient light sensor, proximity sensor, Assisted GPS, and Gyroscope

- 5-megapixel camera with an LED flash

- FM radio tuner

- Six dedicated hardware buttons (Back, Start, Search, 2-stage camera, Power/sleep and Volume Up/Down)

Windows Phone features a new user interface with a home screen, known as Start screen, made up of Live Tiles. These are links to applications, features, functions and individual items (such as contacts, web pages, applications or media items). You can add, rearrange, or remove tiles, which are dynamic and update in real time. For example, the tile for an email account would display the number of unread messages or a tile for a weather app could display the current weather.

Some features are arranged as hubs, which combine local and online content. For example, the Pictures hub might include photos from the phone camera along with albums from your Facebook account. The People hub might include contacts from Windows Live, Facebook and Gmail. Other built-in hubs include Music and Video (which integrates with Zune), Games (which integrates with Xbox Live), Windows Phone Marketplace and Microsoft Office.

Windows Phone 7 uses multi-touch technology. The default user interface has a dark theme, to improve battery life, however you can choose a light theme instead, and also choose your preferred accent color for user interface elements such as tiles.

Don't forget

The example phone being used is the LG Olympus 7 E900, which, with 512 MB RAM and 16 GB Flash memory, meets and exceeds the requirements.

Hot tip

This illustrates the dark default theme versus a light theme, which may be easier to work with but is a bigger drain on the battery power.

Set up Windows Phone

There are a number of tasks you must carry out to set up your Windows Phone before connecting it to your Windows 7 system, including the following:

1 Fully charge the battery in your smartphone

2 Turn on the phone and press the Get Started button

3 Choose your preferred language from those offered

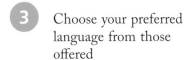

4 Scroll the day, month and year to set the date then press Done (the tick button)

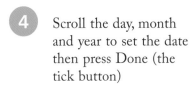

5 Similarly, scroll the hours, minutes and am/pm to set the time

You will be prompted to set up your Windows Live ID. You should choose this carefully, since you can not delete it once it is added to your phone. If you have an Xbox or use a Zune account, you should choose the Windows Live ID associated with those.

You use the onscreen Qwerty keyboard to enter your Windows Live email address and password. Alphabetic section includes the space, comma, period and, for email address entry, the @ and .com. You must switch to numeric mode for other punctuation and for symbols, but both modes have backspace/error correction and the Enter key.

The keyboard also offers predictive assistance, which is useful when entering text into email messages and documents.

Don't forget

Windows Phone supports interface languages of English, French, German, Italian and Spanish.

Beware

You can define more than one Windows Live ID for email, but only the first one can be associated with Xbox and Zune accounts.

Hot tip

As you enter characters of the password using the touch keyboard, the actual values appear momentarily then get replaced by * symbols.

Check out the function of your Windows Phone before attempting to connect to your computer.

1 Select the Phone tile from the set of functions on the Start screen

2 Select the keypad icon to make a call

3 Select the phone number using the touch keypad and make a trial call

Like the Qwerty keyboard, the keypad includes a backspace error correction key. There's also a Call button, and a Save button to save the phone number.

4 Side wipe the Start screen (or click the arrow icon) to display the application list

5 Select an application such as Calculator

6 Use the onscreen keys for numbers and function, to perform calculations

7 Press the Start button to return to Start

295

Windows Phone software

Don't forget

Zune software is required to support Windows Phone for updates and synchronization. It was originally developed to stream music to the Zune MP3 player, but now supports the Windows Phone and also the Xbox and the PC.

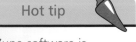

Hot tip

You can sign up for an account at Zune, which allows you to play samples, and download music (at a charge), but you don't need a Zune account to manage your Windows Phone.

Hot tip

Zune software is downloaded and installed on your computer.

1 Connect the smartphone to a USB port on your computer using the supplied mini USB cable

2 Windows identifies the new device and installs the appropriate device driver software

3 You are told that you need Zune software to get updates and add items to your Windows Phone

4 Click Get Software

5 Click Download now, then click Run to begin installation

6 The Zune Setup file is sent to your Downloads folder

...cont'd

7 When the Setup program starts, Accept the license terms

Don't forget

You must disconnect your phone to complete the installation.

8 Click Install, and you are asked to disconnect your phone

Hot tip

There's no activity on the phone, so you could just unplug, but to be sure you may prefer to click Safely remove hardware, and Eject the phone.

9 The Zune Setup program prepares your computer, and then installs the Zune software

10 Click Launch to start and configure the Zune program

Set up software and phone

Don't forget

Zune will use the Windows libraries for music, videos and pictures, and will become the default player for media files. You can change the settings later if required.

Hot tip

You use Quickplay to gather your music, videos, and podcasts in one place, to give quick access without searching through your collections.

1 Select Start to apply the default settings for Zune

2 Skip the artist definitions (unless you set up a Zune account)

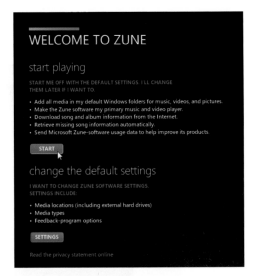

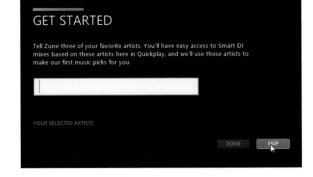

3 Zune starts at the Quickplay panel, but you should select Go to your collection to set up for your phone

4 Connect the phone and click Next to set it up

When you connect the phone, you must specify the name if not already provided, and a check for updates will then be carried out.

5 Edit the suggested name for your phone, then click Next

6 Checks are run for updates, for Zune and for the phone

Make sure that you do not use or disconnect your phone until the checking or updating process has completed.

Choose what to sync

Don't forget

After you connect the phone and apply any updates, the phone is synchronized with your Windows Live account, for email, contacts and calendar.

Zone displays the Summary for the phone.

1 Click Collections to view media files on your computer

Hot tip

Pictures, videos and music that you copy to your phone will be kept in sync, so when you delete a file on the computer, it gets removed from your phone at the next sync.

2 Select a library and drag and drop items to your phone, for example drag an album from your Music library

3 Click the Phone icon to see what has been added

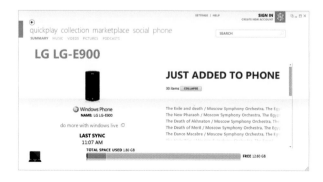

4 Select Music, Videos etc to see what's being synchronized

5 You also find details related to your phone when you sign on to your Windows Live account at www.live.com

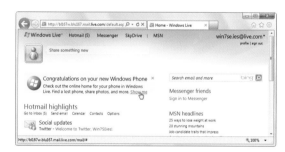

Hot tip

This shows up the first time after you add a new phone. On subsequent occasions, you can display the phone screen by visiting the web page windowsphone.live.com.

301

6 Click Show me, to track a lost phone, or to share photos, calendar events, contacts and other info from your phone

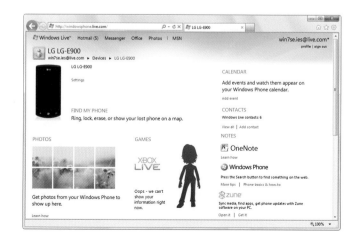

Don't forget

Select Settings if you want to remove your Windows Phone and its details from the Live.com website.

Are you sure?

Remove Cancel

Enable Wi-Fi

Don't forget

If you have wireless networking at home or in the office, you can use this to access the Internet at higher speed than the mobile network.

1 From the application list on your Windows Phone, select Settings, then select Wi-Fi

2 Press the button to Turn on Wi-Fi, and Windows Phone will search for available networks in the neighborhood

3 Select your wireless network and for secure networks enter the required password to complete the connection

4 Connect the phone to your computer and on the Summary screen select View Sync Options (or click Settings at the top of the screen)

5 The Phone Settings will displayed, with Sync Options selected, showing the settings for all the media file types

Hot tip

For each media type, you can specify All, Items I choose, or Manual. You set Manual when you want to keep items on the phone even when they are deleted from the computer.

6 Select Wireless sync, which displays the connection status

Beware

To protect the contents of your phone (and your computer), make certain that you have adequate security set up for your wireless network, and avoid using open networks when traveling.

7 If you want to use a different wireless network, connect using the phone, then click Refresh

8 To accept the network shown as the default, click Next

9 Click Done to confirm the network selection, and Wireless Sync will be enabled

Hot tip

With Wireless Sync enabled, your Windows Phone will automatically sync wirelessly after 10 minutes of charging on mains power, when you are in range of your default wireless network.

10 If necessary, you can open the Phone Settings, select Wireless Sync, and then click Disable Wireless Sync

Networked Windows Phone

1 Open Network and Sharing Center and click See full map

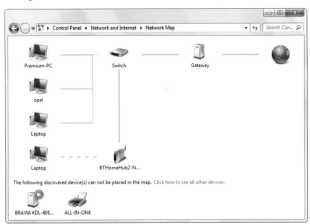

2 There's no Windows Phone, but you will see a network connected TV or other device (if it is powered on)

3 Select Start, Control Panel, View devices and printers, and you again can see the networked TV

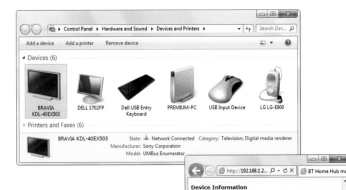

4 You may be able to find out some information about the Windows Phone connection by accessing your wireless router

Play To TV or Computer

The LG-E900 has the Play To app, which lets you play pictures, videos and music on networked TVs and Windows 7 PCs.

1 For a networked TV, just turn it on.

2 For a PC, start Windows Media Player, switch to Library and select Stream, Allow remote control of my Player

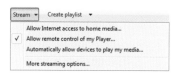

3 Switch to Now Playing to await the media stream

4 Display the phone application list, press Play To, then select the item you wish to play, e.g. an album

5 Press the Device icon, and then the Choose button, and Windows Phone searches for available devices

6 Select the device, for example the networked TV or your PC, and the chosen item will be played

305

Outlook Hotmail Connector

Contacts and Calendars on Windows Phone 7 keep in sync with accounts added to the phone, including Windows Live, Google, Facebook (contacts only) and Outlook with Microsoft Exchange.

1 In Outlook 2010, select File, click Info, then click the Account Settings button and select Account Settings

2 Check the email account type shown beside the name

3 If it's Microsoft Exchange, add the account to your phone

4 For other account types e.g. POP, you need the Outlook Hotmail Connector from http://office.microsoft.com

5 Click the Download now button for the 32-bit version, or click the Download (64-bit) button for the 64-bit version

6 Follow the prompts to download and install the update

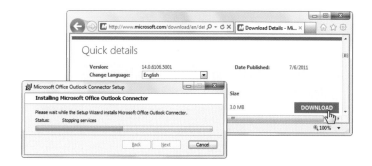

Don't forget

When you have installed the Outlook Hotmail Connector, you can add your Windows Live account to Outlook. If you don't already have a Windows Live account, get one at www.live.com (see page 158).

7 Open Outlook 2010, select File, Info, then click the Add Account button

8 Choose the option to Manually configure server settings or additional server types, and click Next

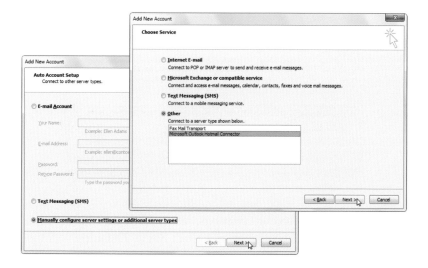

9 Click Other, Microsoft Outlook Hotmail Connector, and Next

10 Enter your name, email address and password, and click OK

Hot tip

Make sure that the box is selected, to allow Outlook to remember the password, since this is needed to sync your information.

Copy Contacts and Calendar

Don't forget

You need to copy your contacts and calendar data from your existing Outlook account to the Windows Live account.

1 Close then reopen Outlook and allow it to download the information for the new account and set up its folders

2 Open Contacts in Outlook in Phone List view, highlight the contacts for the existing account and drag the selection to the new account's Contacts folder

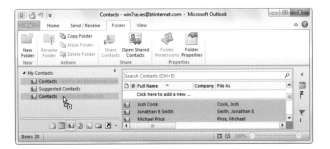

Hot tip

You can also right-click the original Calendar, select Copy Folder, then navigate to the Calendar folder for the new account and click OK to copy the contents there.

3 Similarly you can select and drag calendar entries from the existing account to the new account

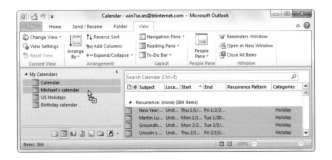

Hot tip

You need to adjust the Account Settings so that Outlook will work from the new account, which will be kept in sync with the online account at Live.com.

4 Open the Account Settings, select the Data Files tab, click the new account and select Set as Default

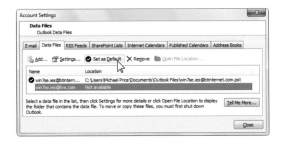

5 Still in Account Settings, select the Email tab, select the new account and click Set as Default

Don't forget

With these changes, you can continue using Outlook to manage your contacts and appointments, and sync your new Windows Phone to your windows live account, to keep everything up to date.

6 Select the Address Books tab, select Outlook Address Books, and click the Change button

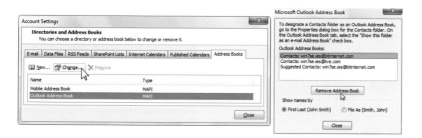

7 Select the Contacts for the original account and click Remove Address Book, then click Close, then Close again

Now you can click Send/Receive to ensure that the local and Internet folders are in sync. Any changes you make on Outlook, or at Live.com will be reflected in the other location.

Hot tip

Contacts on the phone are stored in the People Hub in a single aggregate view. Calendars are stored in a unified view within the Calendar app, where appointments are color coded by account.

Add the Windows Live account to your Windows Phone, if not already defined, and whenever it carries out a sync, contacts and calendar on the phone will be aligned with contacts and calendar in Outlook on your computer and at the Live.com website.

Update Windows Phone

From time to time, you may be reminded that there is an update available for your Windows Phone.

1 Connect your Windows Phone via the USB cable, and you may be told there's an update for your computer and your phone

You need to apply any update for the Zune software on the computer, before the phone update is applied

2 When the phone update is ready to be applied, you'll be told how long it is expected to take

3 Click Update Now, and avoid using or disconnecting the phone while the update is taking place

4 There will be a number of stages, several of which will include rebooting your phone

5 When the update completes, you'll be told that you can now disconnect the phone

Don't forget

Select Applications, Settings and Phone Update, and you can choose to be notified when new updates are available. You can also choose to use your cellular connection for updates, but only do this if you are on an unlimited data plan.

17 Troubleshooting

When errors occur on your computer, Windows attempts to identify solutions. It also provides a set of troubleshooters and a problem step recorder to help investigate problems. Other facilities include allowing a friend to remotely connect to your computer. There is also support for improving program compatibility.

312	Windows error reporting
314	Troubleshooting settings
315	Windows Troubleshooters
316	Troubleshooter in action
317	Problem Steps Recorder
319	View the report
320	Get help from a friend
322	Connecting and sharing
324	Easy Connect
325	System Restore
327	Start in safe mode
328	Safe Boot
329	Program compatibility

Windows error reporting

When an error occurs on your system, Windows collects debug information (a memory dump) and offers to send this over the internet. If you agree, the data goes to a website where the developer of the problem product can review the data and hopefully develop solutions. If a solution already exists, it is sent back so that you can apply it to your system.

To see how Windows checks for problems and provides solutions:

1 Select the flag in the Notification area to click Open Action Center

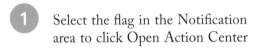

2 Here you can review messages and resolve problems

3 To see what areas are being checked for problems, select Change Action Center settings

4 To choose when to check for solutions to problems, click Problem reporting settings

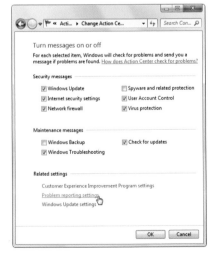

5 Automatically check for solutions is recommended, but you can turn off the check or ask to be prompted

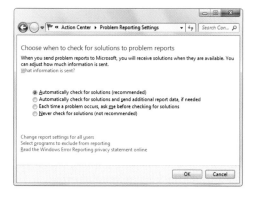

Hot tip

If you are concerned about the information being sent, review the Windows Error Reporting privacy statement to see how the information you send is managed and protected.

6 Specify programs that you want excluded from reporting, for example programs that deal with sensitive information

When there are messages waiting at the Action Center, the Flag icon notifies you.

1 Click the icon for more details and select Action Center to view the full message

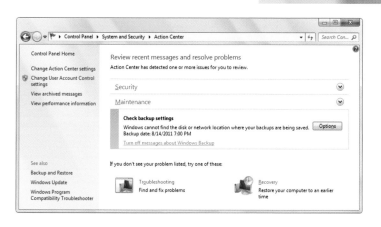

Don't forget

Click Options for the actions. In this case, it suggests Check backup settings, or Try to run backup again (after you re-connect the drive).

2 Select Turn off messages about Windows Backup, if for example you no longer require backups for this PC

Troubleshooting settings

1 Expand the Maintenance section, to review the status of the monitoring that is being applied

2 Click Turn on messages about Windows Backup, if you want to re-establish monitoring for this task

3 Click Change troubleshooting settings to specify the scope of problem analysis allowed on your system

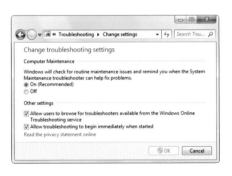

4 By default, Windows will remind you when the System Maintenance troubleshooter can help fix problems, and will also allow users to browse for online troubleshooters

Windows Troubleshooters

1 Open the Action Center and select Troubleshooting

2 This lists categories and the troubleshooters available within these to handle common computer problems

Don't forget

If you encounter a problem, and find no related messages in the Action Center, you can try the troubleshooters provided by Windows.

3 Select a task that appears to match the problem you have

4 If there's no suitable task, click the most appropriate category

5 Windows searches online to find any troubleshooting packs in that category

6 The troubleshooters are listed by their subcategories

Hot tip

Depending on the category you select, you should find one or more troubleshooters online, ensuring that you have the latest support for the problem area.

Troubleshooter in action

1 To illustrate, select Display Aero desktop effects, in the Appearance and Personalization category

Don't forget

This troubleshooting task was selected on a computer that appears unable to display full Aero effects such as transparency.

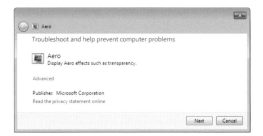

2 Click Next to run the troubleshooter, which carries out a series of checks to detect any problems with Aero

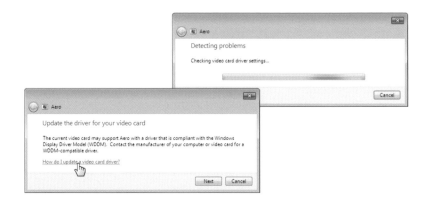

Hot tip

In the specific example, Windows Update was unable to locate a suitable driver, but a Windows 7 compatible driver was located and downloaded from the manufacturer's website.

3 In this case the solution is identified as the need to obtain a driver for the video adapter that supports WDDM

4 Click How do I update a video card driver for advice on the options open to you, to obtain driver updates via Windows Update or manually

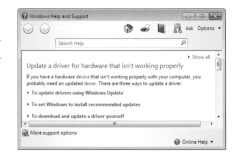

Problem Steps Recorder

If troubleshooting doesn't help, and you need to report the problem, you can use Problem Steps Recorder to automatically capture the steps you take, including a text description of where you clicked and a screen shot during each click. You can save the data to a file that can be used by a support professional or a friend helping you with the problem.

To record and save the steps:

1 Open Control Panel, type record steps in the Search box and press Enter

2 When Problem Steps Recorder open, click Start Record

3 Go through the steps to reproduce the problem. You can pause the recording at any time, and then resume it later

4 You may be told that there are windows on your desktop that are running as administrator

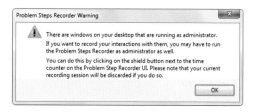

5 Click the Shield on the PSR window to switch modes

Don't forget

You can also select Start, type psr and select the PSR program entry at the top of the Start menu, to open Problem Steps Recorder.

Hot tip

If you want to record any activities that need administrator authority, you must run the Program Steps Recorder as an administrator, in elevated mode.

...cont'd

6 The current recording session will be discarded, and you must restart recording if you elevate to administrator level

7 Click Add Comment whenever you want to make notes about any step in the process you are recording

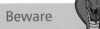
8 Click Stop Record when you have finished all the steps

9 Provide a name and folder for the report and click Save

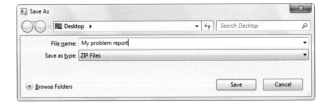

10 The report is saved as a compressed ZIP file in the folder

318

View the report

1 Double-click the compressed ZIP file, then double-click the MHTML document that it contains

2 The report opens in the browser

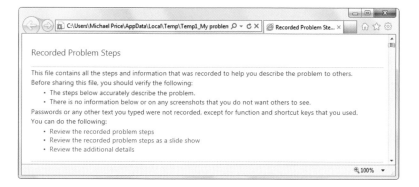

Hot tip

There is a summary of the contents, and links to the individual steps and to additional details, which contain technical information intended for advanced users.

3 Each step has a description of the action taken, plus a screenshot of the full screen at that point

Don't forget

You can view the actions and screenshots as a slideshow, which proceeds automatically, showing a new step every few seconds.

Get help from a friend

Don't forget

You can ask a friend to look at how your system is working, even if they are away from you, by connecting your computers.

Hot tip

You'll need to tell your helper the connection password, perhaps via a separate email message.

1 Open Action Center and select Troubleshooting (see page 315) then select Get help from a friend

2 Click the option to Invite someone to help you

3 Select, for example, Use email to send an invitation

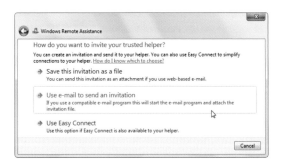

4 Remote Assistance will open your default email program and display a predefined message

5 Amend the message, adding the helper's name and email address, and click the Send button

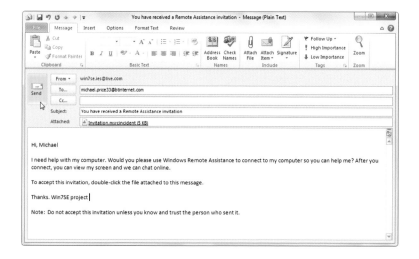

6 Remote Assistance provides a password for you to share, then waits for an incoming connection

7 Your helper receives and opens the message and, if willing to help you, double-clicks the attached invitation file

Connecting and sharing

1 Your helper opens the invitation file and enters the connection password

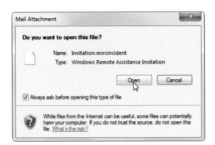 

2 You are notified of the attempt, and to confirm you want your helper to connect to your computer

3 Your helper can now see your desktop on his monitor, and observe any actions that you take

 Don't forget

When your computer is connected this way, you are giving full access, so you should be sure it is a trusted friend that you have contacted.

 Hot tip

You will find that the monitor is switched to the Windows 7 Basic theme, to make it easier to manage the exchange of screen contents.

4 Your helper can click Request control, asking to operate your computer using his mouse and keyboard

5 When you receive the request, click Yes to allow your helper to share control of your desktop

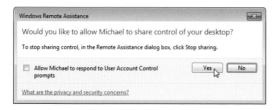

Hot tip

Click the box to allow your helper to respond to User Account Control prompts.

6 Now either you or your helper can operate the computer using mouse and keyboard

323

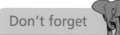
Don't forget

Click Pause if you want to temporarily stop the remote assistance session, for example to carry out a separate task.

7 Click Chat to communicate via instant messaging, or click Stop sharing to retrieve full control

8 Close Remote Assistance when you have finished

Easy Connect

1 Invite someone to help you (see page 320) and select Use Easy Connect

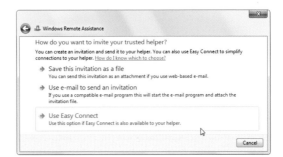

2 Remote Assistance will generate an Easy Connect password which you must supply to your helper

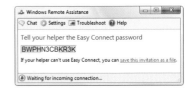

3 Your helper will open Troubleshooting (see page 315) and select Offer Remote Assistance to help someone, then select Easy Connect and enter the password provided

When the connection is made, contact information is exchanged between your computer and your helper's computer that will allow you to quickly connect in the future without using the password.

System Restore

If problems arise due to recently added drivers or updates, you can use System Restore to return the computer to an earlier position.

Don't forget

You can select Start, type System Restore and select the entry at the top of the Start menu to open System Restore.

1 Open the Action Center and select Recovery, then click Open System Restore

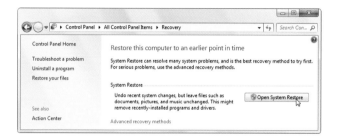

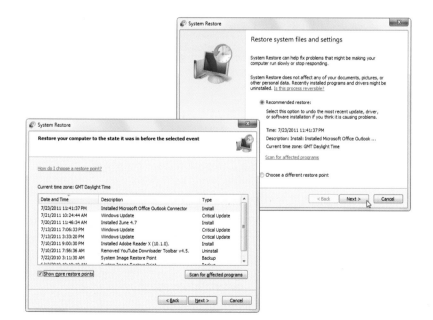

2 Choose the Recommended restore, or Choose a different restore point, to go back to an earlier state, and click Next

Hot tip

System Restore will suggest the option to undo the latest change to your system. Choose this if problems have only just appeared. You can still try another restore point later.

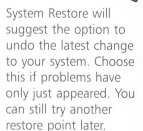

3 If you've displayed more restore points, select the one that predates the problems, and click Next

...cont'd

4 Confirm your restore point and select Finish

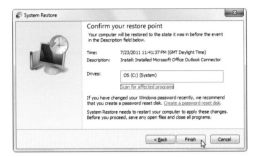

5 Click Yes to continue and carry out the system restore

6 Windows will close down and restart, and the system files are restored to the required versions

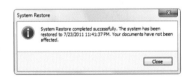

7 If this does not fix the problem, you can Undo System Restore, or Choose a different restore point

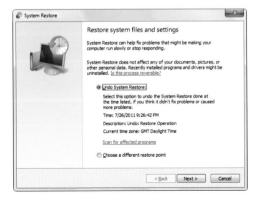

Start in Safe Mode

1 Power on the computer (or click Start, click the arrow next to the Shutdown button and select Restart)

2 Press F8 several times as the computer starts (after the initial PC logo but before Windows itself starts)

3 The Advanced Boot Options menu will be displayed

```
                    Advanced Boot Options

Choose Advanced Options for: Windows 7
(Use the arrow keys to highlight your choice.)

    Repair Your Computer

    Safe Mode
    Safe Mode with Networking
    Safe Mode with Command Prompt

    Enable Boot Logging
    Enable low-resolution video (640x480)
    Last Known Good Configuration (advanced)
    Directory Services Restore Mode
    Debugging Mode
    Disable automatic restart on system failure
    Disable Driver Signature Enforcement

    Start Windows Normally

Description: Start Windows with only the core drivers and services. Use
             when you cannot boot after installing a new device or driver.

ENTER=Choose                                          ESC=Cancel
```

4 Select Safe Mode and press Enter to start Windows

5 Sign on with your user name and password

Hot tip

Safe Mode starts Windows with a limited set of files and device drivers, without the usual startup programs and services. This validates the basic settings.

Beware

Sometimes Windows detects a problem from the previous session and starts up automatically in Safe Mode. Shutdown and restart the system and Windows usually clears the problem and restarts in normal mode.

Don't forget

Use tools such as System Restore (see page 325) to make corrections from within safe mode. To end Safe Mode, restart Windows and allow it to complete normally.

Safe Boot

Don't forget

You can start Safe Mode using the Msconfig Safe Boot option. With this enabled, Windows will continue to start in Safe Mode until you select a different option.

Hot tip

If you suspect one of the Startup items, click Disable All, then Restart and add the items back one at a time, restarting after each addition. In this way, you should be able to determine which item is causing problems.

1 Click Start, type **msconfig** and press Enter

2 Click the Boot tab, click Safe boot and choose Minimal, then click OK and click Restart to start up in Safe Mode

3 When finished with Safe Mode, run **Msconfig,** and choose Normal Startup from the General tab and Restart

4 To control the startup items, run **Msconfig,** click Selective Startup and then select the Startup tab

Program Compatibility

If you have older programs or games that were
written specifically for an older version of
Windows, they might not operate well (or not
operate at all) under Windows 7.

If this situation arises:

① Open Action Center and click Windows
Program Compatibility Troubleshooter

② Click Next to run the Compatibility Troubleshooter

③ The Troubleshooter identifies all the applications that may
have problems. Select the one you want to work with

④ Select Try recommended settings, or select Troubleshoot
program to choose alternative compatibility settings

Beware

Do not try running older
antivirus programs or
system programs, since
using these could cause
data loss or create other
security issues.

329

Hot tip

Return here to try
other settings, if the
recommended settings
don't resolve the
problems.

...cont'd

5 Click Start the program, to try out the program to see if the problems have been fixed by applying the settings

Test the program at this stage or, if more convenient, save the settings and run the program separately. You can still run the Troubleshooter if you need to change settings.

6 Click Next and, if the program had failed, select Try again using different settings, or Report problem to Microsoft

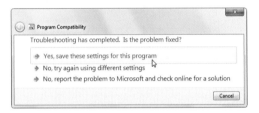

7 If the program worked, select Save these settings for this program, to be automatically applied whenever it is run, then Close the Troubleshooter

If you have Windows 7 Professional, Enterprise or Ultimate editions, you can use Windows XP Mode running under Windows Virtual PC (see page 352) to run older programs.

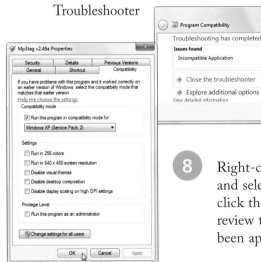

8 Right-click the program icon and select Properties, then click the Compatibility tab to review the settings that have been applied

18 Backup and recovery

You need to keep safe copies of our data and other information so that in the event of problems you can recover your system. Windows provides ways to make backups of the system and data, and helps you restore the copies should it be necessary.

332   Copy files and folders

334   Copy libraries

336   Windows Backup

338   The first backup

340   After the backup

341   Scheduled backup

342   Create a manual backup

343   Manage space

344   Restore files

346   Previous versions of files

347   Recover your computer

349   System repair disc

Copy files and folders

When you create documents or other files on your computer, it is wise to take precautions to protect your work, in case problems arise with the original version.

To illustrate the options and the considerations, we'll look at an example computer (running Windows 7 Enterprise edition).

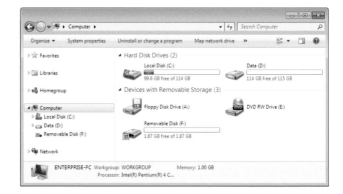

1 Select Start, Computer to view the storage devices:

- Local Disk (C:) containing the system and the library files

- A second hard drive Data (D:) which is initially empty

- Removable Disk (F:) which is also initially empty

- Floppy Disk Drive (A:) and DVD RW Drive (E:) are also available, but with no media

2 Select Start, Control Panel, Add or remove user accounts, to see the accounts

- Michael (Administrator)

- Cathy (Standard user)

- The Guest account is Off

To make a copy of a file on the removable disk:

1 Navigate to the folder containing the file

2 Left-click and drag the file onto the drive name in the Navigation pane, and release it there

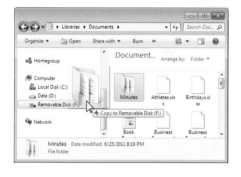

3 You can also drag a folder to copy the whole contents

Repeated copies

Note that a repeated copy at a later date to the same removable drive would over-write the initial copy. To keep a history of changes, you need to copy to a folder, perhaps named for the copy date, or use a separate removable drive each time.

Copy libraries

Suppose you want to save the whole contents of your libraries:

1 Open the Libraries in Windows Explorer

Don't forget

You can Show all folders in the Navigation pane (see page 104) to display the Desktop and the Libraries folder.

2 Click the arrow to the left of Libraries and select Desktop to show the Libraries folder

Beware

Dragging and dropping the Libraries folder creates a link to the original folder, rather than the copy as made for files and folders.

3 Rather than drag & drop, right-click the Libraries folder and select Copy

4 On the Navigation pane, select the removable drive to open it

5 Right-click the Contents pane and select Paste

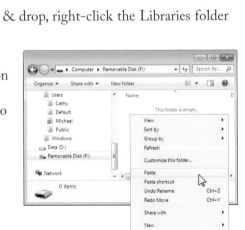

6 The contents of the libraries are copied to the removable drive

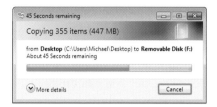

7 Expand the Navigation pane entry for the removable drive, and you'll see how the contents are arranged

Hot tip

The files and folders that are listed in the libraries may be stored in separate locations on your disk.

Note that each Library folder on the copy contains the merged contents of the Current user and the Public libraries. This can lead to difficulties when restoring files and folders.

When you copy libraries, you'll also have problems with over-writing older copies with new copies, as described for files and folders (see page 333).

Other users

You may encounter problems accessing user folders, if you are required to make backup copies on behalf of other users with accounts on your computer.

Beware

You will find that various problems arise when your copying activities are more complex. They can all be resolved, but it may be much easier to use Windows Backup to manage the requirements.

335

Windows Backup

Windows Backup makes copies of data files for all those using the computer. By default, these backups are created on a regular schedule, but you can create backups manually at any time. Windows Backup keeps track of the files and folders that are new or modified and adds them to your backup. To set up Backup:

Hot tip

You can select Start, type backup and click Backup and Restore, at the top of the Start menu.

Alternatively, select Start, Control Panel and click Back up your computer.

You can also select Start, Computer, right-click the drive, select Properties, click the Tools tab and select Backup now.

1 Select Start, All Programs, Maintenance and then click Backup and Restore

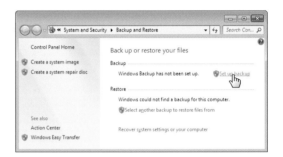

2 Windows Backup starts and searches for available devices

3 The available backup devices are listed, and Data (D:) is recommended

Hot tip

If you add a removable device after starting the Windows Backup setup, click the Refresh button.

336

Choosing the backup device

Windows prefers an external drive if available, or any hard drive other than the system drive. It lists the writable DVD drive, though you'd need multiple discs for a full backup. It also lists the USB flash drive, since it is greater than 1 GB, but this would only be useful for relatively small data backups.

To continue the setup:

You could also select Save on a network and choose a shared folder or drive from another computer on the local network.

4 Select the device you want to use and click Next

5 To help decide what to backup, click the link How does Windows choose what files to backup?

The Help panel explains what Windows does backup (user libraries and a system image) and what it does not backup (program files, deleted files and temporary files).

6 Click Close to end the Help, then select the recommended option Let Windows choose

337

The first backup

When you've chosen what to backup, you can run the first backup:

1 Review the details, and click Save settings and run backup

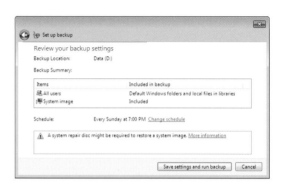

2 Backup commences, and the progress is displayed in the Backup and Restore panel

As indicated, there has been no previous backup, and future backups are scheduled to run weekly, every Sunday at 7:00 PM - though you can change the schedule (see page 341).

3 Click View details for a closer look at the backup actions that are taking place

4 The details panel shows the percent complete and the current action taking place

Copy the libraries and folders for each of the users on the computer

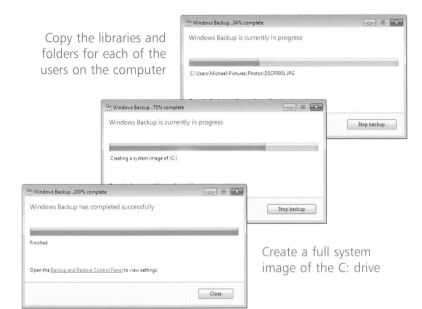

Create a full system image of the C: drive

5 Upon completion, the Backup and Restore panel shows backup size, and date and time for the next backup

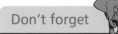

After the backup

1 Select Start, Computer and check the Data (D:) drive

2 There is now only 101 GB free, compared with the initial 114 GB available before Backup was run

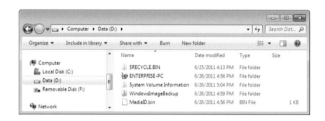

3 Open the drive and you see the contents, but when you move the mouse pointer over the folders, they appear to be empty

4 Double-click a folder and you'll be prompted for permission

5 Open the next couple of folders, and you will eventually find a file of substantial size which is evidently the system image

Hot tip

The contents of the backup drive or folder are protected, and cannot really be dealt with directly. You need the Backup and Restore functions to work with the backup files.

Scheduled backup

1 After the next scheduled update, display the Backup and Restore panel, and you'll see just minor changes

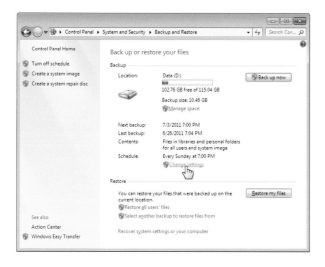

Hot tip

After the first update, Windows Backup only saves changes to the files, and so there is very little to record, especially in the example case, where the scheduled time was just a couple of hours later.

2 To change the schedule, click Change Settings and follow the prompts, until asked to Review your backup settings

3 Select to Change schedule

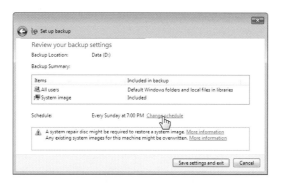

4 Choose How often, What day, What time

Don't forget

You can schedule updates daily, weekly or monthly, and choose any time of day or night.

5 Select OK then click the Save settings and exit button

Beware

If it's time for your regularly scheduled backup and your computer is off, sleeping, or hibernating, Windows Backup skips the backup and waits for your next scheduled backup.

Create a manual backup

If you make changes to your files, and want to ensure you have saved copies, you can run Backup manually.

1 Open the Backup and Restore panel and select Backup now

2 The backup as defined in Setup is initiated, and progress displayed, as described for the first backup (see page 338)

(see page 338)

Don't forget

You can use manual backup if you find that scheduled backups have been missed, for example because the machine was turned off or hibernating at the scheduled time.

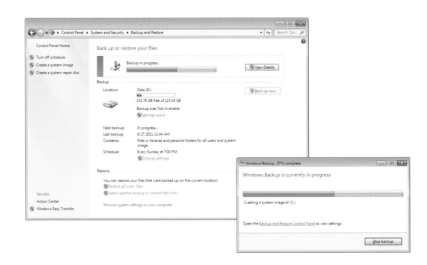

3 The changes to files and the user libraries are copied, then the system image is created

4 When the backup completes, the Backup and Restore panel shows changes in backup size, and next backup date

Hot tip

The backup sizes in the example system change as follows:

First backup	10.30GB
Next backup	10.46GB
Manual backup	10.88GB

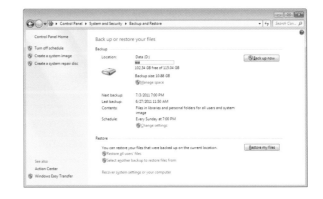

Manage space

Windows Backup allows you to view the way the space on your backup device is used, and how much free space there is.

1 Go to the Backup and Restore panel and select Manage space

2 The summary shows how the backup space is allocated

343

3 Click View backups to see or delete backup periods

4 Click Change settings to say how system images are kept

Don't forget

Windows Backup backs up all selected folders the first time it's run and then it only backs up files that are new or have been modified since the last backup. Periodically, Windows creates a new, full backup, known as a Backup period. You can choose to delete older Backup periods.

Hot tip

If you let Windows manage the space, it will save as many system images as will take no more than 30% of the backup disk, then delete older system images. You can instead choose to keep only the most recent system image. This is always the case for a network backup location.

Restore files

With backups created, you can restore files and folders that have been lost, damaged, or changed accidentally.

The files and folders you select will be restored to their latest versions, unless you click Choose a different date, and select an earlier backup.

You can also click Search to look for files in the backup folders by name. Select Browse for folders, when you want to Add folders to the restore list.

1 Open the Backup and Restore panel, to show the current backup location, and scroll down to the Restore section

2 Select Restore my files, and select Browse for files

3 Explore the backup folders, select files and click Add files

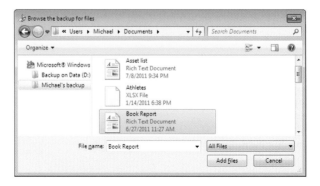

4 You can Remove any files or folders selected by mistake, then click Next to begin restoring your final list

5 Restore to the original location or select another folder

6 The files and folders are restored to the specified location

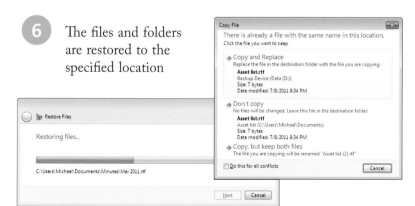

7 The log file shows any problems that might arise

Previous versions of files

If you accidently damage a file, for example save the file with the wrong changes, you can try to restore it from a previous version.

1 Find the current copy of the file, then right-click the icon and select Restore previous versions

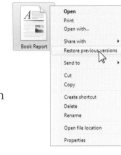

2 The file Properties are displayed, with the Previous Versions tab selected

3 Windows searches your drives for previous versions, and lists those found in restore points and in backups

4 Select a version, click Restore and then confirm

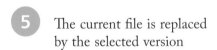

5 The current file is replaced by the selected version

If you accidentally delete a file, you can usually recover it.

1 Double-click the Recycle Bin on the desktop, select the file and press Restore this item

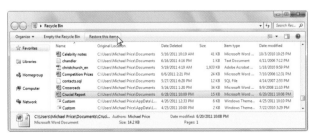

Recover your computer

If major problems arise with your computer, you can recover it using the system image created by Windows Backup.

1 Open Backup and Restore, scroll down and select the option to Recover system settings or your computer

Hot tip

You'd choose System Restore (see page 325) to restore system settings to previous values.

2 Select the option Advanced recovery methods, if you want to recover your computer

3 Use a system image if possible, or otherwise reinstall Windows fully, using the Windows installation disc

Don't forget

If you reinstall Windows you must also reinstall all of the programs that have been installed on your computer, so this is best avoided.

...cont'd

4 You are advised to carry out a data backup (for all users) before applying the system image, so click Backup now

5 Follow the prompts to complete the data backup

6 Restart the computer to continue the recovery

Completing recovery
On restart, you are asked to select the system image. Using the latest system image is the recommended choice. Then follow the prompts to apply the changes and to restore your data files from the backup device.

System repair disc

If problems arise with your computer, you may want to restore the system image from the time when it was operational. However, you could find that Windows is currently unable to start up properly. In that case, you might need a system repair disc, to run the system recovery options

To create the disc:

1 Open Backup and Restore and select Create a system repair disc

2 Insert a writable CD or DVD

The files on the repair disc total about 140 MB so a CD-R would be perfectly satisfactory

3 Click Create disc

4 Windows prepares the files and then creates the disc

5 When the task completes, click OK

...cont'd

Don't forget

The system repair disc is specific to the Windows system type, e.g. 32-bit or 64-bit.

6 You are reminded to label the disc appropriately, in this example as Repair disc Windows 7 32-bit

7 Click Close

8 The AutoPlay panel appears, offering the option to Open folder to view files using Windows Explorer

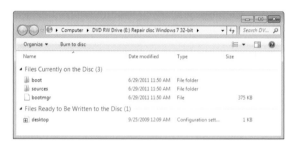

9 Select Start, Computer and you can see how much space is being used, in this case 142 MB

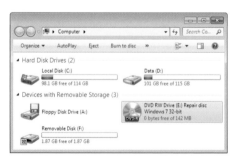

Hot tip

If you are using a Tablet PC or touchscreen, you might need to connect a keyboard and mouse to use the system repair disc and the system recovery options.

Using the system repair disc

Insert the disc and restart the computer. When prompted, press any key to boot from CD or DVD, then follow the instructions that appear, to select your language and display the System Recovery Options, which include System Restore and System Image Recovery.

19 Virtual machines

Sometimes the only application that will do the job is something that needs an older version of Windows such as Windows XP. You can set up a Virtual Machine on your Windows computer that provides the environment needed to run such applications. A full Windows XP system is included, but you can also install other systems such as Windows Vista or Linux.

352	Windows Virtual PC
354	Install Windows Virtual PC
356	Install Windows XP Mode
358	Setup Windows XP Mode
360	The XP Mode system
361	Install an XP application
362	Run the XP application
364	Add existing XP applications
365	Add a virtual system
366	Create the virtual machine
367	Setup the virtual system
368	Install the virtual system
369	Install Vista as guest
370	Install and use Vista
371	Predefined VHD

Windows Virtual PC

Windows Virtual PC is client virtualization software, which can be used under Windows 7 to create multiple Virtual Machines, which can run different operating systems. A virtual machine functions as an additional PC on your Windows 7 desktop, complete with its own Start menu, applications and folders, with access to USB devices, the network, email and the Internet. You can create a new virtual machine using a guest operating system image such as an installation DVD or a downloaded ISO file. This gives you the opportunity to run applications that would otherwise not be supported under Windows 7.

Some editions of Windows 7 (Professional, Enterprise and Ultimate) can take advantage of Windows XP Mode, which is a preconfigured virtual machine running Windows XP SP3. This allows you to run Windows XP applications without the need for a separate licensed copy of Windows XP.

Requirements

- 1 GHz 32-bit/64-bit processor

- 2GB memory or higher recommended

- 15 GB hard disk space per virtual machine environment

- Supported 32-bit/64-bit host operating system
  - Windows 7 (any edition except Starter)

- Supported 32-bit guest operating system
  - Windows XP
  - Windows Vista
  - Windows 7

- Hardware-assisted virtualization (HAV) recommended

To check whether your computer features the hardware-assisted virtualization, go to www.microsoft.com/downloads, and search for HAV detection tool.

1 Select the HAV detection tool web page and scroll to the download section, then download and run the program

2 You'll be told the status for the computer being used

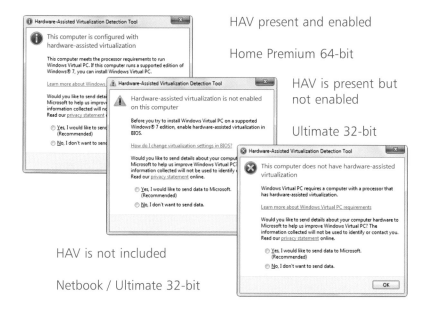

HAV present and enabled

Home Premium 64-bit

HAV is present but not enabled

Ultimate 32-bit

HAV is not included

Netbook / Ultimate 32-bit

If HAV is present but not enabled, you can change the settings in the BIOS. For example, on a Dell computer you would:

1 Restart and press F2 to enter the BIOS Setup mode

2 Expand Post Behavior and select Virtualization

3 Change its setting from Off to Enabled, and Save/Exit

4 Shutdown, power off then power on and restart the PC

Install Windows Virtual PC

1 Go to www.microsoft.com/windows/virtual-pc/, the Home page for the program, and click Download

2 You'll be prompted to allow Windows Validation add-on

3 Select your Windows 7 edition and your language, and choose Download Windows Virtual PC on its own

4 Select Download, and Windows Validation will be run to confirm your system

...cont'd

5 When Windows Validation completes, Open the file to download and install the software

6 The updates from the download are applied to Windows

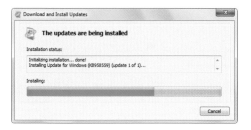

7 When installation completes, you are required to restart the computer to apply the updates

8 The Windows Virtual PC folder is added to the Start menu, with two entries defined

9 Click Windows Virtual PC to open your Virtual Machines, where you can click Create virtual machine

Don't forget
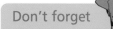

You can also Save the file to your Downloads folder, and double-click the file icon to Run the installation.

Beware

Although there is an entry for Windows XP Mode, clicking this just confirms that this is unavailable in Windows 7 Home Premium.

Install Windows XP Mode

Don't forget

With the Windows 7 Professional, Enterprise or Ultimate editions, you can install Windows XP Mode along with Windows Virtual PC.

1 Go to the Windows Virtual PC home page, select Download and allow the Windows Validation add-on

2 Select Windows 7 edition and language, and Download Windows XP mode with Windows Virtual PC

Hot tip

Note that there is an update that is required if your computer does not have the HAV feature. This update is already installed if your system has Windows 7 SP1.

3 You are advised to print the instructions or send them as an email and to save the web page as a favorite

4 Click the Download for Windows XP Mode

5 Windows Validation will be completed

6 Run (or Save and then Run) the installation file for Windows XP Mode

7 The files are extracted and the Setup runs, installing the virtual hard disk file for Windows XP Mode

8 Select the Download for Windows Virtual PC, then click Open (or Save and then Run) to download the file

9 The updates are installed, and when complete, you are asked to restart the computer

10 Again there is a Windows Virtual PC folder added to the Start menu, and it again has two entries.

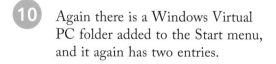

11 Click Windows Virtual PC and you'll see no contents as yet, since Windows XP Mode needs to be configured

357

Setup Windows XP Mode

1 Select Start, All Programs, Windows Virtual PC, and then click Windows XP Mode

2 Accept the license terms, and click Next

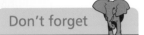
XPMUser is a default account set up with administrator authority and used to manage the Windows XP Mode virtual machine.

You should leave the box selected to Remember credentials, to avoid problems in using the virtual machine.

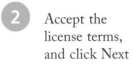

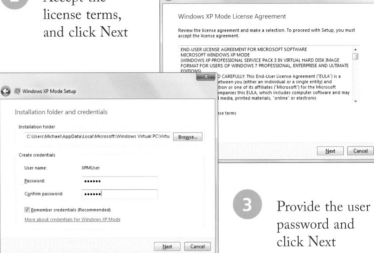

3 Provide the user password and click Next

4 Select to Turn on automatic updates, and click Next

5 Note that drives are shared with Windows XP Mode

6 Click Start Setup to set up Windows XP Mode for first use and start the virtual machine

7 As the setup proceeds, you'll see an outline of Windows XP Mode and how to install and run XP applications

8 The virtual machine starts with a full XP desktop , ready for you to install XP applications

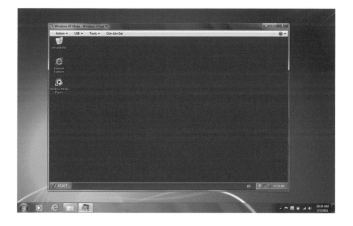

359

9 The Virtual Machines folder now has the entry for the Windows XP Mode virtual machine, with status and size

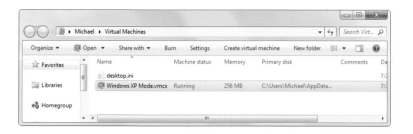

The XP Mode system

1 You can move the mouse seamlessly between the host Windows 7 system and the guest Windows XP system

2 Click Start, My Computer in your XP virtual machine

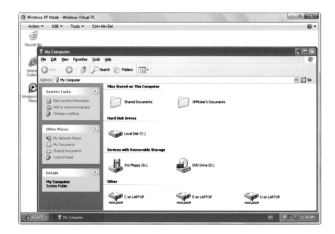

3 It has its own virtual hard drive, floppy drive and DVD drive and shared access to the Windows 7 drives

4 You can access USB devices from the virtual machine

5 When you click Start, you'll see a Log Off button but no Turn Off Computer

6 Click the Action button on the Virtual PC toolbar, or click the Ctrl+Alt+Del button for the options to end the XP Mode session

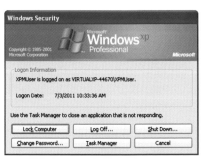

Install an XP application

1 Insert the installation CD or DVD, and Close the AutoPlay screen when it appears

2 Start the Windows XP Mode virtual machine, and select Start, My Computer

3 Double-click the CD/DVD drive to start the installation program

Don't forget

You install an application in Windows XP Mode just as you would on a native Windows XP machine.

Hot tip

To install a program from the Internet, you'd download the installation program then run it from within Windows XP Mode to create a virtual application as with the CD/DVD.

4 Follow the prompts to install the application

Run the XP application

When the installation completes, remove the CD/DVD and locate the application in the Start menu to run it in Windows XP.

1 In this example, you'd select Start, All Programs, and Jasc Software, then click Paint Shop Pro 7

2 The application opens as normal for Windows XP

To run this as a virtual application under Windows 7, you must first logoff and close the virtual machine.

1 In Windows XP Mode, click the Ctrl+Alt+Del button and select Shutdown

2 Select OK and the XPMUser will be logged off and the virtual machine closed

3 In Windows 7, select Start, All programs, and click Windows Virtual PC to expand the folder

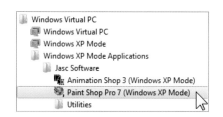

Don't forget

The folder Windows XP Mode Applications is added, to contain virtual applications installed in Windows XP Mode.

4 Click Windows XP Mode Applications and select an application e.g. Jasc Software, Paint Shop Pro 7

5 The application and the virtual machine are started

6 If the virtual machine is still open, or in hibernation with the user logged on, you are warned, but you can Continue

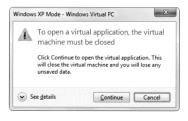

Beware

In either case, you would lose any unsaved data. If this could be a risk, click Cancel, Shutdown the virtual machine fully, then restart the application.

Add existing XP applications

You can add existing applications in Windows XP Mode to the Windows 7 folder as shortcuts in All Users, e.g.

1 Right-click the Internet Explorer 6 icon on the Windows XP Mode desktop and select Create shortcut

2 Right-click the shortcut and select Cut

3 Right-click the Start button and select Open All Users

4 Open the Programs folder for All Users and Paste the shortcut there

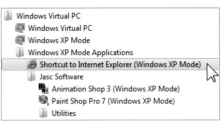

5 Any shortcuts placed here will appear in the Windows 7 Start menu folder for Windows XP Mode Applications

Hot tip

There is a standard Windows 7 style jump list which appears when you right-click the Windows XP Mode Applications taskbar button.

6 The Windows XP Mode applications appear on the Windows 7 taskbar, under a single button, but with program icons rather than preview images

Add a virtual system

You can create other virtual machines for Vista, Windows 7 and even Linux. To illustrate the process with Ubuntu Linux, you start by obtaining the installation disc or an ISO image.

1 Go to www.ubuntu.com and click Download, then select Ubuntu, to get the client rather than the server software

2 Select the version wanted, click Start download and Save

3 The file is downloaded to the default location, usually your Downloads folder

4 Select the file icon, and you have the option to Burn disc image to a CD or DVD

Don't forget

The installation CD or DVD, or a .ISO image of that disc, is needed to create a virtual machine for the guest operating system.

Hot tip

It is usually better to choose the LTS (long term support) version, rather than the latest release. For a Windows Virtual PC, you should select the 32-bit edition.

365

Hot tip

You will use the disc image to create a virtual machine, but the CD or DVD is useful for stand-alone operation of the system.

Create the virtual machine

1 Open the Virtual Machines folder (see page 357) and click Create virtual machine

2 Specify a name and location for the virtual machine

3 Follow the prompts to create a virtual hard disk (VHD)

4 The virtual hard disk and virtual machine are created

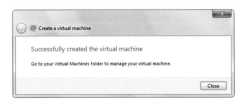

Setup the virtual system

1 Select the virtual machine and click Settings

Don't forget

If you plan to use the installation CD or DVD, rather than the .ISO image, you would specify the physical drive.

2 Select DVD Drive, choose to Open an ISO image, and browse to the downloaded image file, then click OK

367

3 Select the virtual machine and click Open

4 Open Ubuntu from the image file to display the desktop, ready for installation to the VHD

Hot tip

Click on the desktop to assign the mouse to the virtual machine. Press Ctrl+Alt+Left Arrow to restore the mouse to Windows 7.

Install the virtual system

1 Double-click the Install icon and follow the prompts

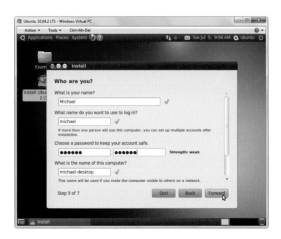

2 The files will be copied and the guest operating system installed in the virtual hard disk

3 Installation is complete so you can carry out any final setup requirements then restart to finalize the system

Install Vista as guest

1 Select Create virtual machine (see page 366) and specify the name, location and memory and create the VHD

Don't forget

In this example, 1 GB memory and 16 GB hard disk space have been assigned to the virtual machine.

2 Select Settings, then DVD Drive, click Access a physical drive, and choose the Windows 7 DVD drive letter

3 Insert the Vista installation disc and Close the AutoPlay panel to cancel any actions

4 Start the virtual machine and it will load files from the DVD

Hot tip

Since the virtual hard drive is initially empty, the virtual machine switches to the DVD Drive to start up.

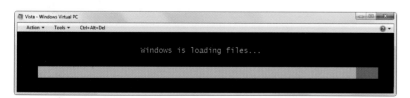

5 Enter your language and your region then click Install now, to begin the Vista installation

Install and use Vista

1 Follow the prompts to install Vista in the VHD, choosing Custom to create a fresh copy of Windows Vista

2 When Vista starts up, you sign in with your user name and password

3 You have access to the full Vista system and all its tools

Predefined VHD

There are predefined VHD files for Windows XP, Vista and Windows 7 available for free at the Microsoft download center.

Don't forget

Go to www.microsoft.com/download and search for Compatibility VPC Image to find this download page.

1 Download the file set for the Windows Vista VHD

2 Run the executable file, and specify your virtual machines data folder

3 The Vista VHD and settings files are extracted

Hot tip

Since the total file size is over 4 GB, the download is split into six parts of 700 MB. The first part is an executable file which assembles the pieces.

```
Extracting Windows Vista.vhd
Extracting from Windows_Vista_IE7.part02.rar
Extracting from Windows_Vista_IE7.part03.rar
Extracting from Windows_Vista_IE7.part04.rar
```

371

4 Open the Virtual Machines folder to view the files

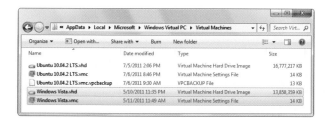

...cont'd

5 Create a virtual machine and specify the name, location and memory, and specify Use an existing virtual hard disk

6 Open the virtual machine, and Vista will start up

7 Logon as Admin/Password1

8 Windows Vista has IE7 installed, but the virtual hard disk also contains installable copies of IE8 and IE9

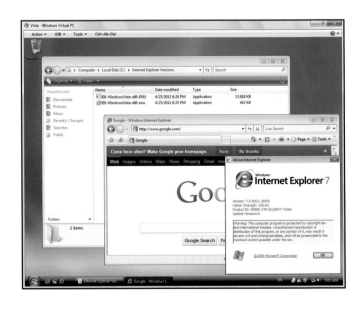

20 Security and Encryption

If your system or your storage devices contain sensitive information, you can protect the data even if the device is lost or stolen, using the various encryption facilities that are included in the advanced editions. You can protect a single file, or the whole system.

374   User account management

376   Set password to expire

378   Hide user list

380   Encrypting files

381   Using EFS

383   Backup encryption key

385   Bitlocker to Go

387   Access the encrypted drive

388   Access from Vista

389   Access from XP

390   Whole system encryption

User account management

There are several ways to manage user accounts on your computer. The primary option is User Accounts (see page 31) in the Control Panel. This is used to create or remove user accounts, change the account types, add or change passwords, or change the pictures associated with accounts.

(see page 31)

If you have several users sharing your computer, you might want to enable Secure Logon. To set this up, you need the alternative User Accounts dialog.

1 Press WinLogo+R to open the run box

2 Type the command control userpasswords2 and press Enter

3 Select the Advanced tab to show Secure Logon

4 Click the box that will Require users to press Ctrl+Alt+Del

---

In Professional, Ultimate and Enterprise editions of Windows 7, you can manage user accounts with the Local Users and Groups policy editor. There are several ways to display this.

1 From the Advanced tab of the second User Accounts option, click the Advanced button

2 Press WinLogo+R, type lusrmgr.msc, press Enter

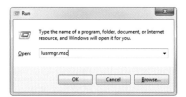

3 Select Start, right-click the Computer button and select Manage

4 When the panel opens, click Users and you will see an extra user Administrator, not shown in User Accounts

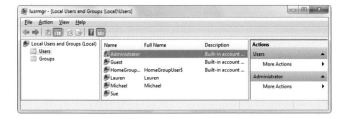

5 Double-click user account Administrator to display its Properties, and you'll see it is disabled by default

6 If you do enable this account, make sure to select More actions, then Set password

Don't forget

If you attempt to open the Local Users and Groups in Home Premium, you'll receive a message saying that this function cannot be used.

Hot tip

This is a built-in account that is automatically created but not normally used. If you do choose to use it, make sure to set a password.

Set password to expire

By default, your password can remain the same for always, but you are recommended to change it on a regular basis. Windows can be set to ensure that this happens.

1 Open Local Users and Groups (see page 375), select your user name and click More Actions, Properties

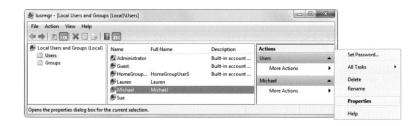

2 Clear the box for Password never expires and click Apply, to find that User must change password at next logon

3 Close Local Users and Groups, then open Local Security Policy (see page 378) and expand Account Policies

4 Select Password Policy, and then Maximum password age

5 When you next sign on to the computer, select your account name as usual and enter your current password

6 You are told your password has expired. Click OK

When you enter a new password, Windows reminds you that you can create a password reset disk (see page 39). However, it is only needed once, not every time you change your password.

7 Enter your existing password, then the new password and then confirm the new password and continue

8 Windows changes the password and confirms the change

Beware

When the specified period has passed, Windows will again notify you that the password has expired and require you to provide a new password.

9 Click OK and Windows starts. The password is reset, and future sign ons will proceed without interruption

377

Hide user list

Whenever you start Windows, logoff or switch users, the Account selection screen displays the list of users defined for that computer.

You might feel it would be more secure for the names to remain hidden, especially if you are using your computer in a public area. You can do this using the Local Security Policy.

1 Press WinLogo+R and type secpol.msc, then press Enter to open Local Security Policy

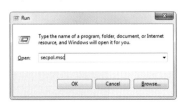

2 Expand Local Policies, select Security Options and locate Interactive Logon: Do not display last user name

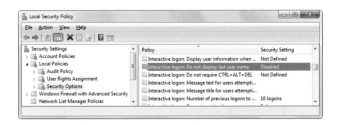

3 Double-click the entry to display the Properties, select Enabled, and then click OK

④ The entry will now be shown as Enabled, so click File, Close to save the change

⑤ The next time you restart, logoff or switch users, the Sign on screen is displayed, with no user name specified

379

⑥ Type your user name and your password to sign on

⑦ If you make a mistake, you are just told The user name or password is incorrect, and you must click OK and try again

Encrypting files

You might be storing personal, financial or other information on your computer that you wouldn't want others to read. Some editions of Windows include encryption tools that can help protect confidential data. There are three components:

- **Encrypting File System (EFS)**
  With this your sensitive files and folders can be encoded so that they can only be read when you log on to the computer with the associated user account

- **BitLocker Drive Encryption**
  This is used to encrypt an entire hard disk volume. The encryption is linked to a key stored in a Trusted Platform Module (TPM) or USB flash drive

- **BitLocker To Go**
  This provides BitLocker encryption for removable media, such as USB flash drives

Windows editions with encryption

EFS is available with the Professional, Enterprise and Ultimate editions of Windows 7. You must have Windows 7 Enterprise or Ultimate to encrypt a drive using BitLocker or BitLocker To Go.

There are no facilities to encrypt files in the Home Premium, Home Basic or Starter editions. However, when you encrypt a USB flash drive with BitLocker To Go, you can add, delete, and change files on that drive using any edition of Windows 7.

Systems running Windows XP and Windows Vista can, with the appropriate authentication, open and read the files on an encrypted drive using the reader program that is included on the drive itself. However, files cannot be changed or added.

Hardware requirements

For Bitlocker drive encryption of the whole system, the Windows partition and the System partition must both have NTFS format.

You can use BitLocker to encrypt additional fixed data drives, and BitLocker To Go to encrypt your removable data drives. These drives must have at least 64 MB available space and can be formatted using FAT or NTFS (unless intended for Windows XP or Windows Vista, when FAT will be required).

Using EFS

You can encrypt individual files, whole folders, or entire drives using EFS. However, it is best to encrypt by folder (or by drive) rather than by individual file. This means that the existing files would be encrypted, and new files that get created in that folder or drive will also be encrypted, including any temporary files that applications might generate.

To encrypt the contents of a folder on your hard drive:

1 Locate the folder in Windows Explorer

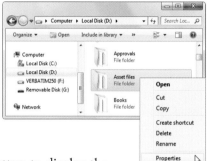

2 Right-click the folder icon and select Properties and the General tab

3 Click the Advanced button to display the Advanced attributes

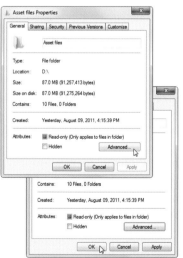

4 Select Encrypt contents to secure data, then click OK

5 Click OK in Properties to apply the change

6 Select the option to Apply changes to this folder, subfolders and files, then click OK to continue

If you allowed encryption of individual files in a folder, temporary files created there would be unencrypted, even though they could contain copies of the information you are trying to protect.

Hot tip

If the folder is on a drive that is not formatted as NTFS, there will be no Advanced button, and EFS encryption will not be available.

Beware

If you choose Apply changes to this folder only, only new files will be encrypted, not existing files.

...cont'd

7 Your encryption certificate is created, and the folder and its contents are encrypted

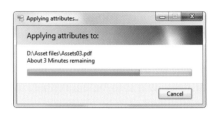

8 As encryption proceeds, a message is displayed, reminding you to Back up your file encryption key

When encryption completes, check the folder in Windows Explorer, and you'll see the name text for the folder and its files has been recolored as Green, whether you display the contents as Tiles, List or any other view.

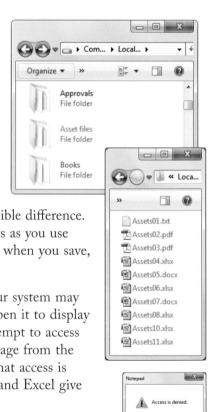

When you work with encrypted files from your user account, that's the only visible difference. Windows will decrypt your files as you use them and will re-encrypt them when you save, and it is all fully automatic.

Another user logging on to your system may be able to see the folder and open it to display the contents. However, any attempt to access the files will give an error message from the associated application, saying that access is denied. For example, Notepad and Excel give these responses.

Similarly, Copy or Move of encrypted files will be denied. Even administrator user accounts will be denied access.

Backup encryption key

1 Press WinLogo+R, and enter certmgr.msc

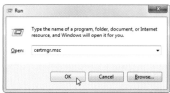

2 Expand Personal and select Certificates

Don't forget

If you lose the certificate, perhaps due to a hard disk failure, you won't be able to use your encrypted files. That's why you are advised to create a backup.

3 Select the certificate for the Encrypting File System

4 Select Action and choose All Tasks, Export

Hot tip

You'll need a removable device such as a USB flash drive, which is not encrypted and which can be kept physically secure.

5 The Certificate Export Wizard starts. Click Next

6 Click Yes, export the private key with the certificate then click Next

7 Select the Personal Information Exchange (PFX) file format, and click Next

...cont'd

8 Provide a password, and re-enter to confirm. Click Next

9 Click Browse to choose the destination drive

10 Select the storage device, enter the file name, and Save

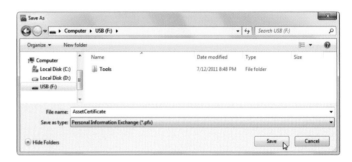

Hot tip

You could use the same device as you used to create your password reset disk (see page 39), since it has the same security requirements.

11 Click Next to confirm name and location

12 Click Finish to complete the Wizard

Beware

Remove the storage media and store it in a safe location, since it can enable anyone to access your encrypted files.

To restore the certificate, you'd insert the backup media, run certmgr.msc to open Certificate Manager, select Personal, and then Action, All Tasks, Import, and follow the prompts from the Certificate Import wizard.

Bitlocker to Go

To encrypt a removable drive:

1 Insert the removable drive and open Computer

2 Right-click the drive icon and select Turn on Bitlocker

3 Choose how you want to unlock this drive - password or smart card

4 Select password and enter your password, enter it again to confirm, then click Next

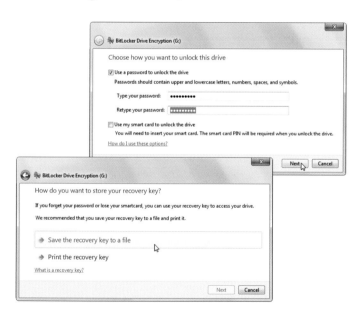

5 Click Save the recovery key to a file, the file name is provided, and you specify the drive and then click Save

Don't forget

If you have Windows 7 Enterprise or Ultimate edition, you can use Bitlocker to Go to encrypt a removable drive, and access it on other systems that do not themselves include Bitlocker support.

Hot tip

Large organizations use smart cards for network authentication and have computers with smart card readers that can access the cards and store information there.

Hot tip

A good choice might be the USB flash drive being used as the password reset disk and for your EFS certificate.

...cont'd

6 You can also choose to print the recovery key

7 When the key has been saved or printed, click Next

8 Click Start Encrypting and the files on the removable device are processed

9 Click Close when encryption completes

10 Open Computer, and you'll see the Lock symbol on the drive icon which indicates it is protected by encryption

Access the encrypted drive

To access the drive from any edition of Windows 7:

1 Insert the removable device and BitLocker will prompt for the password

2 Enter the password, and then click Unlock

3 When AutoPlay runs, click Open folder to view files

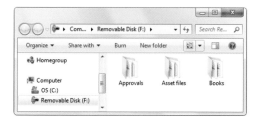

4 You can open, edit and save files or create new files on this drive, and they will be encrypted

5 Use Safely remove hardware when you've finished

Access from Vista

To access the drive from a computer with Windows Vista (and SP1):

1 Insert the removable device and AutoPlay will offer to open the folder to view files

2 Double-click the BitLockerToGo reader program

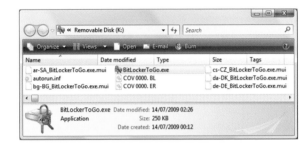

3 Enter the password, and click Unlock, the drive opens and you can see the files and folders

4 You can drag and drop files onto your desktop or into a folder on your hard drive, to view their contents

5 You cannot changes the files on the drive or add new files

Access from XP

1 Insert the removable device and it will open to show the contents as a set of read-only files

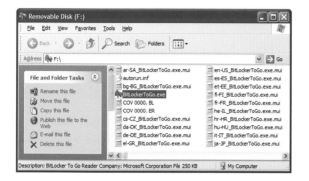

Don't forget

You can also access the encrypted drive from a computer with Windows XP and SP3.

2 Double-click the BitLockerToGo reader program

3 Enter your password, and click Unlock

Hot tip

Whichever way you access the encrypted drive, if needed you can click I forgot my password, and you can provide the recovery key that you saved, and reset the password.

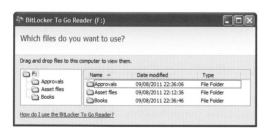

4 Copy files onto your hard drive, to view their contents

5 You cannot changes the files on the drive or add new files

Whole system encryption

Hot tip

To totally protect your computer and prevent access to your data, you can use BitLocker to encrypt the Windows boot drive and internal data drives.

Don't forget

Only the Enterprise and Ultimate editions of Windows 7 support this, and you preferably need a computer with a compatible TPM module.

Beware

You can enable TPM in the BIOS, or you can configure BitLocker to use a USB drive instead. However, problems with BitLocker could make your system inaccessible, so only proceed with this if you have adequate technical support.

 Select Start, Control Panel, System and Security and then BitLocker Drive Encryption

BitLocker Drive Encryption
Protect your computer by encrypting data on your disk
Manage BitLocker

 You'd select Turn on BitLocker for the system or data drive and then follow the prompts to encrypt the drive

3 Any problems with the computer setup would be detected

4 Select TPM Administration to check the level of support, and you may find the TPM module cannot be found

21 Command Prompt

It may not be needed by most

users or for most of the time,

but Command Prompt in

Windows can be very useful

in the appropriate situation.

There's an administrator

mode when necessary for the

tasks being run.

392 Open Command Prompt

394 Select a folder

395 Open as administrator

396 Administrator shortcut

397 Adjust appearance

399 Changing window properties

400 Using the Command Prompt

402 Command line changes

Open Command Prompt

As discussed earlier (see page 132) all editions of Windows 7 include the Command Prompt environment, where you can run commands, batch files and applications by typing statements at the command line.

There are a number of ways to start a Command Prompt session:

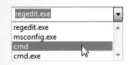
1 Select Start, type cmd and click the Cmd.exe entry at the top of the Start menu

2 Press WinLogo+R to open the Run box, and type cmd.exe then click OK

3 Open the folder C:\ Windows\System32 and double-click the Cmd.exe program icon

4 Double-click a shortcut to the program - with or without the Shortcut suffix and the arrow overlay (see page 459)

All of these methods will start a Command Prompt session, with title cmd.exe, open at the C:\Windows\System32 folder and ready to accept commands.

5 You can open additional, independent Command Prompt sessions, using the same methods

6 Alternatively, from an existing session, type start cmd on the command line and press Enter

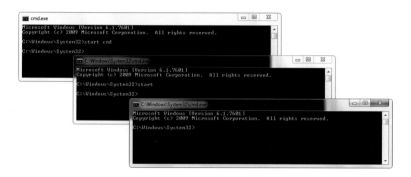

7 The new sessions are given the program path and name as title, and they open in the System32 folder

Using the Start menu
You can also start a Command Prompt session from the Start menu and the Accessories folder.

1 Select Start, All programs, Accessories, and then click Command Prompt

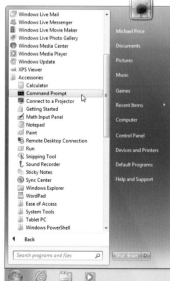

2 This opens a Command Prompt session with the title Command Prompt, and open at the user folder for the current user name

393

Select a folder

You can switch folders in the Command Prompt session using the CD (Change Directory) command. For example, to open the current user's Pictures folder, starting from System32:

1 On the Command Line, type these four CD commands, pressing Enter after each command:
cd \   cd users   cd "michael price"   cd pictures

To avoid problems with long or complex filenames, you can open a Command Session directly at the required folder.

You can use the normal Windows methods for locating folders, and select the required folder from either the contents pane or the navigation pane.

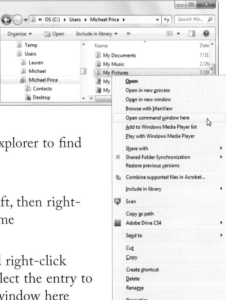

1 Open Windows Explorer to find the desired folder

2 Press and hold Shift, then right-click the folder name

3 From the extended right-click menu displayed, select the entry to Open Command window here

Open as administrator

The Command Prompt session opened has the standard user level of privilege. If some commands that you want to run require administrator privilege, you can open an elevated session, again using a variety of methods:

1. Select Start, type cmd and press Shift+Ctrl+Enter

2. Press WinLogo+R, type cmd and press Shift+Ctrl+Enter

3. Open C:\Windows\System32, right-click Cmd.exe and select Run as administrator

4. Right-click a shortcut to Cmd.exe and select Run as administrator

For each, you reply to a UAC prompt to start a Command Prompt session with the title Administrator: cmd.exe, which opens at the System32 folder.

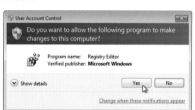

If you right-click the Command Prompt entry in Start menu, Accessories and select Run as administrator, you get a Command Prompt session, entitled Administrator: cmd.exe. Note that this opens at the System32 folder, not the user's folder.

Don't forget

Commands that have system wide effect are restricted to run only in the elevated administrator mode.

Hot tip

You can also type Start or Start cmd on the command line of an existing administrator session to get another administrator session - no UAC required.

395

Hot tip

You can run the entry from the Start menu as administrator.

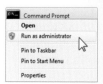

Administrator shortcut

You can configure a shortcut to Cmd.exe to always start in administrator mode.

1 Create a shortcut to Cmd.exe (at C:\Windows\System32\Cmd.exe)

2 Right-click the shortcut and select Properties from the menu

3 Select the Shortcut tab and click the Advanced button

4 Click the box Run as administrator and click OK, then OK again

5 Right-click the shortcut icon, select Rename and give a meaningful name

6 For example, you could have Standard Commands and Elevated Commands

7 Double-click the appropriate shortcut to start the administrator session

Adjust appearance

You can adjust shortcut Properties to control the appearance of the Command Prompt window that is launched by that shortcut.

1 Right-click the shortcut icon and click Properties

2 Select the Options tab

From here you can adjust the size of the flashing cursor, change how the command history is managed, and change edit options.

3 Select the Font tab to choose a different font

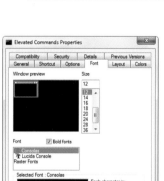

4 The recommended font is Consolas since this is a ClearType font that will be more readable in the window

5 Select Layout to change the buffer size and screen size

Adjust the width if the default 80 characters is not enough, and change the height (in this case from the default 25 lines to 10 rows). A vertical scrollbar allows you to view the whole buffer of information.

Don't forget

You can also adjust the properties from the Command Prompt window.

Hot tip

The fonts for the Command Prompt window must be fixed-pitch. There's a small selection offered, but it is possible to add extras using a Registry update (see page 455) to HKLM\Software\ Microsoft\WindowsNT\ CurrentVersion\Console\ TrueTypeFont.

...cont'd

6 Select the Color tab, to change the colors used for the screen text and pop-up text and their backgrounds

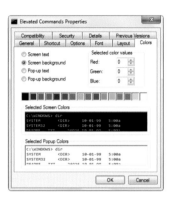 

7 For example, select Screen Background and choose a color from the selection, or enter the required color values

8 Select Apply to apply any changes immediately, and OK to complete any further changes and close the Properties

9 Double-click the shortcut icon to display the Command Prompt session and see all the changes in effect

Repeat the process to adjust the Properties for a shortcut used for a standard level Command Prompt. You might decide to choose a different screen background such as Blue, to distinguish the standard sessions from the Red administrator sessions. Double-click the Standard Commands shortcut to view the effect.

Changing window properties

1 Select Command Prompt using any of the methods

Don't forget

You can also make changes to the properties when you have a Command Prompt session already started.

2 Right-click the titlebar and select Properties

This displays the tabs Options, Font, Layout and Colors for the shortcut Properties. Any changes you make here are for the current session and any future settings started using the same method, in this case the Start menu Command Prompt entry.

Similarly, if you start a session via a shortcut, the changes apply for that shortcut only.

Hot tip

When you start a session via Search box, the Run command or the Cmd.exe program icon, the changes affect the program Properties so apply to all these methods.

3 To make changes that will apply to future sessions, right-click the titlebar and select Defaults from the menu

4 This opens the Console Windows Properties

The changes you make will not affect the current session but will be applied for all future sessions (except for those launched from a shortcut whose properties have been customized).

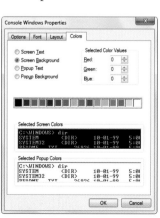

These changes also affect future sessions in character-mode, MS-DOS-based applications that do not have a program-information file (PIF) or store their own settings.

399

Using the Command Prompt

You'll use the Command Prompt to carry out tasks that are not easily achieved using the normal Windows functions.

A typical example is to create a text file containing the names of all the files of a particular type in a folder:

1 Open a Command Prompt at the required folder, using the right-click menu option Open command prompt here

2 Put the following on the command line and press Enter:
dir *.jpg /b >filelist.txt

3 To see what this file contains, use the command:
type filelist.txt

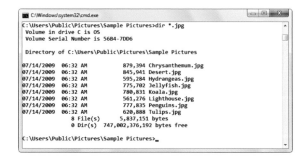

4 To see the normal directory list format, you'd enter:
dir *.jpg

If your Command Prompt session is already open, you'd need to switch directories to get to the required folder. Here you can use Windows features to assist the Command Prompt operation.

1 Open the required folder in Windows Explorer

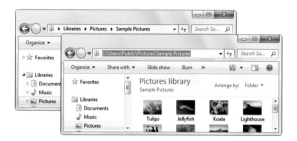

2 Click the Address bar to show the path and press Ctrl+C

3 Switch to the Command Prompt and type the command cd (followed by a single space)

4 Right-click the titlebar and select Edit, Paste`

5 Press Enter to run the command and switch directories

Hot tip

When you select Paste, the contents of the Clipboard are copied to the command line, thus completing the CD command already started.

Command line changes

There are lots of aids you can take advantage of when working on the Command line. This example session illustrates some of these.

1 To switch to a parent directory, enter the command cd ..

2 Click the Up-arrow and press Enter to repeat the command

3 At C:\Users, type cd then press Tab until the required user name appears, then press Enter

4 Change to trial and type copy (followed by space)

5 Right-click the titlebar, select Mark and highlight the path for Sample Pictures, then Copy and Paste

6 A Quote is needed, since there are blanks in the path, so just press Up then edit the command as needed

7 Type a Rename command, using Tab to insert the first of the file names in the directory

8 Use right-arrow and Tab to copy / amend the command

22 Update and maintain

You need to regularly update Windows and other applications on your computer, to ensure the system keeps working effectively and to incorporate the latest security and performance features. Windows Update automates this process. Similarly, you need to manage the storage on the computer.

404 Windows Update

406 Update Settings

408 Microsoft Update

409 Update categories

410 Update History

412 Upgrading Windows

413 Windows Anytime Upgrade

414 Apply the upgrade

416 Disk management

417 Disk cleanup

419 Error checking

421 Defragmentation

Windows Update

The Windows operating system requires frequent updates to keep it secure and fully operational. Updates are provided on an almost weekly basis, and periodically Microsoft issues service packs that consolidate sets of updates.

To see what the update situation is for your computer:

Don't forget

This is one of a number of different ways to ask for the System Properties for your computer to be displayed (see page 424).

1 Click Start, type computer information, and select System from the list at the top of the Start menu

2 This shows the Windows edition, and the latest service pack that has been applied (if any)

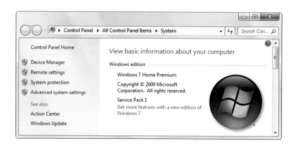

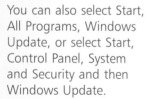

Hot tip

You can also select Start, All Programs, Windows Update, or select Start, Control Panel, System and Security and then Windows Update.

3 To see the status of your system, click Windows Update

4 Click Check for updates, then select important updates

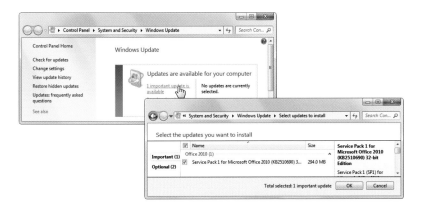

Hot tip

If Automatic Updating has been set (see page 406), the indication of updates waiting appears immediately when you open Windows Update.

5 If there are updates waiting, you can click Install updates and they will be downloaded and installed

6 When installation completes you may be asked to restart the system, so that appropriate files can be updated

Don't forget

You can selectively apply updates in this manner, but it is much easier to let Windows Update do the job automatically.

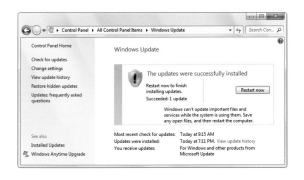

Update Settings

1 Open Windows Update and select Change Settings

2 Choose how you want Windows to install updates on your system

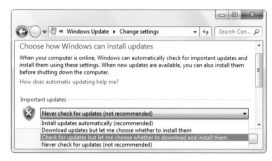

3 Install updates automatically is recommended, and you can choose how often and at what time to run the installs

4 Click OK to apply any changes, and leave your computer running to apply the updates at the specified time

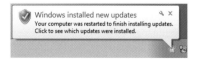

If you turn off your computer before the scheduled time, you will see a reminder that updates are waiting, the next time you turn on the PC.

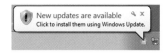

1 You can choose to apply the updates immediately

2 With updates waiting at the end of your session, the flag on Shutdown warns that it installs updates then shuts down

During install and shutdown, progress messages let you know that updating is taking place, and warn you not to power off. There may be similar messages the next time you start up Windows.

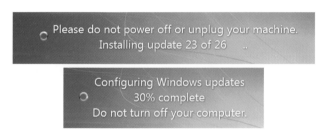

If you like to postpone the updating, but do need to shutdown the computer:

1 Click the arrow next to Shutdown and select the Logoff option

2 Click the arrow next to the Poweroff button and select Shutdown (rather than Install updates and shutdown)

Hot tip

If you leave your PC switched off for a time, the number of updates may grow, and it may take several restarts to clear the backlog.

407

Don't forget

The Poweroff button is displayed on the user account selection panel, and on the Logon panel, on the lower right side.

Microsoft Update

1 Open Windows Update and select Find out more

2 Agree to the terms of use, and click the Install button

3 Updates are detected for supported Microsoft products

Update categories

The updates managed by Windows Update are classified as:

- **Important updates**
  These updates include security and critical updates, as well as reliability improvements, and are automatically downloaded when you enable Windows Update

- **Recommended updates**
  These include software updates and new or improved features, and may be treated as Important updates or Optional updates, depending on your Windows Update settings

- **Optional updates**
  These include updates and software that you install manually, such as new or trial Microsoft software or optional device drivers from Microsoft partners

You must visit Windows Update to check for updates that need to be installed manually. They could include Important updates that require you to accept new terms of use. There are also updates that have an impact on the way your system operates so Microsoft chooses to require confirmation before installation. An example of this is Internet Explorer 9.

Don't forget

These categories apply to Windows updates, and also to updates for other products, if you have enabled Microsoft Update on your system.

Hot tip

If you selected Give me recommended updates in the settings (see page 406), they are treated as Important updates. Otherwise, they are treated as Optional updates.

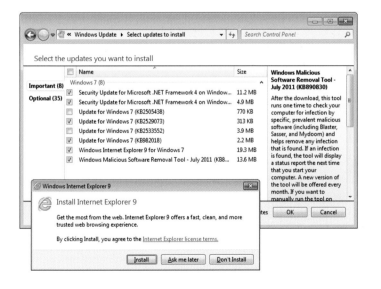

1 Select Install, or Ask me later (to postpone the decision), or Don't Install to remove the update from the list

Update history

Updates may be applied automatically, in the background, but you can review the activities:

1 Open Windows Update and select View update history

2 The updates are displayed, latest first

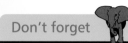
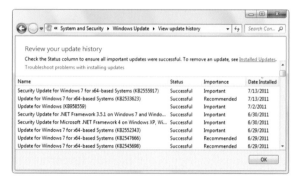

3 Click the Status heading, to review the Failed updates

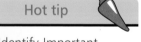
4 Sort in name order to see if the updates ever succeeded

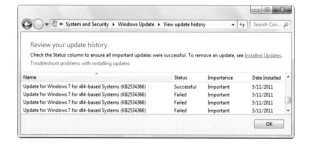

You can review the Windows and other updates that have been installed on your computer, and remove any that may be causing problems.

Don't forget

You'll also find the Installed updates link at the top of the Update history list.

1 Open Windows Update and select Installed updates from the list on the left hand pane

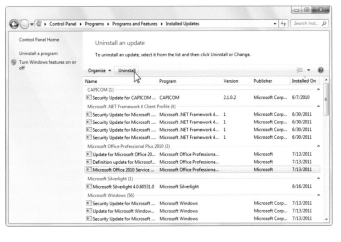

Hot tip

There are some updates that cannot be removed this way. If that is the case, there will be no Uninstall button shown when you select the update.

411

2 Select an update and click the Uninstall button on the toolbar to remove that update

3 You can also select Start, then Control Panel and click Uninstall a program, where you can also View installed updates

Programs
Uninstall a program

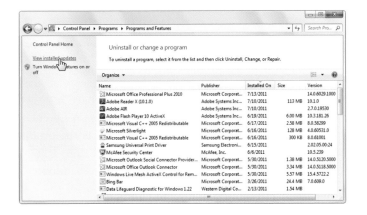

Hot tip

You can switch back and forth between the Updates and the Programs list, using the links in the left hand pane.

Upgrading Windows

Sometimes adding updates isn't enough - you need to upgrade your edition of Windows to an edition that has the extra functions that you need (see page 15), or you may want to upgrade from 32-bit Windows to 64-bit Windows, to take advantage of a larger amount of main memory.

32-bit to 64-bit

This isn't an upgrade in the usual sense - you cannot install the new operating system and retain existing folders and data files. You create a new system, completely replacing the existing system, then install your applications (and apply Windows updates).

You can install any edition of 64-bit Windows on your computer, assuming of course that your computer is 64-bit capable and that you have enough memory to make the transition worthwhile.

Upgrading editions

Changing editions can be carried out as a true upgrade. You update the operating system files, but leave your data files and folders unaffected. The application programs that you have installed will continue to operate.

The following paths are possible:

- Starter → Home Premium
- Starter → Professional
- Starter → Ultimate
- Home Premium → Professional
- Home Premium → Ultimate
- Professional → Ultimate

Starter upgrades are 32-bit only. Home Premium and Professional upgrades are 32-bit to 32-bit editions, or 64-bit to 64-bit editions.

Whichever edition of Windows 7 you currently have installed, its installation DVD and the installed operating system files actually contain all the components of all the editions. It is the product key that unlocks the functions for a particular edition. This is the basis for the upgrading feature incorporated into Windows 7 – the Windows Anytime Upgrade.

Don't forget

You can backup your data files and folders before you make the change, and restore the backup to your revised system. However, you will have to install 64-bit versions of drivers for devices (unless Windows includes a suitable driver), and also reinstall all your application programs.

Hot tip

If you are currently using the Enterprise or Ultimate editions of Windows, then there is no upgrade path, since you already have access to all of the features in Windows 7.

412

Windows Anytime Upgrade

With Windows Anytime Upgrade (WAU), you can upgrade to a more advanced edition of Windows 7 to take advantage of extra features while retaining your current programs, files and settings.

You need Windows 7 Starter, Home Premium or Professional edition, and you must obtain a WAU key for the required edition. You can purchase this from an authorized retail store or online.

To apply the upgrade:

1 Open System Properties and select the option to Get more features with a new edition of Windows 7

2 Alternatively, select Start and click Windows Anytime Upgrade

3 To purchase online choose Go online to choose the edition of Windows 7 that's best for you

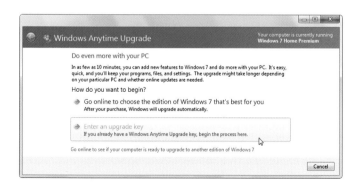

4 If you already have the product key for the new edition, choose Enter an upgrade key

Don't forget

Online purchase of WAU keys is available in Australia, Belgium, Canada, Germany, France, Italy, Japan, the Netherlands, Spain, Sweden, Switzerland, the United Kingdom and the United States.

Hot tip

You can also open Windows Anytime Upgrade from System and Security, in the Control Panel.

413

Hot tip

If you purchase the upgrade key online, after your purchase, Windows will upgrade automatically.

Apply the upgrade

Don't forget

You just follow the prompts to submit your upgrade key and perform the upgrade to the new edition of Windows 7.

1 Enter your 25 character upgrade key and click Next

2 The upgrade key will be verified online

3 Click I accept, to confirm that you agree to the license terms

Beware

Save all documents and data files, and close all open programs, before you click Upgrade. You cannot use your computer while the upgrade is in process.

4 Save files and close programs, then click Upgrade

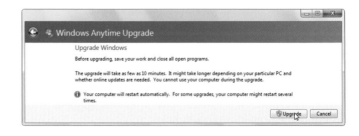

5 The upgrade is applied and the computer will restart

6 Open System Properties and you'll see the new edition

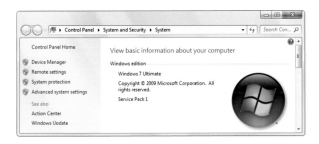

7 Scroll down and you'll see that activation is required

8 When activated, your new edition of Windows is ready

Disk management

The other major component of the computer, alongside the processor and the memory, is data storage. Windows provides several tools to help you manage the disk drives on your system.

Don't forget

You can add Administrative Tools to the Start menu, by changing the Start menu properties (see page 64).

For an overall view of the data facilities of your computer:

1 Select Start, Control Panel, System and Security and then select Administrative Tools

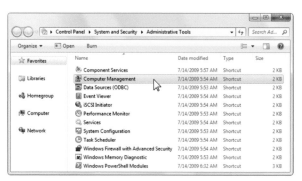

2 Double-click Computer Management (or select and press Enter) and select Storage, Disk Management

Hot tip

Disk Management shows comprehensive details for all the drives, internal, external and removable.

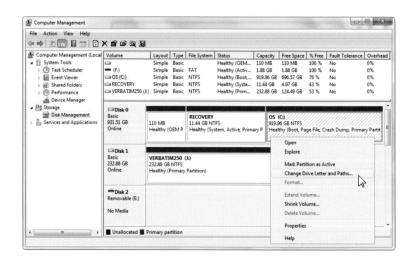

3 Review the details for the drives, or right-click a drive and select a task such as Change Drive Letter and Paths

Disk cleanup

For everyday tasks you can use the tools found in drive properties.

1 Select Start, Computer, select a drive and click Properties

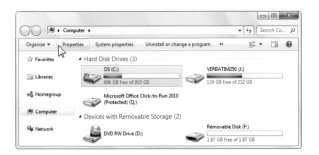

2 In Drive Properties, select the General tab and click the Disk Cleanup button

3 Disk Cleanup calculates how much space you can release

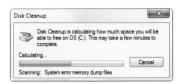

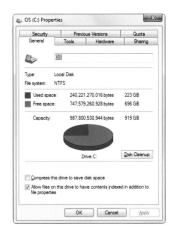

Don't forget

You could select Free up disk space, from the Administrative Tools in Control Panel, System and Security, and then specify which drive to clean up.

Hot tip

Some categories of file are suggested, but you can select others, e.g. Recycle Bin or Temporary Files, to increase the amount of space that will be made available. Select a category and click View Files to see what would be deleted.

4 Select or clear file categories and click OK to proceed

417

5 Click Delete Files to confirm that you want to permanently delete the selected files

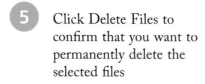

6 Disk Cleanup proceeds to free the space used by those files

7 You may be prompted for administrator permission to remove some file types

8 Click the box to extend the permission to all the items of that type, then click Continue

Clean up system files

If you need more free space, there may be some system files that are not really necessary and can be removed safely.

1 Select Disk Cleanup then click Clean up system files

2 You may for example remove Service Pack Backup Files, if you are sure you won't want to uninstall the service pack

Error checking

1 Open the Properties for a drive and select the Tools tab

This provides three disk tools:

- Error checking
- Defragmentation
- Backup

To carry out error checking on one of your drives:

2 Click Check now, and provide administrator authority if asked

3 To fix file errors on the drive, click Automatically fix file system errors

4 For a thorough check, select Scan for and attempt recovery of bad sectors

5 Click Start

6 Progress messages indicate the stages of the check, and you can use the PC (for tasks not involving that drive)

419

Hot tip

If you clear the box for Automatically fix file system errors, the disk check will report problems but will not correct them.

Don't forget

The sector scan attempts to find and repair any physical errors on the drive itself, and it can take much longer to complete.

Hot tip

You can continue to use the computer (for tasks not involving the drive being checked).

...cont'd

7 When you receive the closing message for Error checking, click See details for the report of the activities

8 Click Close to end

Checking an active drive

1 Select a drive that is in use, for example the drive containing Windows

Don't forget

If the drive is being used, the check must be scheduled for the next start, and run before Windows itself is started.

2 Choose Automatically fix file system errors, and then click Start

3 You are prompted to schedule the disk check for the next time you start the computer

Hot tip

You'll see the report of activities displayed, in this case with three stages since only the check for file system errors was selected.

4 On restart, you have a brief option to cancel

5 If left to proceed, the check will be run before Windows starts

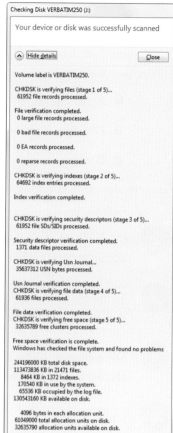

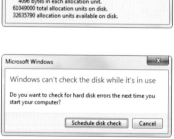

Defragmentation

1 From the Properties, Tools tab for any drive, select Defragment now

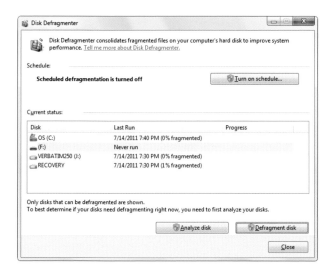

2 All drives that can be defragmented are listed, with the latest information about their fragmentation status

3 Select a drive, for example the removable USB flash drive, and select Analyze disk, to see the current state

4 Select the drive and click Defragment disk, to analyze then defragment the drive

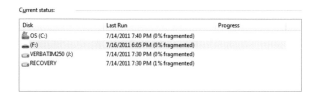

Don't forget

You could also select Defragment your hard drive, from the Administrative Tools in Control Panel, System and Security.

Hot tip

You can choose any drive to defragment, even if you start from Properties for a different drive.

Hot tip

Although this drive may appear to be highly fragmented, it has just a few files that were being simultaneously updated. Defragmentation takes just seconds.

...cont'd

5 Select the drive and click Analyze disk

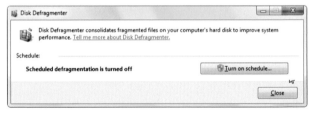

VERBATIM250 (J:)	7/14/2011 7:30 PM (0% fragmented)	Analyze disk
VERBATIM250 (J:)	Running...	78% analyzed
VERBATIM250 (J:)	7/16/2011 6:06 PM (1% fragmented)	

6 Click Defragment disk, to analyze and consolidate

VERBATIM250 (J:)	7/16/2011 6:06 PM (1% fragmented)	Defragment disk
VERBATIM250 (J:)	Running...	88% analyzed
VERBATIM250 (J:)	Running...	Pass 1: 73% consolidated
VERBATIM250 (J:)	Running...	Pass 2: 21% consolidated
VERBATIM250 (J:)	7/16/2011 6:08 PM (0% fragmented)	

Windows can automate the process so that it will happen in the background on a regular basis. To turn this on:

1 Click the button Turn on schedule

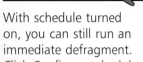

2 Select the frequency, date, time and drives

3 The next scheduled run is now indicated

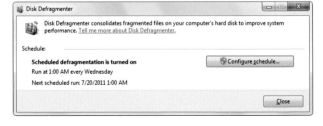

23 Windows performance

Windows provides the tools to help you measure the performance of your system, and identify what may be impacting performance. You can use various monitoring tools and review detailed information about the system. Windows will even help you speed up the system by using USB flash drives or memory cards to act as a cache for system files.

424 System Properties

426 Windows Experience Index

428 Improving performance

430 Data execution prevention

431 Advanced system settings

432 Advanced tools

433 WinSAT and Event Viewer

434 Windows monitors

436 Information on the system

438 Other advanced tools

439 Boosting performance

441 32-bit versus 64-bit

System Properties

System Properties is an important location for reviewing and adjusting the performance of your computer, so Windows provides a number of ways for displaying this panel, so that it is accessible from various areas within the system.

To display System Properties, use any of the following options:

1 Select Start, then right-click Computer and select Properties

2 With the Computer folder open, click System Properties on the toolbar

3 Select Start, Control Panel, click System and Security, and then select System

4 Press the Windows logo key plus the Pause/Break key

5 Whichever method you use, System Properties displays with basic information about your computer

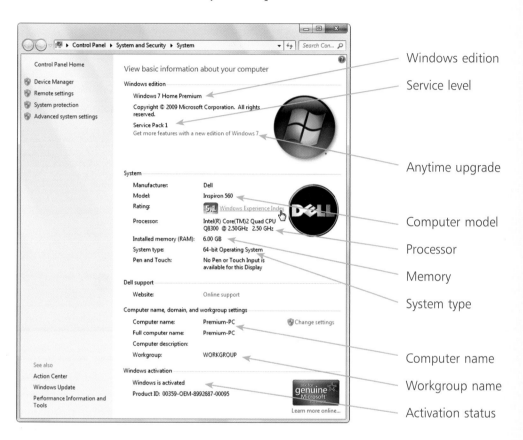

- Windows edition
- Service level
- Anytime upgrade
- Computer model
- Processor
- Memory
- System type
- Computer name
- Workgroup name
- Activation status

The pane on the left provides various links including:

- Device Manager
- Advanced system settings

In the center of the panel, you'll find your System Rating. This is a measure of the capability of the hardware and software in your computer, known as the Windows Experience Index. The higher your score the better and faster your computer performs, especially with advanced or resource-intensive tasks. To see the details:

1 Select Windows Experience Index, or click Performance Information and Tools, which displays the same panel

425

Hot tip

Device Manager provides details of the system components. Advanced system settings provide the full System properties.

Windows Experience Index

The Performance Information and Tools panel shows how the computer hardware has been assessed and the Windows Experience Index established.

Hardware components (processor, memory, Aero graphics, 3D graphics and primary hard disk) are each individually assessed and assigned subscores. The computer's base score is the lowest of these subscores. In the above example, subscores range up to 7.2, but it is the Aero graphics hardware that sets the Windows Experience Index of 5.1.

In another case, a business machine running Windows 7 Enterprise, the base score is only 1.0. This is the subscore for both of the graphics hardware components, but subscores for the processor, memory and disk components are between 3.5 and 4.9.

Reviewing the details in this way makes it clear which machines are suitable for particular tasks. You'd avoid using the second machine for any tasks with graphics requirements, for example, but it should cope well with word processing or spreadsheets.

1 For a detailed report, select the link View and print detailed performance and system information

Don't forget

The report spells out in more detail the characteristics of the system, memory, storage, graphics and network components, showing for example how much of the system memory is shared with the graphics adapter.

Hot tip

Note that these reports only evaluate the primary hard drive and graphics adapter. There may be greater performance benefits than indicated, if you have secondary devices for either.

2 Click Print this page to save a copy of the report

The equivalent report for the second machine, in particular the Graphics section, illustrates why the Graphics subscores are so low, since the adapter is DirectX 8, where Windows 7 recommends at least DirectX 9 capability, and preferably DirectX 10.

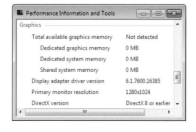

Beware

If any of these reports do encourage you to upgrade hardware components, you'll need to rerun the assessment to get the new rating.

Improving performance

Don't forget

You don't need to change hardware, you can use Performance Options to make changes to the settings to get more efficient operation.

Hot tip

Removing all visual effects will apply the Windows Classic theme, with the traditional Windows styling.

Don't forget

You can also display Performance Options using Advanced system settings.

1 From Performance Information and Tools, select Adjust visual effects

2 The default Let Windows choose will have most of the effects selected

3 Choosing Adjust for best appearance means **all** the effects would be selected

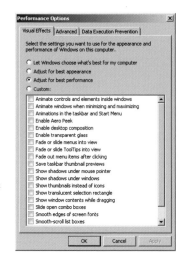

4 You get **no** effects if you Adjust for best performance

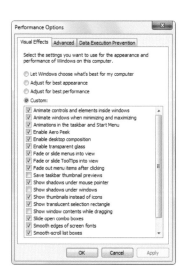

5 The best balance is to select Let Windows choose, click Apply, then deselect effects you can manage without

6 Click Apply, and your choices of effects become the Custom setting

Processor scheduling

1 Click the Advanced tab, and you can choose to prioritize Programs or Background services

The usual choice is Programs, but you might choose Background for a computer that acts as a print server or provides backups.

Virtual memory

Windows creates a Page file to supplement system memory. To review or change the settings:

1 From the Advanced tab, click the Virtual memory Change button

By default, Windows will automatically manage the paging file for your drive or drives. To choose the values yourself:

1 Clear Automatically manage paging file

2 Choose an initial size, and a maximum size then click the Set button to apply

Setting the initial size the same as the maximum will avoid the need for Windows to adjust the size of the paging file, though this may not necessarily improve performance.

With multiple drives, choose the one with most space available.

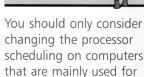

Don't forget

You should only consider changing the processor scheduling on computers that are mainly used for background tasks.

Hot tip

By default, Windows 7 sets the initial size of the page file to 1.5 times the amount of RAM in your system, and it sets the maximum size of the page file to 3 times the amount of RAM.

Hot tip

Make sure you always have at least one drive with a paging file, even on a large memory PC, since some programs rely on the paging file.

Data execution prevention

The third tab in the Performance Options is for Data execution prevention or DEP. This is a security feature intended to prevent damage to your computer from viruses and other security threats, by monitoring programs to make sure they use system memory safely. If a program tries executing code from memory in an incorrect way, DEP closes the program.

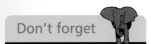
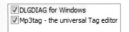
1 By default, Windows will Turn on DEP for essential programs and services only

2 You can choose to Turn on DEP for all programs and services

3 Click Add to select programs for which you want to turn DEP off

If DEP keeps closing a particular program that you trust, and your antivirus software does not detect a threat, the program might not run correctly when DEP is turned on. You should check for a DEP-compatible version of the program or an update from the software publisher before you choose to turn off DEP for that program.

Hardware-based DEP

Some processors use hardware technology to prevent programs from running code in protected memory locations. In this case, you will be told that your processor supports hardware-based DEP.

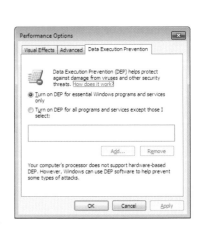

If your processor does not support hardware-based DEP, your computer will still be protected because Windows will use software-based DEP.

Advanced system settings

Windows provides another way to display the Performance Options:

1 Open System Properties and select Advanced system settings

2 In the Performance section click the Settings button

3 Performance Options display, with Visual Effects selected

4 Select a tab and adjust settings (see page 428)

System Properties also gives access to Device Manager.

5 Click the Hardware tab, then click the Device Manager button (or click the Device Manager link in the System panel)

(see page 428)

The Performance section refers to memory usage. However, this setting, which was in Windows XP, is not included in Windows 7.

431

Don't forget

The Device Manager lists all the hardware devices installed on your computer, and allows you to change their properties.

Advanced tools

1 From Performance Information and Tools, select Advanced tools

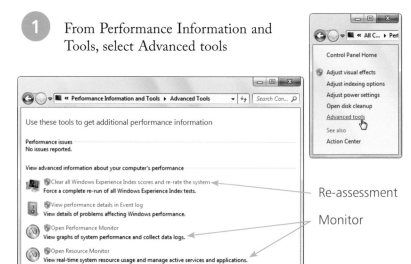

Re-assessment

Monitor

Info on system

Visual Effects

Manage disks

Health report

The Performance issues section will list any problems that have been identified that might impact performance. For example on a laptop computer, Advanced Tools indicates two issues:

1 Select an issue to display the details

2 Click help for more guidance, click Remove from list, or click OK

WinSAT and Event Viewer

1 Clear all Windows Experience Index scores

This runs WinSAT, the Windows System Assessment Tool, to repeat the assessment of the computer and generate new subscores and base score based on the latest system status.

2 View performance details in Event Log

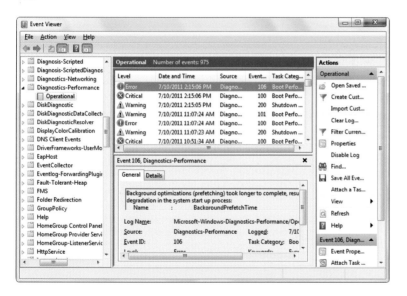

Windows identifies significant events on your computer, for example when a program encounters an error or a user logs on. The details are recorded in event logs that you can read using the Event Viewer. The Advanced Tools link opens the viewer with the Windows Diagnostics - Performance, Operational event log, but there are many other logs available.

You can also open Event Viewer from Administrative Tools, in the Control Panel, Systems and Security.

Don't forget

This re-run will take into account any hardware changes or adjustments to settings such as the virtual memory page file.

Hot tip

Advanced users might find the information helpful when troubleshooting problems with Windows or other programs. For most users, the Event Viewer will only be used when directed by technical support staff.

Windows monitors

 Open Performance Monitor

The program starts with an overview and a system summary, plus links to learn more about using the program. There's also a link to open the Resource Monitor program.

2 Expand Data Collector Sets or Reports to view log details

3 Expand Monitoring Tools and click Performance Monitor to display the graph of processor activity

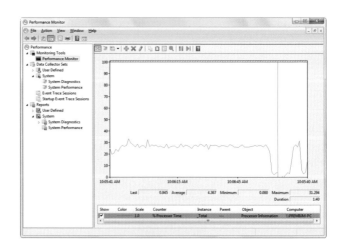

4 Open Resource Monitor

With this you can view systems resource usage in real-time, and manage the active applications and services.

5 Click Overview for a summary of computer activity

6 Click CPU for processor details

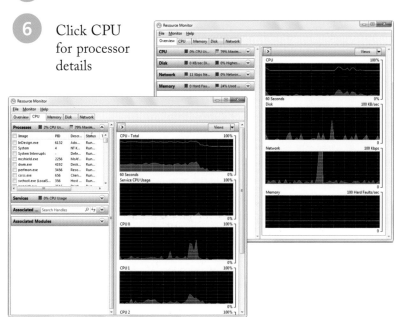

Don't forget

You can open the Resource Monitor utility from Advanced Tools, Performance Monitor or Task Manager, or select Start, type resource mon and press Enter.

7 Click Memory for the allocation of physical memory

8 Click Disk for disk activity by process

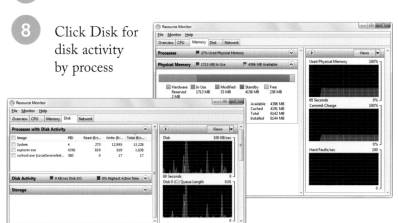

Hot tip

Resource Monitor also includes graphs for network data transfer activity (see page 272).

Information on the system

Don't forget

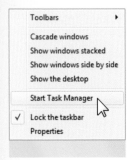

You can also open Task Manager by pressing the keyboard shortcut Ctrl+Shift+Esc, or by right-clicking an empty area on the taskbar and then selecting Start Task Manager.

1 Open Task Manager

This allows you to get information about the programs and process that are currently running on the computer.

2 Click Applications for a list of all open programs, or click Processes for a list of individual tasks for the current user

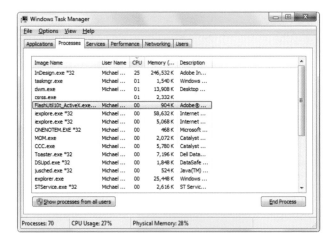

3 Click the button to Show processes from all users

4 Click Performance for graphs of processor and memory usage. There are also Networking graphs (see page 272)

Hot tip

Note that Task manager provides a button to press that will open Resource Monitor.

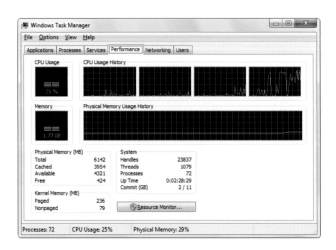

5 View advanced system details in System Information

This opens the System Information program MSinfo32.exe which shows details about the computer hardware configuration, components, software and drivers.

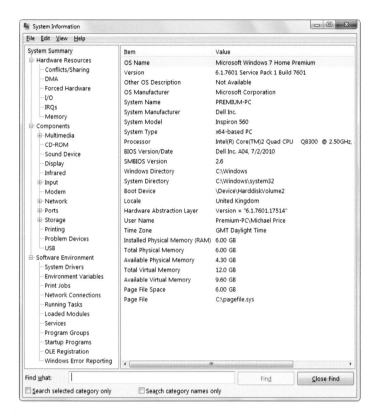

Don't forget

You could also select Start, All Programs, Accessories, System Tools and then System Information.

Hot tip

To find a specific detail, type keywords in the Find what box, choose Search selected category only (if appropriate) and then click Find.

System Information lists the details in four categories:

● System Summary - operating system, computer name, type of BIOS, boot device, user name, amount of memory etc

● Hardware Resources - technical details of the computer's hardware, intended for IT professionals

● Components - details of disk drives, sound devices, modems and other devices

● Software Environment - shows information about drivers, network connections, and other program-related details

Other advanced tools

1 Adjust the appearance and performance of Windows

This will display Performance Options to adjust visual effects, processor scheduling, virtual memory and DEP.

2 Open Disk Defragmenter

This will allow you to modify the schedule for automatically defragmenting your hard disk.

3 Generate a health Report

Don't forget

See page 428 for details of the performance options, and page 421 for more on the disk defragmenter.

This will collect data for sixty seconds then provide a report detailing the status of the hardware resources, response times and processes, with suggestions for ways to maximize performance and system operation.

Hot tip

To get useful results and meaningful statistics, you should use the system as normal while the reports are being generated.

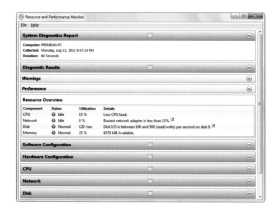

Boosting performance

There's another way to boost the performance of your computer, without having to make major upgrades to the hardware. You can add USB components such as an external drive or a flash drive. These won't be included in the Windows Experience Index, but they can still enhance the computer's capability.

1 Connect a second hard disk, for example the Verbatim 250 GB portable drive

2 The first time you do this, Windows installs the device driver software

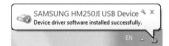

SAMSUNG HM250JI USB Device
Device driver software installed successfully.

3 Windows assigns a drive letter and runs AutoPlay, so you can select the option required, or click Close

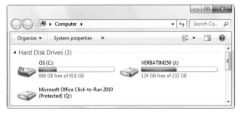

The USB drive is listed in the Computer as a hard disk drive, even though it is removable.

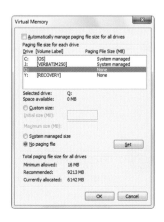

4 Open Advanced settings (see page 429) to assign a page file

5 Restart the system to apply

(see page 429)

Don't forget

Connect the drive to the mains supply via its power adapter (if required), then connect the USB cable to one of the USB ports on the computer.

Beware

Avoid removing the drive while the system is active, if you have created a page file on it.

...cont'd

Don't forget

ReadyBoost is disk caching that uses flash memory to boost your system performance. It can use any form of flash memory such as a USB 2.0 drive, SD card or CompactFlash.

Hot tip

Verbatim's Netbook USB Drive provides up to 32 GB storage, with Readyboost capability, in a tiny format that is ideal for use with netbook computers.

If you add a USB Flash Drive to your computer, you may be able use ReadyBoost to improve the overall performance.

1 Insert the USB drive into an available USB port

2 Windows installs the device driver if required, then assigns a drive letter and displays the AutoPlay options

3 Select Speed up my computer

4 Dedicate the whole or part of the drive to ReadyBoost

In this case, the drive is fully assigned to ReadyBoost.

Sometimes, you may be told that a particular drive is not suitable for ReadyBoost. In this case there is insufficient space, but in other cases it may be that the device is too slow to support the use of ReadyBoost.

5 Click OK to end the request

6 The drive space remains available for data

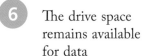

32-bit versus 64-bit

Windows 7 editions (other than Starter and Home Basic) are available as either 32-bit or 64-bit. This refers to the addressing structure used by the processor. Desktop computers generally have a 64-bit processor that can run either version of Windows. Some laptop and netbook computers have 32-bit processors, and so can only run the 32-bit Windows.

To check the processor level and the current operating system:

1 Open System Properties, and select Windows Experience Index, or click Performance Information and Tools

2 Select the link View and print detailed performance and system information

- Asus Netbook - 32-bit Windows, 1 GB, not 64-bit capable

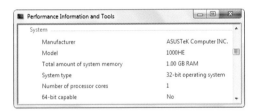

- Dell Laptop - 32-bit Windows, 2 GB, 64-bit capable

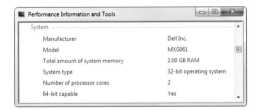

- Dell Desktop - 64-bit Windows, 6 GB, 64-bit capable

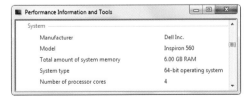

Don't forget

You should note the amount of memory as well as 64-bit capability. You need at least 5 GB memory to benefit from the 64-bit version of Windows.

441

Hot tip

When the computer already has a Windows 64-bit operating system installed, the report doesn't specify the 64-bit status, because it is implicitly capable.

...cont'd

It may improve the performance of your 64-bit capable computer if you install the 64-bit operating system, but only if there is sufficient memory to make this worthwhile. You'll need at least 4 GB and more if possible.

There's no information report to tell you how much memory you can add to your computer, but you can visit www.crucial.com, and download the Scanner tool to check your system.

1 Go to www.crucial.com and click Scan my computer

2 Follow the prompts to download the Scanner tool, and it will check your system

In the first system, current memory is 2 GB, and maximum memory is 4 GB. Switching to 64-bit Windows is possible, but will be of marginal benefit only.

The second system already has 6 GB, but can take a maximum of 8 GB.

With 64-bit Windows installed, you will find two Program File folders, one for 32-bit (often called x86) and one for 64-bit applications.

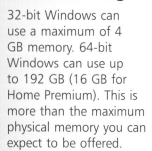

24 Windows Registry

The heart of the Windows system is the Windows Registry. Windows provides the facilities for working with the Registry, and this may let you carry out tasks that are not otherwise supported. However, do be aware that errors in making such changes could leave your system unusable.

444 The Windows Registry

446 Registry backup

447 Open Registry Editor

448 Example Registry change

450 Finding a key

451 Backup before changes

452 Change a value entry

453 Using a standard account

455 Scripted updates

456 Applying an update

457 Resize taskbar thumbnails

458 Remove shortcut suffix

460 Adjust Aero Peek

The Windows Registry

Arguably the most important component in the Windows system, since it records everything about your hardware and software, the Windows Registry is something that in normal circumstances you never need to deal with directly.

The Registry is a structured database that stores the configuration settings and options for applications, device drivers, user interface, services, and all kinds of operating system components. It also stores all the counters that are used to provide the performance reports and charts.

Installation programs, applications and device software all deal directly with the Registry, so all the updates happen in the background. However, the Registry stores user-based settings in a user-specific location, thus allowing multiple users to share the same machine, yet have their own personal details and preferences. The Registry also makes it possible to establish levels of privilege, to control what actions a particular user is permitted to carry out.

Changes to the Registry Editor

When you make changes to the setup for your user account, Windows writes the necessary updates to the Registry for you. Similarly, when you install new programs or hardware devices, many Registry modifications will be applied. Normally, you won't need to know the details.

Registry Editor

However, there will be times when the developers have failed to provide a necessary change, and the only way (or the quickest way) to make the adjustment is by working directly with the Registry. Windows includes a Registry Editor that you can use, with caution since the Registry is a crucial part of your system, to browse and edit the Registry.

The Registry is made of a number of separate files, but you never need to be concerned with the physical structure, since the Registry Editor gives you access to the full Registry, displaying the logical structure and taking care of the specifics of updates.

Before you browse or edit the Registry, you should have an understanding of the structure and how changes get applied, and especially how the original values can be saved - just in case changes get applied that have unwelcome effects.

The structure of the Registry

The data in the Windows Registry is organized in a hierarchical or tree format. The nodes in the tree are called keys. Each key can contain subkeys and entries. An entry consists of a name, a data type and a value, and it is referenced by the sequence of subkeys that lead to that particular entry.

There are five top level keys:

- HKEY_LOCAL_MACHINE   HKLM
  Information about the computer system, including hardware and operating system data such as bus type, system memory, device drivers, and startup control data

- HKEY_CLASSES_ROOT   HKCR
  Information about file types, shortcuts and interface items (alias for parts of HKLM and HKCU)

- HKEY_CURRENT_USER   HKCU
  Contains the user profile for the currently logged on user, with desktop, network, printers, and program preferences (alias for part of HKU)

- HKEY_USERS   HKU
  Contains information about actively loaded user profiles and the default profile

- HKEY_CURRENT_CONFIG   HKCC
  The hardware profile used at startup, for example to configure device drivers and display resolution (alias for part of HKLM)

Sections of the Registry are stored in the System32 and User folders, each subtree having a single file plus a log file, for example Sam and Sam.log, or System and Sytem.log. Subtrees associated with files are known as Registry hives. They include:

HKEY_LOCAL_MACHINE\SAM	Sam
HKEY_LOCAL_MACHINE\SECURITY	Security
HKEY_LOCAL_MACHINE\SOFTWARE	Software
HKEY_LOCAL_MACHINE\SYSTEM	System
HKEY_CURRENT_CONFIG	System
HKEY_CURRENT_USER	Ntuser.dat
HKEY_USERS\.DEFAULT	Default

Beware

Some products available on the Internet suggest the Registry needs regular maintenance or cleaning. Although problems can arise, in general the Registry is self-sufficient and such products are not necessary.

Hot tip

Applications read the Registry to check that a specific key exists, or to open a key and select entry values that are included.

445

Don't forget

The tree, subtree, alias, hive and file structure can be very complex, but the view taken via the Registry Editor is fortunately more straightforward.

Registry backup

Before using the Registry Editor, you should create a restore point using System Restore (see page 336). The restore point will contain information about the Registry, and you can use it to undo changes to your system.

To create a manual restore point:

1 Open System Properties (see page 325) and select System protection

2 Select the System Protection tab and click Create to create a restore point immediately

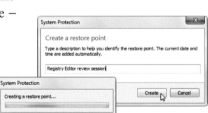

3 Type a description, to remind you of the reason for the restore point

4 When the restore point completes, click Close – no restart is required

5 Just to check, open System Properties and click the System Restore button

Open Registry Editor

Registry Editor is not accessible via the Start menu, Control panel, Administrative tools or through any shortcuts. You must run program Regedit.exe by name.

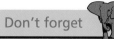
1 Select Start, type regedit and press Enter to run the Regedit.exe program

2 Assuming you have an administrator account, click Yes, to allow Registry Editor to start with full administrator privilege

3 Registry Editor starts, and the first time it runs, you'll see the five main subtrees, with all their branches collapsed

4 Select a key e.g. HKEY_LOCAL_MACHINE (HKLM) and double-click to expand to the next level

Example Registry change

Before exploring the Registry further, it will be useful to look at a typical Registry update, used to make changes for which Windows has no formal method included.

One such requirement is to change the registered organization and registered owner for the computer. These names will have been set up when Windows was installed. The names chosen may no longer be appropriate, perhaps because you've changed companies, or because the computer was passed on or purchased from another user.

To see the registration details:

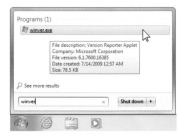

1. Select Start, type winver and press Enter to run the Winver.exe program

2. The details of the installed version of Windows are shown, along with the registered owner and organization

3. Assume that these details need to be revised to Sue Price and In Easy Steps

4. Search the Internet for advice on changing registered owner

You will find that this particular change included in a number of Windows hints and tips lists. You'll even find a solution at the Microsoft website www.microsoft.com. All the suggestions follow a similar pattern. They advise you to run Regedit.exe and find the Registry key named HKEY_LOCAL_MACHINE\SOFTWARE\Microsoft\Windows NT\CurrentVersion, where you can change the owner and organization. Some of the websites also discuss the need for administrator authority, and they usually warn about taking backups before making changes.

To locate the key, you can step through the path, subkey by subkey, double-clicking each one in turn.

1 Locate the subkey SOFTWARE and double-click

2 Scroll down to subkey Microsoft and double-click

You can double-click a subkey, or select it and press enter, to expand it to the next level.

3 Scroll down to subkey Windows NT and double-click

Although the subkeys are shown in capitals or mixed case, as displayed in the Registry, they are in fact not case sensitive.

4 Select subkey CurrentVersion and scroll through the list of entries to select RegisteredOrganization

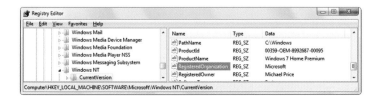

Finding a key

Don't forget

Rather than stepping through the path, you could use the Find command in Regedit.

Hot tip

Pressing F3 carries out the Find Next operation, to locate the next match.

Beware

You'll soon discover that subkey names are not unique, and also the same text could appear in the data content of Registry entries.

Don't forget

Find is more effective if you restrict the search, for example putting a Value entry name, and clearing the Key and Data boxes. You could also search for known text in the data content.

1 Select the highest level key Computer, and then click Edit, Find (or press Ctrl+F)

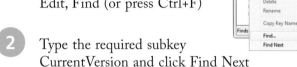

2 Type the required subkey CurrentVersion and click Find Next

3 The subkey is in the wrong branch, so keep pressing F3

4 This is the wrong section, and matches data content

5 Search instead for the Value entry name RegisteredOrganization

Backup before changes

1 Select the subkey, or a value entry within the subkey, and then click File, Export

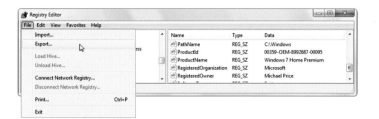

Don't forget

You should make a backup of the branch at the subkey within which changes are required.

2 By default your Documents folder will be selected, but you can choose a different folder if desired

Hot tip

You can create a backup of the whole registry, but it is sufficient to backup just the branches being changed.

451

3 Provide a file name for the Registration File (.reg) that is being created and choose Selected branch

Hot tip

The .reg file will have all the subkeys, value entries and data contents for everything within the subkey selected for Export.

4 The Registration file is written to the selected folder

Change a value entry

1 Select the Value entry to be changed and double-click

This entry has text data. The value data for other entries could be binary or numbers. You must replace existing contents with the same type of data values.

2 The Value entry is opened with Value data displayed ready for Edit

3 Replace the existing contents with the required information

4 Click OK to apply and save the change. It is immediately in effect

If you change your mind part way through, you cannot just close Registry Editor - you must restore the original values using the branch backup, or else reverse the changes individually.

5 Repeat for any other values to be changed

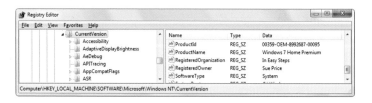

6 Close Registry Editor when you have finished - no Save is required, since changes are dynamically applied

Using a standard account

Logoff and switch to a Standard user account, making sure no other accounts are active.

1 Select Start, type regedit and press Enter to run the Regedit.exe program

2 There's no UAC interception, Registry Editor starts up at Computer (or at the last key referenced by this account)

3 Locate the Value entry RegisteredOrganization in the Windows NT subkey, and double-click the name

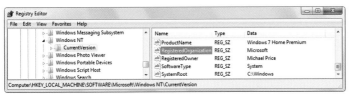

Beware

The standard account can edit and create Registry keys under HKEY_CURRENT_USER, but not entries under HKEY_LOCAL_MACHINE. Some registry entries are even blocked for reading.

4 The current value is shown

5 Change the value to the required text and click OK

6 Registry Editor displays an error message to say it is unable to edit the entry

453

...cont'd

If you are signed in with a standard user account but you need full Registry Editor access, you must run Regedit as an administrator.

1 Select Start, type regedit

2 Right-click Regedit.exe at the top of the Start menu and select Run as Administrator

3 Provide the password for the administrator account displayed and click Yes, to allow Registry Editor to start with full administrator privilege

As an alternative, you can open the Command Prompt as an administrator, and start Regedit.exe from there.

1 Select Start, type cmd.exe and press Shift+Ctrl+Enter

2 Respond to the UAC prompt, then type regedit.exe and press Enter, and the full Registry Editor will start

Scripted updates

You'll find that some websites offer scripted versions of Registry updates that you can download and run. These are similar to the Registration files that you create when you backup a branch of the Registry. To illustrate this method, you can create your own script to update the Registered owner details.

Don't forget

Using scripts that are provided can make it easier to apply updates, as long as you trust the source websites.

1. Open Notepad and type the Registry Editor header, the subkey path and the Value entries required

2. Select File, Save and choose a folder if required, or accept the default, normally Documents

Hot tip

This .reg file automates the process followed to find the subkey and amend the Value entries for Organization and Owner.

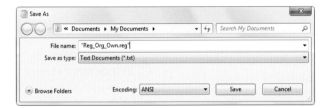

3. Type the file name and file type e.g. "Reg_Org_Own.reg"

The quote marks ensure that the file type .reg will be used, rather than Notebook's default file type .txt.

4. Click Save and the Registration file will be added to the specified folder

Applying an update

Don't forget

You use this same process to apply the backup Registration file, if you decide to reverse the changes you have made.

1 To apply an update, double-click the Registration file

2 There will be a UAC prompt, and then you will be warned of the potential dangers of updates

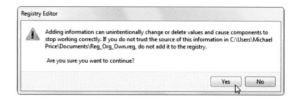

3 If you are happy with the update, click Yes

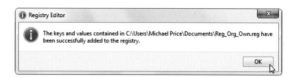

Hot tip

The update is applied without any requirement to run Regedit or open the Registry.

4 The keys and values included are added to the Registry

5 Confirm the update by running Winver (see page 448)

6 You can also open the Registry and check the subkey and its Value entries

Beware

It is well worth repeating that you must change the Registry with care. Only use trusted sources when you do make changes. And make sure you have a Registry Backup before you make any change.

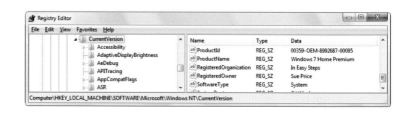

Resize taskbar thumbnails

When you move the mouse cursor over a Windows 7 taskbar button, you'll see a small version of the application window.

To make this larger in size:

1 Open Regedit.exe, and locate the subkey HKEY_CURRENT_USER\Software\Microsoft\Windows\CurrentVersion\Explorer\Taskband

2 Right-click the right hand pane and select New, DWORD Value, then name the value MinThumbSizePx.

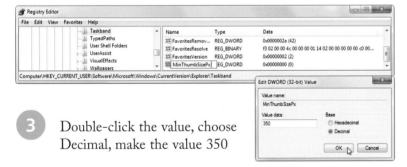

3 Double-click the value, choose Decimal, make the value 350

4 Logoff and logon again to put the change into effect

5 View a taskbar thumbnail to see the results

Remove shortcut suffix

When you create a shortcut on the desktop, Windows insists on adding the word Shortcut to the name.

For example:

1 Locate the Notepad.exe program file, which is usually found in C:\windows\system32

2 Right-click the program icon and select Create shortcut

3 The shortcut cannot be added to the program folder, so Click Yes to place it on the desktop

4 The shortcut is created and given the program name followed by - Shortcut

If you find yourself editing the name to remove this addition, you might like to edit the Registry to avoid the suffix for all future shortcuts you create (this change won't affect existing shortcuts).

1 Open Regedit.exe, and locate the subkey HKEY_
CURRENT_USER\Software\Microsoft\Windows\
CurrentVersion\Explorer

2 Select Value entry Link, then click File, Modify (or double-click Link)

3 Change the first part of the number (19) to 00 to give a value of 00 00 00 00

4 Click OK to update the value, then close Regedit.exe

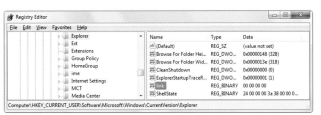

Don't forget

Using scripts that are provided can make it easier to apply updates, as long as you trust the source websites.

You must logoff and logon again for the change to take effect. Now when you create a shortcut, it will just receive the program name with no suffix.

Remove shortcut arrows

You can also use Registry updates to change the shortcut icons, avoiding the shortcut arrow overlay, or using a different perhaps smaller arrow to overlay the shortcut icons.

There are a number of different methods suggested for this. They involve adding a reference to an alternative icon file in a value entry in subkey [HKEY_LOCAL_MACHINE\SOFTWARE\Microsoft\Windows\CurrentVersion\explorer\Shell Icons].

You can search the Internet for articles using a search term such as "Windows 7 remove shortcut arrow," and choose your preferred website. Note that the instructions provided may differ for Windows 32-bit versus Windows 64-bit systems.

As with all Registry updates, make sure that you back up first, before making any changes.

459

Hot tip

Sometimes changes such as this have unexpected side effects, so a backup or restore point will be particularly important.

Adjust Aero Peek

When the mouse moves over the box at the bottom right of the screen, all open windows are replaced by empty frames. This can be distracting, when you are just moving the mouse to a corner to help locate the pointer.

You can change the time delay before Aero Peek reduces the screen to the desktop.

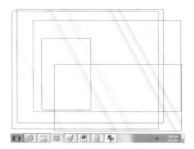

1 Open Regedit.exe and find the subkey HKEY_CURRENT_USER\ Software\Microsoft\Windows\CurrentVersion\Explorer\ Advanced

2 Right-click the right-hand pane and select New, DWORD Value (see page 457) and name the value DesktopLivePreviewHoverTime

The default is 500 (half a second), 1000 is one second, and 0 is instant. To return to the default, set the value to 500 or delete the Value entry.

3 Double-click to edit, select Decimal and enter a value in milliseconds, for example 2000 (two seconds) then click OK

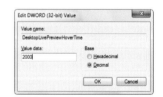

As usual, you must logoff, and then logon again, to reload the HKCU subtree portion of the Registry, to put the Registry update into effect.

25 Where next for Windows

The Windows and Internet environment is constantly changing. However, if you want to keep up to date with developments, and find out what new ideas are planned, explore the Microsoft team blogs.

462 Internet Explorer 10

464 Preview IE 10

466 Windows Live Essentials

468 Windows Blogs

469 Windows 8

Internet Explorer 10

Don't forget

For many users, Internet Explorer 9 is still a new product, perhaps not yet even installed on their computers. However, Microsoft is hard at work developing the follow-on version.

If you'd like to know what is coming for Internet Explorer in future, Microsoft offers a preview.

1 Go to www.microsoft.com, type Internet Explorer, and click the spy glass to Search Microsoft.com

2 Click the link for the Internet Explorer 10 Test Drive

Hot tip

The results for the search will differ over time, but you should always find information here about the latest version of Internet Explorer.

3 View the demos, or click Download to obtain the Preview

4 Click the button marked Download Preview

5 Select Run and follow prompts to download and install

Hot tip

You'll be asked to accept the license terms before the software is actually installed on your computer.

6 Internet Explorer 10 opens with the TestDrive web page

Preview IE 10

1 From the Test Drive page, select Preview's User Guide

2 Review the contents of the User Guide and click the arrow to return to the Test Drive web page

3 Select Release Notes for the latest status of the Preview

4 For technical details, view the Guide for Developers

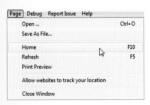

5 From the Test Drive web page select Blog to read the posts in the IEBlog at the MSDN website

6 To end the session, click the Close button or select Page, Close window

7 To start a session, select Start, All Programs, and Internet Explorer Platform Preview, or double-click the Preview icon on the desktop

8 To switch to another website, select Page, Open, then type the website address and click OK

9 The selected website is displayed in Internet Explorer 10

Windows Live Essentials

At this time, the latest version of this suite of applications is Windows Live Essentials 2011. If you check the Microsoft Downloads site, you may find an updated release.

1 Go to www.microsoft.com/downloads and search for Windows Live Essentials 2011

2 This shows two recent updates, so select the later release

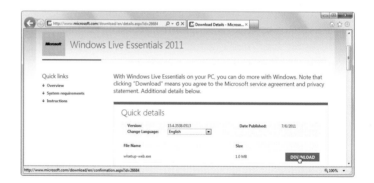

3 The update is to version 15.4.3538.0513

4 Open any Windows Live program, click the Application button and select About

5 The current version is 15.4.3508.1109

6 Click the Download button to start the transfer

7 When prompted, choose to Run the Setup program, and Windows Live Essentials prepares to install

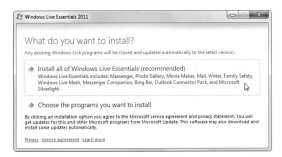

Don't forget

You can choose the individual programs that you want to install or update, but you are recommended to install all of Windows Live Essentials.

467

8 Choose to install all the applications, updating the existing ones, and adding any new ones

9 The files are downloaded, and installed

10 When installation completes, select Restart now to finish the process

When the system has restarted, open one of your Windows Live applications and select the About option as before, to check that the level has been updated.

Hot tip

Check periodically at the Microsoft Downloads website for any new updates. You'll also get reminders from the Inside Windows Live blog (see page 468).

Windows Blogs

A useful way to keep up to date with changes and new facilities is to make use of the various Blogs supported by the Windows development teams. To see what blogs are available:

1 Visit the website windowsteamblog.com

2 You'll get the latest news for Windows related topics

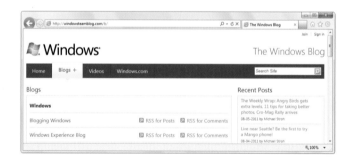

Windows Live:
Follow us on Twitter (@windowslive)

SkyDrive:
Like us on Facebook
Follow us on Twitter (@skydrive)

Hotmail:
Like us on Facebook
Follow us on Twitter (@hotmail)

Messenger:
Like us on Facebook
Follow us on Twitter (@messenger)

3 Click the Blogs button for links to the blogs currently available, with RSS buttons for posts and comments

The blogs are from Microsoft teams for Windows, Windows Live, Internet Explorer, Windows Phone, Office, Bing and Zune.

Windows	Windows Phone
Blogging Windows	Windows Phone Blog
Windows Experience Blog	Windows Phone Developer Blog
Extreme Windows Blog	Windows Mobile 6 Developer Blog
Windows for your Business	**International**
Developing for Windows	Konsumencki rzut oka – Windows Polska
Windows Security Blog	Windows Phone中文官方开发者博客
Springboard Series Blog	El blog de Windows para América Latina
Windows Home Server Blog	O Blog do Windows para o Brasil
	Блог Windows для России
Windows Live	**Other Microsoft Team Blogs**
Inside Windows Live	The Microsoft Office Blog
Windows Live for Developers	Bing Community
Internet Explorer	Major Nelson
Exploring IE	Zune Insider

Windows 8

There's little information as yet about the next version of Windows. Microsoft representatives have talked about the product at developers conferences, and Microsoft has even posted a video on YouTube that shows Windows 8 in action.

1 At www.youtube.com search for Building Windows 8, and locate the item published by Microsoft

2 This video illustrates the Tablet user interface, which is optimized for touch as well as mouse and keyboard

The new user interface incorporates a tile-based Start screen which replaces the Start menu in previous versions of Windows, with a customizable, scalable full-screen view of apps. The tiles are live, showing notifications and up-to-date information.

...cont'd

New applications for Windows 8 can be built using HTML5 and JavaScript, and will be full-screen and touch-optimized, and work with or without a keyboard and mouse on a broad range of screen sizes and pixel densities, from small slates to laptops, desktops, all-in-ones, and even wall-mounted displays.

Examples of applications on the Start screen include a weather application, Windows Store, Investments, RSS news feeds, user's Personal Page, and user's Windows Live Account.

The new interface is particularly designed for wide-screen 16:9 resolution, with 1366×768 and larger screens able to display two Windows 8 applications side by side using Snap. You can also adjust the sizes of the snapped applications. Of course, if you prefer you'll still be able to work in the familiar Windows 7 style.

When the time does come to make your upgrade to Windows 8, you'll be glad to know that the memory, graphics and processor requirements of the new version are no greater, and perhaps less demanding than the Windows 7 requirements, so your existing hardware should be adequate.

Index

Symbols

32-bit processor	12, 15, 441
64-bit processor	12, 15, 179, 412, 441
μTorrent	154

A

Abort	77–78
Access from XP	389
Accessories	118
Account password	32
Account picture	31
Account selection	16, 34
Action Center	13, 26, 247, 313
Address bar	21, 102
Adjust	
Llibrary properties	97
Screen resolution	44
UAC settings	38
Administrative Tools	135
Administrator account	30, 36, 42
Adobe Reader	42, 145
Advanced sharing	271
Advanced system settings	431
Aero	17, 19
Aero themes	52
All-in-one computer. *See* Portable computers	
All-in-one printer	24
All Programs	18
AppData folder	60
Applications Carousel	290
Arrange library contents	95
Aspect ratio	44
Asus	282, 286, 288, 441
Attachments	166
Audio Bar	287
Audio connections	222
Audio file formats	224
Authorisation	42
Automated shutdown	76
Automatic logon	75
AutoMovie themes	219
AVG Antivirus Free Edition	146–147

B

Backup and recovery	
Choose backup device	337
Copy files and folders	332
Copy libraries	334
Manage space	343
Manual backup	342
Previous versions	346
Recover computer	347
Repeated copies	333
Restore files	344
Scheduled backup	341
System repair disc	349
Windows Backup	336
Backup encryption key	383
Battery meter	278
BitLocker	14, 380
BitLocker To Go	14, 380, 385
Blocked senders	169
Browser	23
Browsing history	182, 191

C

Calculator	126
Canon Image Gateway	204
Cell phone. *See* Smartphone	
Center	
Action	13, 26
Network and Sharing	22, 24
Change account picture	33, 34
Change folder view	88
Change search provider	184
Change shortcut icon	78
Change theme	52
Chrome	23
Classic theme	62, 280, 428
ClearType	50
Collapse folder list	21, 104
Color depth	200
Combine tasks	66
Command prompt	132, 392
Adjust appearance	397
Administrator shortcut	396

Command line changes	402
List of commands	132
Open	392
Open as administrator	395
Select a folder	394
Using	400
Windows properties	399
Command Prompt	132
Compatibility View	198
Compression algorithms	200
Computer folder	64, 83
Computer search	100
Configure taskbar	66
Connecting and sharing	322
Connect to the Internet	22
Contacts	168
Control Panel	26, 36, 52, 64
Controlled account	42
Convertible. *See* Portable computers	
Copy CD tracks	224
Copy files and folders	332
Create account	31
Create HomeGroup	260
Create library	96
Create movie from photos	218
Create network	258
Create panoramic image	209
Create theme	56
Create Windows Live ID	158
Customize Start menu	64

Wireless printer	246
Dictate to computer	234
Digital camera	202
Canon Image Gateway	204
Create panoramic image	209
Import images	206
Install software	203
PhotoStitch	209
Transfer more images	208
Transfer photos	205
Untransferred images	206
View imported images	207
Digital images	200
Color depth	200
Compression algorithms	200
Digital zoom	200
Image file formats	200, 201
Image resolution	200
Import with Windows	211
Optical zoom	200
Digital zoom	200
Disable transparency	57
Disc Image Burner	129
Disk cleanup	417
Disk management	416
Display as link	64
Display as menu	64, 65
Download media files	226
Download theme	55
Drag with left mouse button	116
Dual network access	266
Duplicate displays	48
DVD Maker	128

D

Data execution prevention	430
Dell	282, 283, 441
Defragmentation	421–422, 438
Desktop background	30, 55, 65
Desktop Gadgets	30, 136
Devices and Printers	205
Add a printer	238
Add a scanner	254
Audio Bar	287
Generic/text only printer	251
Location aware printing	253
Network printer	245
Share printer with XP	244
Sharing the printer	242
Updating device drivers	240
USB printer	239
Using the scanner	256
Virtual printers	249

E

Easy Connect	324
Editions of Windows 7	14
Edit photos	213
Edit video clip	217
Email	28, 156
Add email accounts	159
Create Windows Live ID	158
Email programs	156
Junk email	161, 169
Microsoft Outlook	156
Web mail	156
Windows Live Mail	157
Enable transparency	57, 281
Enable Wi-Fi for Smartphone	302
Encryption	109, 380

Ending Windows   17
Enhanced search   110
Enterprise   14
Error reporting   312
Event Viewer   433
Expand folder list   21, 104
Experience Index. *See* Windows Experience Index
Explorer. *See* Windows Explorer
Extend displays   48

F

Facebook   172
Family safety   36, 40
Fast user switching   35
FAT   82, 98
Favorites   189
Fax and Scan   125, 256
Features of Windows 7   15
File system   82
File types   109
Find folder   21
Fine-tune ClearType   50
Firefox   23
Flag icon   26
Flash drive   14, 20, 39, 101, 287
Floppy disk   39
Folders
  Address bar   102
  Customize   98
  Folder and search options   106
  Folder contents   87
  Folder path   21
  Location path   102
  Move and copy   115
  Show hidden files   106
  Structure   82
  View   106
Force move or copy   116
Fragmentation   82

G

Generic/text only printer   251
Get help from a friend   320
Get themes online   54
Getting Started   28, 31, 36

Group folder contents   90
Guest account   30, 34, 36

H

Hardware-assisted virtualization (HAV)   352
Help and Support   18, 79
Hide icon and notifications   68
Hide user list   378
Hide window contents   19
Home Basic   14
HomeGroup   13, 14, 25, 61, 225
  Create a HomeGroup   260
  Home network   261
  Join   261
  Share files   260
  Status   262
HomeGroup status   262
HomeGroup versus Network   268
Home media streaming   230
Home network   22, 25, 259, 261
Home page   179, 188
Home Premium   14
HP   274–275, 283, 288, 290
Hyperlink   181

I

IBM PC   12
Identify displays   49
Image file formats   200, 201
Image resolution   200
Import images from camera   206
Import with Windows   211
Include folder   20
Indexing
  By properties   109
  Contents plus properties   109
  Encrypted files   109
  Fast searches   108
  File types   109
  Locations   108
  Options   108
  Settings   109
Index settings   109
InPrivate Browsing   195
Input Panel   289

Insert files in message   167
Install Windows Virtual PC   354
Instant messaging   28, 172
    Facebook   172
    Privacy setting   172
    Send an invitation   173
    Video call   173
Internet Explorer
    Browsing history   182, 191
    Change search provider   184
    Choose add-ons   142
    Compatibility View   198
    Favorites   180, 189
    Gallery   184
    Home page   179, 188
    Hyperlink   181
    InPrivate Browsing   195
    Manage add-ons   142
    Managing add-ons   194
    Microsoft Bing   183
    New Tab button   187
    No add-ons   179
    One box   181
    Open in new window   185
    Page back and forward   182
    Pinned sites   190
    Quick Tabs   187
    RSS feeds   192
    Search for web page   183
    Shrink to fit   197
    Start   179
    Tabbed browsing   186
    Turn on suggestions   183
    Use tab set   188
    Web slices   192
    Window   180
    Zoom and print   196
Internet Explorer 8   13, 23
Internet Explorer 9   13, 23, 178, 462
Internet Explorer 10   462
    IEBlog   465
    Preview   463, 464
Internet radio   228
Internet TV   13
Irfanview   148

J

Join HomeGroup   261
Jump lists   73
Junk email   161, 169

K

Keep changes   44
Keyboard shortcut   79, 122, 188, 282, 436
Keystroke combinations   79

L

Landscape   44
Language bar   70
Laptop. *See* Portable computers
Launchpad   18
Library   20, 82
    Add a location   92
    Adjust properties   97
    Arrange contents   95
    Create   96
    Include folder   20, 92
    Library pane   91
    Location unavailable   94
    Removable drives   93
    Type   20
Live Essentials. *See* Windows Live Essentials
Live Mail. *See* Windows Live Mail
Local Security Policy   376, 378
Local Users and Groups   375, 376
Location aware printing   253
Location bar   66, 102
Logoff   35, 78
Logon screen   16

M

Maintenance   26
    64-bit Windows   412
    Apply upgrade   414–415
    Defragmentation   421–422
    Disk cleanup   417
    Disk management   416
    Error checking   419
    Microsoft Update   408
    Service packs   404
    Windows Anytime Upgrade   412–413
    Windows Update   404

Installed updates   411
Install updates   405
  Settings   26, 406
  Uninstall update   411
  Update categories   409
  Update history   410
Make text larger   46
Managing
  Accounts   37
  Add-ons   194
  Audio devices   222
  Wireless networks   267
Math Input Panel   127, 289
Maximize button   19
Media Center   14
Media files   25
Media Player Library   225
Menu bar   85
Messenger   28
Microsoft
  Bing   183
  Outlook   156
  Silverlight   143
  Surface Globe   290
  Update   408
Mini computer. *See* Portable computers
Mobile phone. *See* Smartphone
Mobility Center. *See* Windows Mobility Center
Monitor network   272
Most Recently Used list   18, 64
Mouse settings   80
Move and copy   115–116
Move window   19
Movie Maker. *See* Windows Live Movie Maker
MS-DOS   12, 132
Multiple displays   48
Multiple input languages   70
Multitouch. *See* Touch
Music. *See* Sound

N

Navigation pane   21, 83, 104, 333
  Collapse folder list   104
  Expand folder list   104
  Favorites   113
  Move and copy   115
  Show all folders   105
Netbook. *See* Portable computers
Netbook display   286
Network adapter   14, 258

Network and Sharing Center   22, 24, 262
Network Firewall   27
Networking   24
  Advanced sharing   271
  Create a network   258
  Dual network access   266
  Home network   259
  Manage wireless networks   267
  Monitor network   272
  Network adapter   258
  Network and Sharing Center   262
  Network location   258
  Network status   22, 24, 262
  Public network   259
  Resource Monitor   272
  Sharing folders   270
  Smartphone   304
  Task Manager   272
  Wireless network   264
  Work network   259
Network map   24, 269
Network Meter   272
Network printer   245
Network versus HomeGroup   268
Newsgroup
  Subscribe   175
Newsgroups   174
New Tab button   187
Notebook. *See* Portable computers
Notepad   119
Notepad++   149
Notification area   17, 26, 68, 287
NTFS   82, 98

O

Office 2010   250
Open Command Prompt   392
Open file location   101
Open in new window   83, 185
OpenOffice.org   150–151
Opera   23
Operators   110, 112
Optical zoom   200
Order prints over the Internet   215
Organize button   86
Original Images folder   214
Other Windows Essentials   144
  Adobe Reader   145
  AVG Antivirus Free Edition   146–147
  Irfanview   148

Notepad++ 149
OpenOffice.org 150–151
Paint.NET 152–153
µTorrent 154
Outlook Express 28

P

Page file 429
Page back and forward 182
Paint 123
Paint.NET 152–153
Parental controls 36, 40
Password hint 16, 32, 39
Password protection on wakeup 277
Password reset disk 39
PC-DOS 12
Peek 19, 67, 460
Performance 13
  32-bit versus 64-bit processors 441
  Adjust visual effects 428
  Advanced system settings 431
  Advanced tools 432
  Data execution prevention 430
  Defragmentation 438
  Event Viewer 433
  External drive 439
  Performance Monitor 434
  Processor scheduling 429
  ReadyBoost 440
  Resource Monitor 435
  System Information 427, 437
  System Properties 424
  Task Manager 436
  Virtual memory 429
  Windows Experience Index 426
  WinSAT 433
Performance Monitor 434
Permission 42
Personalization Gallery 54
Personalize 52
  Aero theme 52
  Change theme 52
  Create a theme 56
  Desktop background 55
  Disable transparency 57
  Download theme 55
  Enable transparency 57
  Get themes online 54
  High-contrast theme 62
  Home Basic 62

Save theme 60
Screen saver 59
Share theme 61
Sound scheme 58
Starter 62
Themepack file 61
Windows 7 basic theme 62
Windows 7 theme 56
Windows Classic 62
Windows color 57
Phishing 169
Photo Gallery. *See* Windows Live Photo Gallery
Photos. *See* Digital images
PhotoStitch 209
Photo Viewer. *See* Windows Photo Viewer
Pinned sites 190
Pin to
  Jump list 74
  Start menu 18, 72
  Taskbar 71
Play CDs 223
Play to device 231, 305
Pointer schemes 80
Pointer speed 80
Pointer trails 80
Portable computers 274
  Audio Bar 287
  Battery meter 278
  Enable transparency 281
  Input Panel 289
  Math Input Panel 127, 289
  Netbook display 286
  Power management 276
  Screen brightness 276
  Tablet PC 14, 44
  Touch PCs 288
  User interface 280
  Windows Mobility Center 278, 282
Portrait 44
Power button 64, 275
Power management 275
PowerShell 133
Predefined VHD 371–372
Presentation settings 284
Preview pane 107
Previous versions of files 346
Printers. *See* Devices and Printers
Print your photos 215
Privacy setting 172
Problem Steps Recorder 317
Professional 14
Program Compatibility 329
Programs 143
Public network 25, 259

Q

Quick Tabs 187

R

ReadyBoost 440
Recently Used list 18, 64
Recovery. *See* Backup and recovery
Registry Editor. *See* Windows Registry
Remote Assistance 321
Resource Monitor 272, 435
Restore button 19
Restore files from backup 344
Revert to original 214
RSS feeds 176, 192
Run box 76

S

Safari 23
Safe Boot 328
Safe senders 169
Save and publish your movie 220
Save searches 114
Save theme 60
Save your video project 219
Scanner 254, 256
Scheduled backup 341
Screen brightness 276, 284
Screen orientation 44
Screen resolution 44, 46
Screen saver 59
Searches 114
Search filters 110, 112
Search for web page 183
Searching
    Computer folder 100
    Enhanced search 110
    Filters 110, 112
    Keywords 112
    Open file location 101
    Operators 110, 112
    Save searches 114
    Search results 101

Start menu 101
Second monitor 48
Secure desktop 37
Security 26
    Access encrypted drive 387
    Access from Vista 388
    Backup encryption key 383
    Bitlocker to Go 385
    Encrypting files 380
    Hide user list 378
    Local Security Policy 376, 378
    Local Users and Groups 375–376
    Set password to expire 376
    Trusted Platform Module (TPM) 14, 390
    User account management 374
    Using EFS 381
    Whole system encryption 390
Security shield 36
Send an invitation 173
Set custom text size (DPI) 46–47
Set password to expire 376
Set up a network 22
Set up Windows Phone 294
Shake 19
Share printer with XP 244
Share theme 61
Sharing folders 270
Sharing the printer 242
Shortcut on desktop 77
Show
    All folders 105
    Desktop 67
    Hidden files 106
    Hidden icons 18, 68, 279
    Icon and notifications 68
Shrink to fit 197
Shutdown 17, 35, 77–78
Small icons 66
Smartphone 292
    Enable Wi-Fi 302
    Functions 295
    Networked 304
    Operating systems 292
    Play to device 305
    Set up 294
    Software 296
    Sync 300
    Windows Phone 7 292–293
    Zune software 296
Snap 19
Snipping Tool 130
Sort folder contents 89
Sound
    Audio connections 222

Audio file formats 224
Copy CD tracks 224
Dictate to computer 234
Download media files 226
Home media streaming 230
Internet radio 228
Manage audio devices 222
Media Player Library 225
Play CDs 223
Play to device 231
Speakers 222
Speech recognition 234
Text to speech 236
Visualization 223
Soundcard 222
Sound Recorder 130
Sound scheme 58
SPDIF 222
Speech recognition 234
Standard account 30, 36
Starter 14
Starting Windows 16
Start in Safe Mode 327
Start Internet Explorer 179
Start menu 18, 31
Use default settings 64
Start menu properties 64
Start menu search 101
Sticky Notes 122
Streaming music 230
Strong password 32
Subscribe to newsgroup 175
Switch user 35
System Information 437
System
Monitor 272
Properties 424
Repair disc 349
Restore 325
Tools 134

Themepack file 61
Thumbnail 84
Toolbars on taskbar 69
Touch 13, 14
Applications 290
Input Panel 289
Math Input Panel 127, 289
Multitouch 13, 288
Touch PCs 288
Transfer more images 208
Transfer photos 205
Troubleshooting 27
Categories 315
Connecting and sharing 322
Easy Connect 324
Get help 320
In action 316
Problem Steps Recorder 317
Program Compatibility 329
Remote Assistance 321
Safe Boot 328
Settings 314
Start in Safe Mode 327
System Restore 325
View report 319
Windows error reporting 312
Trusted Platform Module (TPM) 14, 390
Turn on guest account 34
Turn on suggestions 183
Turn system icons on or off 68

T

Tabbed browsing 186
Tablet PC. See Portable computers
Tab set 188
Taskbar 18
Taskbar properties 66, 69, 286
Task Manager 272, 436
Text size 46–47, 122
Text to speech 236

U

UAC prompt 37–38, 42
Ultimate 14
Unlock taskbar 66
Untransferred images 206
Updating device drivers 240
Upload photos. See Digital images
USB flash drive 14, 20, 39, 101, 287
USB printer 239
Use large icons 66
User account 16, 30
Active 47
Adjust UAC settings 38
Change picture 33–34
Create an account 31
Family safety 36
Manage another account 37
Management 374
Password 32

Password hint	32, 39
Password reset disk	39
Picture	31
Switch user	35
Types	30
UAC prompt	37–38, 42
User Account Control (UAC)	27, 36–37
Users folder	31
Utilities	
Snipping Tool	130
Sound Recorder	130

V

Verbatim	287, 439–440
Versions of Windows	12
Video call	173
Video clips	216
Video file format	216, 220
Virtual memory	429
Virtual PC	
Existing XP applications	364
Hardware-assisted virtualization (HAV)	352
Install	354
Install XP application	361
Linux virtual machine	366
Other virtual machines	365
Predefined VHD	371
Requirements	352
Run XP application	362
Virtual Machines	355
Vista virtual machine	369
Windows XP Mode	356
XP Mode system	360
Virtual printers	249
Vista. *See* Windows Vista	
Visual Effects	219, 281, 431–432
Visualization	223

W

Web slices	192
Welcome message	16
Welcome screen	31
Whole system encryption	390
Windows 7 basic theme	62
Windows 7 editions	14

Enterprise	14
Home Basic	14
Home Premium	14
Professional	14
Starter	14
Ultimate	14
Windows 7 features	15
Windows 7 libraries	91
Windows 7 theme	52
Windows 8	469
Building Windows 8 blog	469
Examples	470
Windows 95	12, 16
Windows Anytime Upgrade	15, 412–413
Windows applications	118
Accessories	118
Adobe Creative Suite.	118
Calculator	126
Disk Image Burner	129
DVD Maker	128
Math Input Panel	127
Microsoft Office	118
Notepad	119
Paint	123
Sticky Notes	122
Windows Fax and Scan	125, 256
Windows Live Essentials programs	118
Windows Photo Viewer	124
WordPad	120
XPS Viewer	121
Windows Backup	336
Windows classic theme	62, 280, 428
Windows color	57
Windows desktop	17
Windows error reporting	312
Windows Experience Index	
	286, 425–426, 433, 439, 441
Windows Explorer	82
Change folder view	88
Folder contents	87
Group folder contents	90
Layout	85
Libraries	91
Navigation pane	104
Organize button	86
Preview	85
Sort folder contents	89
Toolbar	86
Windows Fax and Scan	125, 256
Windows Live	13
Windows Live Calendar	171
Windows Live Essentials	28, 138
Choose add-ons	142
Choose programs	141
Descriptions	139

Download	140
Getting started	138
Install	138, 140
Restart	142
Select	140
Updates	466
Website	139
Windows Live	143
Windows Live Mail	157
Add contacts	168
Add email accounts	159
Attachments	166
Calendar	170
Create Windows Live ID	158
Insert files	167
Junk email	161, 169
Newsgroups	174
Phishing	169
Reading pane	163
Reply	165
RSS feeds	176
RSS subscriptions	176
View messages	164
Window	162
Windows Live Movie Maker	
AutoMovie themes	219
Create movie from photos	218
Edit video clip	217
Save and publish your movie	220
Save your project	219
Video clips	216
Video file format	220
Windows Live Photo Gallery	212
Edit photos	213
Group images	212
Import pictures	212
Original Images folder	214
Print your photos	215
Revert to original	214
Video clips	216
Windows Mail	28
Windows Media Center	232, 290
Windows Media Player	223
Windows Mobility Center	278, 282
Audio Bar	287
Enable on desktop	283
Functions	284
Presentation settings	284
Windows NT	12
Windows Phone 7	292–293
Windows Photo Viewer	124
Windows PowerShell	133
Windows Registry	283, 444
Adjust Aero Peek	460
Backup	446, 451

Change value entry	452
Finding a key	450
Open Registry Editor	447
Registry change	448
Registry Editor	444
Remove shortcut arrow	459
Remove shortcut suffix	458
Resize taskbar thumbnails	457
Scripted updates	455
Structure	445
Windows team blogs	468
Windows Touch. *See* Touch	
Windows Update. *See* Maintenance	
Windows Vista	12, 28, 268, 352
Predefined VHD	371–372
Virtual machine	365, 369–370
Windows XP	12
Windows XP Mode	14, 356
WinSAT	433
Wireless network	264
Wireless networking	13
Wireless printer	246
WordPad	120
Work network	25, 259

X

XP Mode system	360
XPS Viewer	121

Y

Yahoo	184
YouTube	206, 220, 469

Z

Zune software	296